Sonia Gallico

ROME

AND VATICAN CITY

A COMPLETE GUIDE WITH ITINERARIES

ats
italia
editrice

Contents

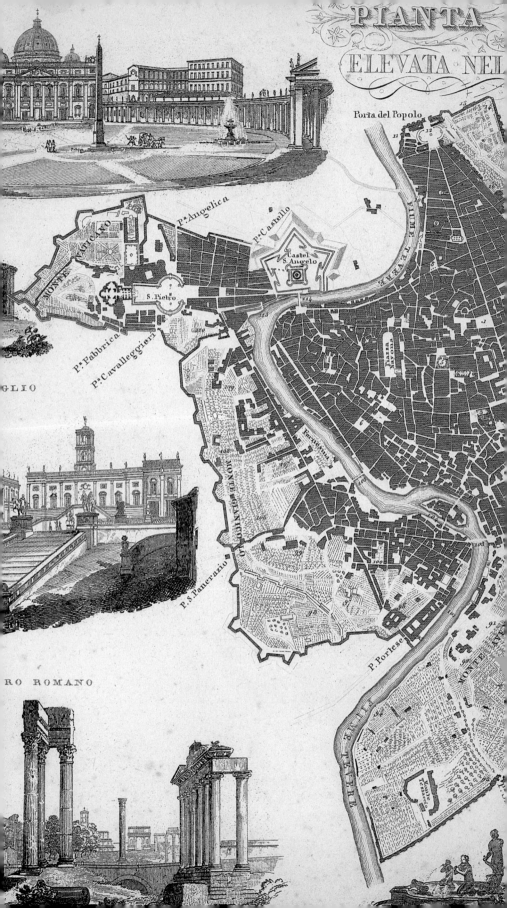

PIANTA
ELEVATA·NEI

Porta del Popolo

FIUME TEVERE

P.a Angelica

P.a Castello

Castel
S. Angelo

MONTE VATICANO

S. Pietro

P.a Fabbrica

P.a Cavalleggieri

GLIO

MONTE GIANICOLO

P. S. Pancrazio

P. Porlese

MONTE

RO ROMANO

FIUME TEVERE

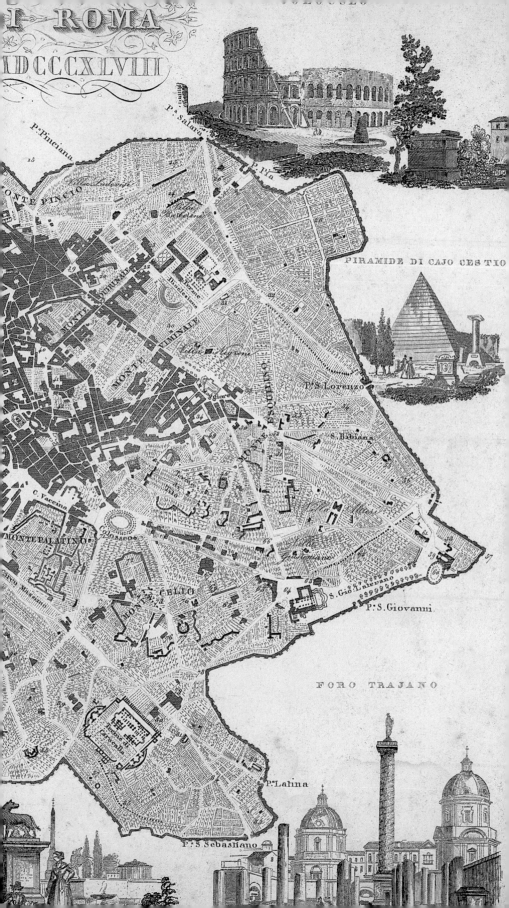

INTRODUCTION

The ancient legend concerning the birth of Rome (the mythical date of its foundation being 21 April 753 BC) associated the origins of the eternal city to the famous destruction, by the Greeks, of the city of Troy on the coast of Asia Minor. The hero Aeneas, son of the goddess Venus, fleeing Troy with his father Anchises and his little son Ascanius, began a long roving journey which eventually took him to the shores of Lazio where he founded the city of Lavinium. One of his descendants, Rhea Silvia, a priestess of Vesta, was loved by the god Mars and gave birth to twins, Romulus and Remus, who while still babies were abandoned and set adrift on the waters of the Tiber River. Discovered by a shepherd, they were subsequently raised in a cave and suckled by a

Rooms of the Conservatori, Cavalier d'Arpino, Discovery of the She-Wolf, detail

she-wolf. Having reached manhood, they decided to found a city and dug a square trench on the Palatine Hill to mark its boundaries, agreeing that the name would be given by which of the two saw the most birds flying in the sky. Romulus won having seen twice as many birds as his brother and decided to call the city Rome but Remus, out of spite, leapt across the newly-dug trench and Romulus to avenge such an insult, slew him on the spot. The city was subsequently governed by seven kings (Romulus himself, Numa Pompilius, Tullus Hostilius, Ancus Marcius, Tarquinius Priscus, Servius Tullius, Tarquinius Superbus), of whom the last three were of Etruscan origin. In the year 509 BC, the monarchy fell and the Republic was established.

Aerial view of the Palatine Hill

ORIGINS Archaeological discoveries seem not to contradict the tradition, in fact scholars agree that the Palatine Hill was the first area of Rome to be inhabited. Excavations undertaken in the area since 1950 have brought to light traces of primitive dwellings dating back to the 9-8C BC; these consist in holes dug into the rock used to hold poles that supported simple huts, and channels to carry away the rainwater. There must also have been other settlements of Latin peoples on the surrounding hills; of these, however, practically no trace has thus far been found. About the 8C BC, on the left side of the river near the Isola Tiberina and the river port, perhaps located behind the modern city registry office (*anagrafe*), a market was founded, an area for the exchange of goods which, being outside the inhabited area, took the name of forum (*foras*, outside). This was the so-called *Forum Boarium*. Over the course of the 7C and 6C BC - in the period of Eturscan dominance - Rome underwent a period of great development during which little by little another forum, the *Forum Holitorium*, came into being slightly to the north of the first, between the Theatre of Marcellus and via della Consolazione. Also in this period a great temple was built on the Capitoline Hill, dedicated to three divinities who were often worshipped together in the Latin world (Jupiter, Minerva and Juno). Traces of the temple remain inside Palazzo Caffarelli. The valley slightly to the east, later occupied by the Roman Forum, was used at the time as a burial ground. At the end of the 6C, it was drained with the construction of the *Cloaca Maxima*, and became the heart of Republican and Imperial Rome.

REPUBLICAN AGE In the first years of the Republic, the dominance of Rome already extended north as far as Veio, and south as far as Capua, and the city itself continued to expand. In the mid 5C BC, development and construction work came to an abrupt halt as conflicts arose between patricians and plebeians, but urban growth later continued and was not impeded by the wars of expansion in the Mediterranean in the 3C and 2C (Taranto was conquered in 272 BC and Carthage destroyed in 146 BC). However few traces of buildings from this period remain, it being the custom among the Romans, unlike our modern practice of conservation, to rebuild the monuments of the past while leaving their original dedication intact.

In the course of the 2C BC, the Roman Forum became the main public area of the city, and was adorned with temples

Aerial view of the Roman Forum

and basilicas. At the beginning of the 1C BC, the *Tabularium* was built (later incorporated into Palazzo Senatorio), while between the 1C and the 2C BC the temples of Fortuna Virilis and of Vesta (both in the *Forum Boarium*) were erected. During the 1C BC, under Julius Caesar the conqueror of Gaul, the city acquired new splendour: he ordered the building of another square next to the old forum so as to expand the centre, by then too small to accommodate the needs of late-Republican Rome. The Theatre of Marcellus also dates from a similar period.

IMPERIAL AGE Augustus' monumental plans were even greater than those of Caesar, and were not just limited to the area of the Roman Forum. His new constructions included, among other things, another forum with an immense temple bigger than Caesar's, public baths dedicated to Agrippa, an amphitheatre and public libraries. The area of the Campo Marzio was also developed, where a monumental tomb was built destined to hold the remains of the emperor, his relatives, and his successors, who continued his policy of great building projects. Nero (54-68), after the fire of 64 AD that destroyed a large part of the city, ordered a vast reconstruction plan of his own. A new *piano regolatore* was implemented with straight streets, wider than before, and a market, the *Macellum Magnum,* on the Caelian Hill. The baths of Nero were built in the Campo Marzio and, over the Esquiline, Oppian and Palatine Hills, the emperor's splendid new residence was constructed, the *Domus Aurea*, the only surviving part of which, on the Oppian Hill, has recently been restored and opened to the public. Rome was also affected by great fires (69 AD on the Capitoline, and 80 AD on the Capitoline and in the Campo Marzio) under the Flavian dynasty (Vespasian, 69-79; Titus, 79-81; Domitian, 81-96). This was the period in which the Flavian amphitheatre was built, begun by Vespasian and completed by his son Titus in

Temple of Vesta in the Forum Boarium

Coliseum

80 AD. Tradition has it that the inauguration ceremony lasted 100 days and involved the death of 500 wild beasts and many gladiators. Under Nerva (96-98) the forum that bears his name was built next to that of Augustus, while under the emperor Trajan (98-117) Rome was endowed with the greatest complex of squares, basilicas and markets it had ever seen, a work attributed to the architect Apollodorus of Damascus. Unfortunately, part of these grandiose Imperial Fora was destroyed with the creation of via dei Fori Imperiali, inaugurated in 1932 during the Fascist period to connect piazza Venezia to the Coliseum. The old layout of the city made up of adjoining squares perpendicular to one another was thus broken in two, one of the great town-planning mistakes of modern Italian history. There has been a long discussion, still on-going, as to the feasibility of eliminating this road, which today carries a heavy traffic, and rejoining the Imperial Fora to these of the Republican age.

Other Roman emperors made important modifications to the city, Under Hadrian (117-138) the temple of Venus was built (facing the Coliseum) and the Pantheon restructured. Later, while the early Christian communities were organising their underground cemeteries (the catacombs) and places of worship inside their homes (the *domus cultae*), with the Severian dynasty building projects were given fresh impulse. Septimius Severus (193-211) restored the palaces on the Palatine Hill, began work on grandiose new baths and raised a great triumphal arch in the Roman Forum to celebrate his victories against the Parthians, a people inhabiting modern-day Iran. These projects were completed by his son Caracalla (211-217). Further great bath complexes were built during the reign of Diocletian (284-305) the biggest ever constructed (near what today is Termini Station). Roman building prowess was then at its height. The trend continued under Maxentius (306-312), to whom is due the famous basilica near the Roman Forum, and under Constantine (306-337) who built his great arch near the Coliseum using marble taken from earlier buildings.

Aerial view of the Imperial Fora

PALAEO-CHRISTIAN AND MEDIAEVAL ROME

In the city of Milan in the year 313 Constantine proclaimed his famous edict legalising the Christian faith which, despite many persecutions, had firmly established itself throughout the empire. Numerous places of worship were subsequently built, known as "basilicas" because they were similar to the Roman buildings of that name. Some of these, such as St. Mary Major, St. John and Santa Sabina, were located inside the city walls, others lay outside: St. Peter's in the Vatican, St. Paul Outside-the-Walls and San Lorenzo fuori le Mura. Almost all of them were built using *spolia*, in other words materials, particularly columns and marble, taken from ancient buildings in ruins. This practice became so widespread that in the 4C and 5C various proclamations were made calling on the population not to destroy the great glories of a relatively recent past.

Aerial view of the
basilica of Santa Sabina

However, in 330 the capital of empire was moved from Rome to Constantinople, and in the late 4C – early 5C, with the division of the empire ordered by Theodosius, first Milan (in 395) then Ravenna (in 402), became the seat of the Roman empire of the West. And it was Ravenna that, for nearly two centuries, witnessed the wonderful flowering of Byzantine art.

Partly abandoned, Rome entered into a period of decline. In 410 it was invaded by the Visigoths of Alaric, and again in 455 by the Vandals. The most critical moment came during the Gothic Wars of 535-553 which resulted from the attempt by the emperor Justinian (527-565), who resided in Constantinople, to regain control over the lands of the West. Hunger, plague and destruction brought complete ruin and, according to historians of the time, almost all the inhabitants would flee to the countryside leaving the city deserted for days at a time.

The scourge of the Gothic Wars having passed, during the 7C the city underwent a slow but significant recovery. As the buildings of pagan and Christian worship fell into ever greater ruin, over the course of the years groups of low houses began to rise up around them, mostly constructed using *spolia* and with gardens of various dimensions between one house and another. The more important interventions of this period include the conversion of the Pantheon into a church in the year 609, and the construction of the basilica of Sant'Agnese fuori le Mura (7-8C) on the via Nomentana.

During the 8C and the 9C, at the same time as the Carolingian Reniassance in France, the city of Rome began to take on a new role, that of capital of the Western Christian world, and the pope began to acquire a new "power", that of proclaiming the emperors of the Holy Roman Empire. Thus it was that, on Christmas night in the year 800, Pope Leo III crowned Charlemagne, king of the Franks, as emperor. The city of Rome was clearly on the rise and around St. Peter's there slowly arose, thanks mostly to Pope Leo IV (847-855), a fortified citadel that would become the nucleus of the future Vatican City.

Santa Maria in Cosmedin

The Comune of Rome was only founded in the year 1144 and it never achieved great power, as Comunes in other Italian cities did, because of the continual struggles between the papacy, the representatives of the people, and the feudal nobility who were a powerful force in the city. One result of this was that, while the great cathedrals (first Romanesque then Gothic) were being built in the rest of Europe, artistic activity in Rome was subdued, with the construction of the church of Santa Maria in Cosmedin, and the restoration of various palaeo-Christian structures such as Santa Maria in Trastevere and San Clemente. Another important development, around the year 1200, was the birth of a school of mosaicists whose work had great influence throughout Italy. Just one Gothic church was built, Santa Maria sopra Minerva (near the Pantheon), work on which began around 1280.

After the first Jubilee Year in history, called in 1300 by Pope Boniface VIII, from 1309 to 1377 the headquarters of the papacy moved from Rome to Avignon, and the city sank to one of its lowest points of demographic and economic decline.

RENAISSANCE ROME Until beyond the mid 1400s, while in other Italian cities such as Florence, Milan, Venice, Urbino, Ferrara and Mantua the early Renaissance was already well underway, Rome still offered a desolate spectacle with the ruins of ancient pagan temples and Christian churches towering over an abandoned landscape, as may be seen in later 16C prints. It has been calculated that the population at the time was no more than 40,000.

Only in the mid 15C did Pope Nicholas V (1447-1455) begin a policy of renovation which sought to rescue those ancient monuments still in a condition to be used, such as Hadrian's mausoleum, which became a castle (Castel Sant'Angelo), the *Tabularium* on the Capitoline Hill over which a new structure was built, the headquarters of the local city authorities, and the ancient basilica of St. Peter's, which some attempt was made to repair.

Sixtus IV (1471-1484) continued along the same path, beginning the transformation of the Vatican Palaces with the construction of a great hall of gigantic proportions (40.23 metres long, 13.4 wide and 20.7 high; probably a reproduction of the dimensions of the Temple of Solomon in Jerusalem) and calling in famous Florentine artists to decorate it: Botticelli, Perugino, Ghirlandaio and Signorelli.

The end of the 15C saw an increase in the production of buildings and works of art, probably in preparation for the Holy Year 1500, but the real turning point in the artistic history of Rome came with the election to the pontifical throne of Julius II (1503-1513), nephew of Sixtus IV. An ambitious man, he immediately set himself a precise political design, that of restoring to Rome, the new capital of Christianity, the ancient glory of the Caesars. To this end, he called in the most accomplished artists of the time who, coming to his court from

Piazza del Campidoglio

various Italian cities, gave life to an extraordinary period of artistic production known as the "mature Renaissance" during which the city once again became the virtual artistic capital of Europe. Among the artists active in Rome in this period was the architect Donato Bramante (1444-1514) to whom was entrusted the task of designing the great new shrine of the Christian world, the basilica of St. Peter's, to be built by razing to the old Constantinian basilica to the ground. Others included Michelangelo Buonarroti (1475-1564), originally called to build Julius II's own funerary monument and subsequently to create the great fresco cycle on the ceiling of the Sistine Chapel (1508-1512), and the youthful Raphael (1483-1520), to whom was given the task of painting the rooms of the papal apartments, which later came to be known as the *Stanze* of Raphael.

Aerial view of the basilica of St. John Lateran

This ambitious programme of revitalisation changed with the death of the pope in 1513 and of Bramante in 1514. The new pontiff, Leo X (1513-1521) a member of the Medici family, divided his interests between Florence and Rome. Raphael dominated the artistic scene of the time, directing a multitude of apprentice painters who executed extraordinary fresco cycles. But in 1520 Raphael died suddenly at the age of just 37 and soon afterwards the political climate in the Roman Curia also changed, with Luther's Protestant schism and increasing imperial pressure following the election of Charles V in 1519 creating uncertainty and disquiet.

In 1527 Rome and the Vatican were occupied by a Protestant army under the orders of Charles V, and the city was devastated as it had not been since the Barbarian invasions. This was the famous Sack of Rome during which innumerable works of art were lost. Recovery took place slowly over the following decades. Pope Paul III (1534-1549) commissioned Michelangelo to redesign the Campidoglio, complete St. Peter's (1546) and fresco the end wall of the Sistine Chapel (1536-1541).

Piazza Navona, Fontana dei Fiumi

Pope Sixtus V (1585-1590) continued in his predecessors' footsteps and in just five years, thanks also to the efforts of the architect Domenico Fontana, the face of Rome changed completely. During this period, the famous via Sistina was laid down, four Egyptian obelisks were erected in four different squares, the dome of St. Peter's was completed, part of the Vatican Palaces was constructed and the façades of St. John Lateran and of the adjoining palazzo were restructured.

BAROQUE ROME At the beginning of the 1600s, Rome again became a centre of great artistic excellence in which famous painters from all over Italy were active, such as the Carracci brothers, Domenichino, Guido Reni and Caravaggio. But the 17C was characterised above all by the art of Gian Lorenzo Bernini (1598-1680) to whose powerful personality three popes submitted. Thanks to him Rome acquired the Baroque appearance that still predominates

in the city today. Among his principal works are the Fontana dei Fiumi in piazza Navona (1647-1651) and the colonnade of St. Peter's Square (1656-1667).

His great rival was Francesco Borromini (1599-1667) who created such wonderful architectural monuments as the churches of Sant'Ivo alla Sapienza and San Carlo alle Quattro Fontane. During the 1600s, Rome also attracted many foreign artists, such as the Flemish Rubens, the Spanish Velázquez and the French Poussin, all of whom came to the city to study the artists of the Renaissance whom they considered as their great masters.

Spanish Steps

ROME IN THE 1700S AND 1800S In the first half of the 18C, the artistic culture of papal Rome was still dominated by the Baroque which, between 1720 and 1740, was given new life through the activities of a number of young architects who "completed" the appearance of the 17C city. Among their more important contributions, some of which still exist today, are the river port of Ripetta (1703-1705) by Alessandro Specchi, demolished following a law passed in 1875 to make way for the *muraglioni*; the Spanish Steps (1723-1726) by Francesco De Sanctis; the Fontana di Trevi (1732-1762) by Nicola Salvi; the façade of the church of Sant'Ignazio and the lovely little square in front, both the work of Filippo Raguzzini between 1727 and 1728; and the monumental frontage of St. John Lateran by the Florentine Alessandro Galilei in 1735.

Beginning in the second half of the century, and particularly during the papacy of Clement XIII (1758-1769), the new neo-classical culture came to be established, thanks to the ideas of Winckelmann (1717-1768) and the works of Antonio Canova (1757-1822). The most famous architect of this period was Giuseppe Valadier (1762-1839) whose name is linked to the restructuring of piazza del Popolo (1816-1824) and to the restoration of, among others, the Coliseum (completed in 1826) and the Arch of Titus.

Many Romantic painters, writers and poets came from abroad to spend extended periods in Rome, where the remains of the ancient past left a deep impression upon them. They included the German Goethe, the French Ingres, Corot and Stendhal, and the English Byron, Shelley and Keats. The latter two are also buried in Rome, in the non-Catholic cemetery near the Pyramid of Caius Cestius.

In 1870 Rome became the capital of the newly unified Italy and many areas were pulled down with the aim of creating a "monumental" city. Among the more important buildings dating from this period is the Monument to Victor Emanuel II, king of Italy, also known as the *Altare della Patria*, work on which began in 1885 and was completed in 1911.

Via della Conciliazione

ROME FROM THE 1900S TO THE 21ST CENTURY

During the twenty tragic years of Fascist rule, via dei Fori Imperiali and via della Conciliazione were created. Later, following the Second World War and over the rest of the 20C, the city underwent a period of great expansion and today, including the outer suburbs, has more than three million inhabitants. One of the most important neighbourhoods dating from this period is certainly EUR, which was completed in the 1960s and contains residential buildings as well as ministries and large company headquarters. Also in EUR are some of the great monuments of modern architecture in Rome such as the Palazzetto dello Sport, designed at the end of the 1950s by the engineer Pier Luigi Nervi.

A lot of work was done to the city for the occasion of the 22nd Olympic Games (1960), including the building of the Leonardo da Vinci international airport. This was followed by a period of vast and completely uncontrolled urban expansion.

Another phase of redevelopment of the city coincided with the Great Jubilee Year 2000, during which 25 million pilgrims from all over the world descended upon Rome. Important changes were made to the historical centre where many public buildings were restructured and restored. New constructions of these years include: the Auditorium *Parco della Musica* by the architect Renzo Piano, the new wing of the Capitoline Museums by Carlo Aymonino and the controversial protective shell over the *Ara Pacis Augustae* by the American architect Richard Meier.

Many of the urban and social problems facing the city today are shared by a lot of other big cities of our time: regulating the expansion of the outskirts, controlling traffic and limiting pollution; others are specific to Rome, such as the conservation of the ancient city over its various stages of development. It is perhaps for this latter reason that so little space has been given to modern architectural and urban development projects. Now, however, the city is projected towards Europe, and remains committed, on the one hand, to a rigorous protection of its ancient ruins, but open, on the other, to new experiences that can, and indeed must, coexist with the past.

Auditorium
Parco della Musica

itinerary

CAPITOLINE HILL

CAPITOLINE HILL

The Capitoline Hill (Campidoglio) as it appears today is the result
of a design by Michelangelo in the mid 16C, later implemented
over various stages. The square, with at the centre the famous
statue of *Marcus Aurelius* (161-180), is linked to the city below
by the *cordonata* (a ramp of wide low steps). At the far end of
the square is Palazzo Senatorio, main headquarters of the local
authority of Rome, to the right is Palazzo dei Conservatori to the
left Palazzo Nuovo, home of the Capitoline Museums.
From earliest Roman times, the Capitoline was the most
important hill in the city, its most sacred site but also the place
where the most important civil ceremonies were held and where
triumphal processions would end. It had two summits, the *Arx*
and the *Capitolium*, separated by a hollow, the *Asylum*. The *Arx*
was occupied by the temple of Juno "Moneta" ("who warns")
over which the mediaeval church of Santa Maria in Aracoeli was
later built. The *Capitolium* was the seat of the city's greatest
temple, dedicated to the Capitoline Triad of Jupiter, Juno and
Minerva, dating from the 6C BC. Fragments of this temple remain
in the Palazzo dei Conservatori, in the gardens behind it and, as
recently discovered, in the nearby Palazzo Caffarelli. Towards
what is now piazza della Consolazione, the *Capitolium* ended
in a sheer drop known as the Tarpeian Rock, from the name
of the young Roman girl who, according to tradition, was flung
from there by the Sabine invaders, despite the fact that she had
opened the gates of the city to them.
Between the two temples, which faced out over the Forum,
lower down was the *Tabularium*, the building in which the tables
of the Law were kept; parts of it are still visible behind Palazzo
Senatorio, great blocks of peperino marble dating from the
beginning of the 1C BC. In Roman times, the Capitoline was

linked to the Palatine by the Via Sacra, the city's most important artery along which official cortèges would pass.

With the decline of Rome, beginning in the 5C AD, the Campidoglio lost its status as a sacred hill and became a pasture for grazing animals, whence comes the name of Via di Monte Caprino, which lies behind Palazzo dei Conservatori. About the 12C, there are records of markets and fairs of livestock, an indication of the growth of a civil hub in the city, as distinct from the religious hub which had already come into being around St. Peter's Basilica. These separate vocations were destined to last over the centuries.

The ancient *Tabularium* (upon which Palazzo Senatorio was built during the course of the 16C) was modified over time with mediaeval structures that shifted its orientation towards the current square of Campidoglio. From the end of the 1300s and during the first half of the 1400s it was fortified with corner towers, still visible today. Some old 16C prints show a building with a portico that would later be incorporated into the Renaissance structure.

Anonymous, a view of piazza del Campidoglio before Michelangelo's modifications, mid 16C

Étienne Dupérac, Michelangelo's design for piazza del Campidoglio, 1569

PIAZZA Michelangelo's first design probably dates from 1536, but no documentation survives. The statue of the emperor *Marcus Aurelius*, on the other hand, was placed in the centre of the square in the year 1538, as recalled in an inscription on the base. The statue, from the area of the Lateran, was placed here as homage to the world of classical Rome, marking the devotion and admiration for the past that characterised the men of the Renaissance. Made in bronze covered in a thin layer of gold leaf, the statue was removed in 1981 and, following years of patient restoration work, put on display inside Palazzo dei Conservatori. Its place in the square is taken by a faithful copy.

In a famous print dating from 1569, the French engraver Étienne Dupérac shows all the details of Michelangelo's project: in the background Palazzo Senatorio with its bell tower, flanked by two similar buildings to form a trapezium that gives the illusion of a larger and deeper space than really exists.

The layout is connected by a design in the paving of a star enclosed within an oval, with the equestrian statue in the centre, and a wide and imposing *cordata* linking the square to the city.

Michelangelo died in 1564 and saw the completion only of the fountain of Palazzo Senatorio. The rest was carried out by his followers Giacomo Della Porta, and Girolamo and Carlo Rainaldi. The star design was made only in 1940.

CORDONATA Planned by Michelangelo, it was built by his pupil Giacomo Della Porta who completed the job in 1582.

The desired aim, of Baroque inspiration, was for the steps to come into people's view suddenly as they passed the surrounding buildings, but this scenic effect was irredeemably lost when, in 1929, the urban setting was altered to create piazza dell'Aracoeli.

At the base of the *cordonata*, or stepped ramp, are two *Egyptian Lions*. Transformed into fountains in 1588, they originally came from a Roman temple dedicated to the oriental goddess Isis, located near the Pantheon.

Cordonata with Palazzo Senatorio in the background

Halfway up the ramp on the left, resting on a plinth made of ancient fragments, is the 19C statue of *Cola di Rienzo*, a famous tribune killed in the square by the people of Rome during a revolt of 1354.

On the balustrade are two colossal statues, the *Dioscuri* (the twins Castor and Pollux, sons of Zeus; according to mythology they achieved immortality by spending one day in the Underworld and one on Earth), found nearby in the Ghetto. The missing parts were restored, and they were placed at the top of the ramp in 1585.

The so-called *Trophies of Marius* were put in place in the final years of the 16C; they are late 1C AD statues from an old Roman nymphaeum of the time of Alexander Severus (222-235).

Further along are statues of *Constantine* and his son *Constans* taken from the baths of Constantine on the Quirinal Hill.

Piazza del Campidoglio

PALAZZO SENATORIO The façade overlooking the square was designed by Michelangelo after 1538. His plan was not to destroy the pre-existing mediaeval building, but to cover it with a frontage that, as is evident from the aforementioned engraving by Étienne Dupérac (1569), consisted of two floors of equal height over an elevated base, with a double staircase to the front. The building was to have been completed with a balustrade topped with enormous statues, almost overwhelming the visitor.

Michelangelo lived to see only the stairway to the building, the niche of which he flanked with 2C AD statues representing the river *Nile* and the river *Tiber*. The goddess *Minerva*, a 1C AD sculpture with a porphyry mantle representing the goddess of Rome, was placed here in 1589.

The rest of the façade was completed by Giacomo Della Porta between 1564 and 1602. He made considerable modifications to the original plan, keeping the pilasters, but opening square widows in the second floor, flattening the mouldings, introducing festoons and making the statues on the balustrade smaller. Particularly beautiful is the central portal with a curved and broken pediment, typical of Michelangelo's architecture.

The campanile from 1579-1582 is the work of the Lombard architect Martino Longhi the Elder, who probably sought to recreate the motif of the central arch of Michelangelo's fountain, with its double pilaster strips to each side.

Statue of Marcus Aurelius, copy

PALAZZO NUOVO It was built in the mid 17C by Girolamo and Carlo Rainaldi to a design by Michelangelo against the rise of the Aracoeli in the place where, in 1595, Giacomo Della Porta had placed the Roman statue of *Marforio* (representing a river god and dating from the 2C AD; the name derives from *Martis* = Mars, and *forum*), which also incorporates a fountain and is one of Rome's "talking" statues.

Palazzo Nuovo

It became a museum (the first public museum in Europe) in 1734, the year in which Pope Clement XII (Lorenzo Corsini 1730-1740) decided to open to the public a collection of Roman statues begun

Palazzo dei Conservatori

Capitoline Museums,
Capitoline Venus

in 1471 under Pope Sixtus IV (Francesco della Rovere 1471-1484),
merged with another collection acquired the preceding year by cardinal Albani. This fact is mentioned in the inscription over the *Marforio*.
- The Capitoline Museums contain Roman works from the Imperial
age with reproductions of Greek originals from the third and second
centuries BC. Among the finest exhibits are, on the ground floor, the
sarcophagus of Alexander Severus from the 3C AD with depictions
of Greek myths; on the first floor, the *Dying Gaul*, a copy of a Greek
sculpture, the original of which was from Pergamon, showing a soldier's final minutes of life; a bust of the Empress Helena from the beginning of the 4C; and copies of Greek statues by the sculptors Skopas and Praxiteles (4C BC), including the famous *Capitoline Venus*
unearthed in the mid 17C near the church of San Vitale between the
Quirinal and Viminal Hills.

PALAZZO DEI CONSERVATORI So called because it was
the headquarters of the magistrates whose job it was to ensure ob-
servance of the Statutes, it was designed by Michelangelo who,
as with Palazzo Senatorio, covered a pre-existing building with a
new frontage. It was completed with very few modifications by
his greatest pupil Giacomo Della Porta, who followed the work
up to 1586.
It has two floors, of which the lower has a portico, framed within
a giant order. At the top, a balustrade with statues lightens the
façade.
The courtyard, with a façade from 1720 by Alessandro Specchi
(the architect of piazza di Spagna) holds, among other things, fragments of a colossal statue of *Constantine*, which in Roman times
was located in the basilica of Maxentius. Dating from the 4C AD,
the statue was around twelve metres high and had a wooden
body covered in a thin layer of plaster and marble, while
the head, hands and feet were in solid marble.
The building was decorated in the1600s by artists who
created wall frescoes, beautiful carved walnut doors
and wooden ceilings. It is home to a vast museum divided as follows:
- The Rooms of the Conservatori. The first room is decorated with frescoes representing the *Orazi* and the *Curiazi*
(according to tradition, the outcome of a war between
Rome and neighbouring Alba Longa was entrusted to
three heroes from each side, all triplets, the three Orazi
of Rome, and the three Curiazi of Alba. After the Curiazi
had eliminated two of the Orazi, the survivor managed
to face each of his foes separately, killing all three. This
marked the beginning of the 8C BC expansion of Rome
into Lazio). The work, from 1595, is by Giuseppe Cesari
known as Cavalier d'Arpino. Against the walls are statues

Pinacoteca Capitolina,
Caravaggio,
The Fortune Teller

of Popes *Urban VIII* (Maffeo Barberini 1623-1644) and *Innocenzo X* (Giovanni Battista Pamphilj 1644-1655) by, respectively, Gian Lorenzo Bernini and Alessandro Algardi, both famous sculptors of the Roman Baroque.

The following rooms contain important sculptures from antiquity including: the *Capitoline Brutus* (3C BC), a splendid example of early Roman portraiture; the *Spinario* (a Greek work from the 3-2C BC); and the famous *Capitoline She-Wolf*, the symbol of Rome, (believed to be an Etruscan work until a recent restoration identified it as mediaeval because of the particular techniques used to cast the bronze), to which the twins *Romulus* and *Remus* were added in the second half of the 1400s by the Florentine sculptor Antonio Pollaiolo.

- The Museum of Palazzo dei Conservatori. The Gallery *dei Fasti Moderni*, inscribed with the names of the administrators of the city of Rome from 1640 to the present, gives access to:
- A room with sculptures from the *Horti Lamiani* on the Esquiline Hill, including the bust of *Commodus as Hercules*.
- Various rooms with Greek and Roman exhibits.
- A great semicircular glass hall designed by the architect Carlo Aymonino containing the original of the equestrian statue of *Marcus Aurelius* and the remains of the colossal statue of the emperor *Constantine*, including the head, left hand and globe.

Rooms of the
Conservatori, Spinario

- A section of the temple of Capitoline Jupiter, built by the last king of Rome, Lucius Tarquinius Superbus, at the end of the 6C BC.
- Areas surrounding the rooms of the Conservatori containing the collection of Greek and Etruscan vases brought together by Augusto Castellani.
- The Pinacoteca Capitolina on the second floor. It was set up around 1750 under the pontificate of Benedict XIV (Prospero Lambertini 1740-1758), and contains several important works including canvases by Titian (*Baptism of Christ*), Caravaggio (*The Fortune Teller* and *St. John the Baptist*), Guido Reni (*St. Sebastian*), Pieter Paul Rubens (*Romulus and Remus*) and Pietro da Cortona (*Triumph of Bacchus*). The final room contains views of Rome by the Dutch painter Gaspard Van Wittel who Italianised his name to Gapare Vanvitelli.

The underground gallery built in 1939 to link Palazzo dei Conservatori with Palazzo Nuovo has recently been reopened to the public. It contains the Gallery of Inscriptions and the remains of a Roman temple dedicated to Veiovis (a divinity of Etruscan origin), and also gives access to the portico of the *Tabularium* which affords a magnificent view over the Forum.

CAPITOLINE MUSEUMS

☐ Capitoline Museum
☐ Museum of Palazzo dei Conservatori
☐ Rooms of the Conservatori
☐ Pinacoteca Capitolina
☐ Capitoline Medal and Coin Collection
☐ Palazzo Clementino Caffarelli
☐ Tabularium
☐ Gallery of Inscriptions

BASEMENT

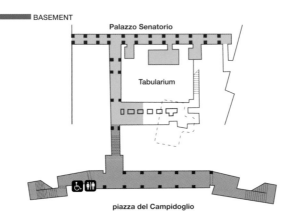

Palazzo Senatorio

Tabularium

piazza del Campidoglio

Palazzo Nuovo   Palazzo dei Conservatori

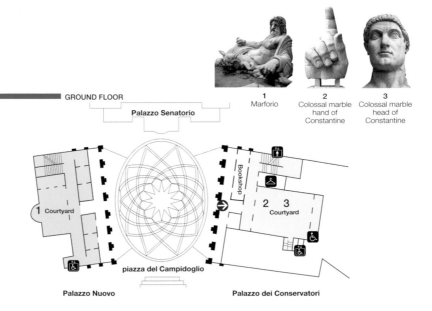

GROUND FLOOR

Palazzo Senatorio

1
Marforio

2
Colossal marble
hand of
Constantine

3
Colossal marble
head of
Constantine

1 Courtyard

Bookshop

2 3
Courtyard

piazza del Campidoglio

Palazzo Nuovo   Palazzo dei Conservatori

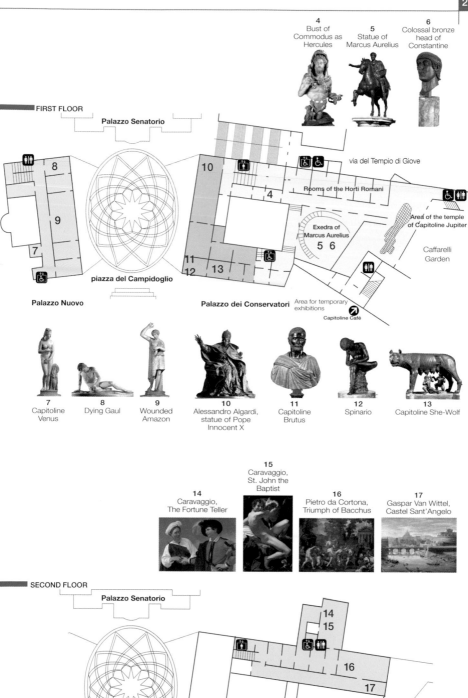

4
Bust of
Commodus as
Hercules

5
Statue of
Marcus Aurelius

6
Colossal bronze
head of
Constantine

FIRST FLOOR

Palazzo Senatorio

8

9

7

via del Tempio di Giove

10

4

Rooms of the Horti Romani

Exedra of
Marcus Aurelius
5 6

Area of the temple
of Capitoline Jupiter

Caffarelli
Garden

11
12   13

piazza del Campidoglio

Palazzo Nuovo

Palazzo dei Conservatori

Area for temporary
exhibitions

Capitoline Café

7
Capitoline
Venus

8
Dying Gaul

9
Wounded
Amazon

10
Alessandro Algardi,
statue of Pope
Innocent X

11
Capitoline
Brutus

12
Spinario

13
Capitoline She-Wolf

15
Caravaggio,
St. John the
Baptist

14
Caravaggio,
The Fortune Teller

16
Pietro da Cortona,
Triumph of Bacchus

17
Gaspar Van Wittel,
Castel Sant'Angelo

SECOND FLOOR

Palazzo Senatorio

14
15

16

17

piazza del Campidoglio

Palazzo dei Conservatori

Capitoline Café

Panoramic
terrace

PIAZZA DELL'ARACOELI

The piazza dell'Aracoeli is a fairly recent work. It was created in 1929 by pulling down, not without controversy, the old Roman neighbourhood around which Michelangelo had designed the piazza of Campidoglio. The new square opened a wider vista towards piazza Venezia, *Trajan's Column* and its two adjacent churches, and all the way to the Quirinal Hill. The neighbourhood that was pulled down covered the area occupied by the current square's central garden, so it is still possible to imagine how it must have looked before.

In the same period, the old Baroque church of Santa Rita da Cascia, which used to be located at the foot of the stairway leading to Aracoeli, was "dismantled" and faithfully reconstructed between the Theatre of Marcellus and piazza Campitelli. The ruins of a Roman *insula*, however, were left in place, a five-storey apartment block dating from the first centuries of the empire, partly reconstructed in the 4C, and during the Middle Ages when the small campanile on the right was added.

The fountain, dating from 1589, is by the architect Giacomo Della Porta who completed the work during the pontificate of Pope Sixtus V (Felice Peretti 1585-1590). It was later remodelled in the mid 1600s under Pope Alexander VII (Fabio Chigi 1655-1667).

SANTA MARIA IN ARACOELI

SANTA MARIA IN ARACOELI The church of Aracoeli, built in the 10-11C over a pre-existing structure perhaps dating from the 5C, was greatly modified during the 1200s and again in the Baroque.

The stairway, with its 124 marble steps, came from a Roman temple and was, according to tradition, put in place in 1348 at the behest of the people of Rome to thank the Virgin Mary for having spared their city from the great plague, which devastated Italy and was described by Boccaccio in his famous work, the *Decameron*.

The façade, which is almost square, was built in 1280, and the portal is believed to belong to the same period, later restored in the 1400s and 1500s. Also from that time are the traces of frescoes on the inside of the lunettes, while the central window, built to replace the original, was put in place by order of Pope Urban VIII whose heraldic symbol, the bee of the Barberini family, appears three times on the glass. In the Middle Ages, it is probable that the façade was covered in mosaics.

The interior has three naves, a transept and an apse. Almost all the columns come from old buildings and have splendid Ionic and Corinthian capitals; the floor too, of marble paving with mosaic strips, dates from the 9-10C. The transept was added at the end of the 1200s by Arnolfo di Cambio, one of the greatest artists of the Middle Ages.

The ceiling dates from 1575, and was built to thank the Virgin Mary for having guided the Christians to victory against the Turks in the battle of Lepanto in 1571. Of the side chapels, the first on the right is particularly noteworthy: it has frescoes by Pinturicchio (mid 15C), and over the late 17C altar is a 10C painting of the *Madonna and Child*.

In the left-hand section of the transept is an aedicule dating from the 17C in the form of a small temple, dedicated to St. Helen, under which is an urn re-evoking the legendary apparition of the Virgin Mary to the emperor Augustus, following which he is said to have ordered the building of an altar dedicated to the son of God. In the adjoining chapel is the statue of the *Santo Bambino*, the Infant Jesus, dating from 1400. According to tradition it was carved from the wood of an olive tree from the Garden of Gethsemane. The original was stolen in 1994, and has been substituted with a copy. The statue was said to have therapeutic powers for the sick and women in childbirth. Also worthy of attention are two 12C pulpits decorated with mosaics on the two pillars nearest the main altar, rebuilt in their present form in the first decades of the 20C, and the fresco of *St. Anthony and two angels* by Benozzo Gozzoli. Recent restoration work has uncovered late 13C frescos attributable to Pietro Cavallini, in the last chapel on the right.

Santa Maria in Aracoeli, central nave

Wooden ceiling, coat-of-arms of Pope St. Pius V (Michele Ghislieri)

Wooden ceiling, Madonna and Child

PIAZZA VENEZIA

One of the nerve centres of Rome, an important hub of city traffic and an obligatory stop off point for tourists. Its construction, in 1911, involved a series of demolitions that sacrificed the north part of the Capitoline Hill and razed to the ground a 15C palace, subsequently rebuilt near the basilica of San Marco. Piazza Venezia is dominated by the huge mass of the *Vittoriano*, the monument to Victor Emanuel, which closes the visual axis from piazza del Popolo along via del Corso. On the right of the square is Palazzo Venezia, a Renaissance structure mirrored by the Palazzo delle Assicurazioni di Venezia, which was completed in 1911 and gives symmetry to the whole. At the centre of the

façade of the latter is a winged lion, the symbol of Venice, dating from the 16C.
In the area between Palazzo delle Assicurazioni di Venezia and via dei Fori Imperiali, at the base of the Quirinal Hill, are two beautiful churches: the 16C Santa Maria di Loreto, attributed to Donato Bramante and Antonio da Sangallo il Giovane, and the 18C Santissimo Nome di Maria. From this point of piazza Venezia begins via dei Fori Imperiali which ends at the Coliseum, on the opposite side is piazza dell'Aracoeli which leads directly up to Campidoglio.

Monument to
Victor Emanuel II

Grave of the Unknown Soldier

Statue of Victor
Emanuel II

MONUMENT TO VICTOR EMANUEL II Also known in Italian as the *Vittoriano*, it was built to celebrate the Unification of Italy, achieved in 1860. Work began in 1885 under king Umberto I (l878-l900) who personally laid the first stone, but the inauguration took place only in 1911 and the *four-horsed chariots* were added in 1930. Throughout this period controversy raged over the plans of the architect Giuseppe Sacconi who had cut away part of the Capitoline Hill destroying Roman remains, churches and convents, as well as Renaissance buildings including a tower built in the mid 16C by Pope Paul III (Alessandro Farnese 1534-1549).

The first king of the united Italy, *Victor Emanuel II* (1861-1878), father of Umberto I and considered as the Father of the Country, appears at the centre of the monument sitting astride a horse on a high plinth, with two fountains, one to either side, recalling the *Tyrrhenian Sea* (to the left) and the *Adriatic Sea* (to the right).

Following the First World War (1918), the monument also became the Altar of the Nation and the Grave of the Unknown Soldier, where an eternal flame burns over the tomb of the nameless combatant. It has never truly found favour among the Romans (due to its shape, it is also ironically known as the "typewriter"), because of its bogus classicism and the overly-pompous use of white marble. Nonetheless, it has now been accepted as a testimony of early 20C art. It contains the Museum and Institute of the Italian Risorgimento and the *Sacrario delle Bandiere*.

The terraces at the bottom of the colonnade afford a magnificent view over the Forum and the city.

PALAZZO VENEZIA The building, completed between 1455 and 1470 by cardinal Pietro Barbo who later became Pope Paul II (1464-1471), was destined to become the official residence of the pontiffs. It was completed after his death by his nephew, cardinal Marco.

It was built in the period of transition from the medieval style (angular blocks with battlements) to the Renaissance (proportionality, windows with cross frames, courtyards). The new building incorporated the old basilica of San Marco, which dates back to the 9C and has splendid mosaics from the early Middle Ages in the apse and stuccowork from

Palazzo Venezia

Palazzo Venezia, cloister and internal courtyard

Internal courtyard, fountain of the Marriage of Venice and the Sea

the 18C (access is from piazza di San Marco), and a medieval tower, completely restructured during the 15C. Headquarters, in the mid 16C, of the embassy of the Venetian Republic, whence the building gets its name, during the twenty years of Fascist rule Palazzo Venezia became the seat of the Italian government. Mussolini used to appear at the central balcony - an 18C addition in the middle of the main façade - to address the crowds gathered in the square below.

The building currently houses the library of the National Institute for Archaeology and History of Art. The frescoed rooms on the top floor are used for important temporary exhibitions. The magnificent internal courtyard (access in via del Plebiscito) has octagonal columns with original capitals some of which are decorated with *cornucopias* (a symbol of plenty during the Renaissance) and papal insignia from the 15C.

The *Lion of St. Mark* on the corner of via del Plebiscito dates from the first twenty years of the 20C.

SANTI APOSTOLI Not far distant, in the square of that name, is the basilica dei Santi Apostoli, dedicated to Sts. Philip and James. Originally from the 6C, it was restructured in the first half of the 15C by Pope Martin V (Oddone Colonna 1417-1431) and again, at the end of that century, by Sixtus IV who added an external portico with octagonal pillars in the lower part and slim Ionic columns above. This façade, perhaps the work of the architect Baccio Pontelli, was modified in the 1600s by Carlo Rainaldi with the addition of the windows and balustrade with statues representing *Christ and the twelve Apostles*. The rest of the façade was done by the 19C architect Giuseppe Valadier. Inside, the basilica bears the mark of the architect Carlo Fontana who, from 1702, completely restructured the interior by order of Pope Clement XI (Giovanni Francesco Albani 1700-1721). It contains interesting frescoes by Giovanni Battista Gaulli known as il Baciccia (1707) and Giovanni Odazzi (1709). However, the most important thing to see is the *funerary monument to Clement XIV* (Lorenzo Ganganelli 1769-1774), work of the neo-classical sculptor Antonio Canova (1789), depicting, apart from the pontiff, the figures of *Meekness* and *Modesty* afflicted with mourning.

Santi Apostoli, façade

Santi Apostoli, cloister and fountain

itinerary

THE FORA

FORUM BOARIUM
AND HOLITORIUM

The first public spaces in ancient Rome came into being on the left bank of the Tiber near the Isola Tiberina, in the area between Santa Maria in Cosmedin, San Giorgio in Velabro and the theatre of Marcellus, where ever since the 8C BC a lively exchange of goods had been taking place between the peoples occupying the nearby hills. This was the site of the *Forum Boarium*, a name (perhaps from the Latin *bos, bovis* = ox) that would suggest the existence of a livestock market. Archaeologists have pinpointed its location to the area in front of the church of Santa Maria in Cosmedin. In the 6C BC, a little further north, arose the so-called *Forum Holitorium* (probably from *oleum* = oil), a vegetable and oil market near the church of San Nicola in Carcere.

Of all the temples built in that period only two remain standing today, both from the 2-1C BC: the temple of Vesta and the temple of Fortuna Virilis.

The current appearance of the area is due to work undertaken in the years 1920-1930 by the architect Antonio Muñoz, who destroyed the old mediaeval quarter in order to expose the ancient buildings.

TEMPLE OF VESTA

TEMPLE OF VESTA It dates back to the time of the Roman conquest of Greece (mid 2C BC), replicating the circular form of the temple of Delphi, with parts in marble from Mount Pentelicus near Athens.

Slightly raised above ground level, it has a round cella surrounded by a portico of twenty columns of the Corinthian Order. The entablature is missing, having collapsed. It was assumed that this temple was dedicated to Vesta (divine protectress of hearth and home, and therefore of the city of Rome) because of its likeness to a similar temple in the Roman Forum; however, it is likely that it was in fact the place of worship of the divinity Hercules Victor.

In the Middle Ages it became a church and, by the time of the Renaissance, had assumed the name of Santa Maria del Sole. About the year 1920 the temple was restored to its presumed original form. Recent restorations have sought to integrate the missing parts of the capitals.

Inside is a late 15C fresco of the *Madonna and Child*.

Nearby is the *Fontana dei Tritoni* (1717), built by order of Pope Clement XI (Giovanni Francesco Albani 1700-1721). His heraldic emblem of three mounts and an eight-pointed star is visible on the base of the water conduit.

Temple of Vesta

TEMPLE OF FORTUNA VIRILIS

TEMPLE OF FORTUNA VIRILIS Incorrectly called "Fortuna Virilis", it was in fact probably dedicated to the god Portunus, protector of activities in the fluvial port. One of the oldest temples of Rome, in its current form it dates from 1C BC, however there are traces of it as early as the 5C BC, and evidence has been found of its restructuring in the 3C BC.

It has the typical form of ancient Roman temples: resting on a high base and reached by a flight of steps (reconstructed), it has a cella preceded by an open pronaos (porch or atrium). The columns at the front and the pilasters along the sides are of the Ionic Order and made of tufa, the same material being used for the perimeter walls. The top sections are made of travertine. The entire building was covered in plaster, of which some traces remain on the columns.

Its excellent state of repair is due to the fact that in the 9C, and perhaps even earlier, it was transformed into a Christian church, which during the Renaissance was dedicated to Santa Maria Egiziaca. Traces of this transformation may be seen on the side of the building facing the Tiber where large rectangular windows were created. From the 16C on it became the object of study by artists, including such famous names as Serlio, Palladio and Piranesi. Its restoration began in the 1800s, being completed in 1925 by the architect Antonio Muñoz who incorporated "simplified" (i.e., undecorated) forms

Giovanni Battista Piranesi, *View of the temple of Fortuna Virilis*, etching from *Vedute di Roma*, 1748-1774, detail

Giovanni Battista Piranesi, *View of the temple of Cybele at Piazza della Verità*, etching from *Vedute di Roma*, 1748-1774, detail

Temple of Portunus, known as Fortuna Virilis

so as to facilitate the distinction of the "ancient" from the "new" (for example, the mouldings on the architrave over the columns).

SANTA MARIA IN COSMEDIN

It was built in various stages over pre-existing Roman remains. In the 6C a community, perhaps from Constantinople where there existed a church with a similar dedication ("Cosmedin" is a Greek word meaning "the beautiful, the ornate"), ordered the building of a small structure with a single nave and an apse to serve as the centre for a deaconry.

That church was later restructured under Pope Hadrian I (772-795), with the addition of two side aisles and two smaller apses. At the beginning of the 12C, Pope Callistus II (1119-1124) made further modifications, particularly in the atrium, and added the campanile. Remodelled during the 1600s and 1700s, from 1890 the church was restored to what was thought to be its Romanesque form.

Bocca della Verità

The exterior has the characteristic porch with dissimilar columns that were already present in the 8C, over which subsequent transformations were built.

Inside the atrium is the famous *Bocca della Verità*, a Roman drain covering around which a legend arose, already popular in the Middle Ages, according to which it has the power to unmask lies, and whosoever puts his hand in the mouth and tells a lie will have it bitten off.

Ciborium

The three naves, divided by wide piers alternating with columns in groups of three (all from ancient buildings with late Corinthian capitals), are illuminated by small windows. The stone floor inlaid with geometric patterns is from the 12C while the ceiling is modern. The screen of the *schola cantorum* (the area reserved for the cantors) is from the 12C, while the tabernacle over the altar and the choir date from the 13C.

Santa Maria in Cosmedin with the Fontana dei Tritoni in the foreground

In the right-hand chapel is a famous *Madonna and Child* taken from the apse of the church and placed here in 1898. Some historians attribute it to Cimabue (13C), others believe it could date from as early as the 5C. In the space on the right is a mosaic from the 8C. The counter-façade incorporates columns taken from old Roman monuments.

Arch of Janus

ARCH OF JANUS The name comes from *ianus* (a covered passage) and it was built at the beginning of the 4C AD, probably commissioned by Constantine (306-337) or by his son Constantius II (337-340). It has four arches supported by four massive piers inset with niches that once contained statues. The inside has a cross vault.

Having been incorporated into a mediaeval fortress, it was restored to its "original" state in the 1920s and 1930s when the entire area was modified.

SAN GIORGIO IN VELABRO Part of a more unusual but no less intriguing Rome, a Rome made up of small churches and hidden corners, San Giorgio in Velabro is a site not to be missed. Located in the valley of the *Velabrum*, an ancient stream that once crossed the Forum and emptied into the Tiber, it is one of the oldest churches in the city.

It was built at the end of the 7C and enlarged around the year 830 under Pope Gregory IV (827-844) who ordered the addition of the two side aisles, giving the building its current form. The portico, from the 1200s, includes earlier remains and the typically Romanesque bell tower also dates from the 13C.

The interior has columns taken from ancient buildings, each one different from the others. One element worthy of note is the raised altar, which marks a stylistic tendency that would become more accentuated during the Romanesque period. The wall on the left runs at a slightly oblique angle with respect to the one on the right because it was built on pre-existing remains that were used as a foundation. In the early Middle Ages it was common for buildings to be constructed in haste, without showing too much respect for laws of symmetry or for coherence between the various parts.

The ciborium (the structure over the altar) is from the late 1100s. The much-restored fresco in the apse is by Pietro Cavallini (13C).

San Giorgio in Velabro

Abandoned during the 1500s, the church was restored, beginning in 1610, with the addition of Baroque decorations. Later, in the 1700s, it became a storehouse for oil and wine. In 1824, a plan by Giuseppe Valadier sought to revive the church but the project was never realised. In 1926, radical restorations directed by the architect Antonio Muñoz returned the building to its supposed "primitive" state.

A bomb attack in July 1993 destroyed the front right of the portico, also damaging part of the interior of the church. Under the direction of the *Soprintendenza ai Beni Architettonici e Storici di Roma*, it was rebuilt exactly "as it had been", not without some controversy.

ARCUS ARGENTARIORUM The Arch of the Money-Changers. It was built in 204 as a homage from the money-changers (*argentarii*) and livestock merchants (*negoziantes boarii*) to the emperor Septimus Severus, and gave access to the commercial quarter.

AREA SACRA DI SANT'OMOBONO Excavations undertaken during the 1930s in front of the church of Sant'Omobono, brought to light two archaic temples, believed to date from the time of king Servius Tullius (6C BC). They are probably the temples of Fortuna and of Magna Mater, each with an altar in front.

Alongside the excavations are the remains of a portico with Tuscan Order columns dating from the late Republican era (1C BC).

SANTA MARIA DELLA CONSOLAZIONE This church
stands on the place where, according to tradition, a mother weeping for her son who was in prison awaiting execution had a vision of the Virgin Mary predicting his miraculous salvation. The original church from the late 15C was part of a hospital complex that now no longer exists. It was completely rebuilt at the end of the 16C to a design by Martino Longhi the Elder, the architect who also designed

San Nicola in Carcere, Roman columns

the bell tower of the Campidoglio. The upper part of the façade is from 1826, but was built following the original model. Inside are late 16C paintings by Taddeo Zuccari, Antoniazzo Romano and Cristoforo Roncalli known as il Pomarancio.

SAN NICOLA IN CARCERE On the opposite side of via Luigi Petroselli is the church of San Nicola in Carcere, so called because a prison was believed to have existed nearby.

Its outer walls incorporate remains of columns taken from three Roman temples, the bases of which are still partly visible. It dates perhaps from the 8C but was rebuilt in the 12C and remodelled during the Renaissance. The façade by Giacomo Della Porta dates from 1599 and has a giant Ionic Order framing the portal and the round window. Above is a jutting entablature decorated with garlands and festoons upon which rests the tympanum.

San Nicola in Carcere

The tower, which dates from the Middle Ages, has recently been much restored.

THEATRE OF MARCELLUS Begun by Julius Caesar in 46 BC, after his assassination in 44 BC it was completed by Augustus who, in 22 BC, dedicated it to Marcus Claudius Marcellus, the son of his sister Octavia. Marcellus was Augustus' designated successor but died prematurely at the age of just 19. The theatre was inaugurated in 21 BC, or according to some historians in 13 BC, with the killing of 600 wild beasts.

The name of the architect remains unknown, although the theatre follows the "rules" laid down my the famous theoretician of antiquity, Vitruvius Pollio.

The theatre is semicircular and its external façade in travertine is 32 metres high characterised by tiers of arches one over the other with columns of the Doric, Ionic and Corinthian Orders (the top, Corinthian, tier no longer exists). This motif, used here for the fist time, soon became typical for the façades of Roman theatres and amphitheatres, such as the Coliseum.

The cavea, 130 metres in diameter and with space for 15,000 spectators, and the orchestra, 37 metres wide, have both been lost. The stage was destroyed by a great fire in 64 AD, and was rebuilt, first by Vespasian (69-79 AD) and then by Alexander Severus at the beginning of the 3C.

The theatre was used until the end of the 4C (circa 370), after which it was gradually abandoned. By the 12C it had been transformed into a fortress, later enlarged by the Savelli family in the 13C and 14C.

It was much admired by Renaissance architects who incorporated into their own buildings the idea of three overlying tiers in different orders. In 1523-1527 it was remodelled by Baldassarre Peruzzi, a sophisticated artist from Siena. He walled in the upper floor and created the elegant windows that can still be seen today. In the 1700s it passed to the Orsini family and in the 1800s shops and houses were built around it.

The restoration of the theatre, which began in 1926 and was completed in 1932, involved the demolition of the shops and workshops that had sprung up on the lower floor as the level of the land had become higher, and

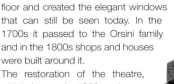

Theatre of Marcellus

the building of a prop and buttresses to support the building. Baldas-sarre Peruzzi's additions, however, were kept in place in order to leave visible traces on the building of the "passage of time".

TEMPLE OF APOLLO SOSIANO In 1940, three columns and a fragment of entablature were re-erected to the right of the theatre of Marcellus. They come from the so-called temple of Apollo *Sosiano*, the name of which derives from the consul Caius Sosius who ordered it to be built in 34 BC. It has been calculated that the temple was 29.2 metres high. The travertine columns were once covered in plaster. Of particular importance were the sculptures in the temple façade, be-ing Greek originals from the 5C BC, imported to Rome at the end of the 1C BC as spoils of war from the Greek region of Euboea. These statues have recently been restored and put on display in the old Giovanni Montemartini power station, which has been transformed into a museum.

In the same area are a number of mediaeval buildings, much restruc-tured during the first decades of the 20C and today the headquarters of local government offices. Behind, are the remains of the Porticus of Octavia.

ROMAN FORUM

Originally (9-7C BC) the isolated graveyard of a city that had come into being near the Tiber (see *Forum Boarium* and *Forum Holitorium*), the area of the Forum (from the Latin *foras*, meaning outside the inhabited centre) was drained some time towards the end of the 7C BC by the building of a great drain, the *Cloaca Maxima*, which gathered the waters from the surrounding hills such as the Quirinal and the Capitol.

In the Republican era (6C BC), the Forum became the city's most important square, the political and commercial heart of Rome, and so it remained during the Imperial age (from 1C BC) when the other adjoining public areas were built. Rectangular in shape, linked to the Palatine and the Capitol by the via Sacra, the Forum was subject to constant modifications and transformations as politicians and emperors, seeking to leave a trace of themselves in the most important area of Rome, would reconstruct the buildings and monuments which, for this reason, all date from different periods. Only time has rendered them all alike, hiding their diversity under the patina of the centuries.

Because of a lack of maintenance and the consequent blockage of the *Cloaca Maxima*, in the 7-8C AD the appearance of the valley of the Roman Forum began to change. Slowly, the buildings began to be covered with layers of mud and sedimentation, causing the level of the ground to rise by some six metres.

In the Middle Ages and the Renaissance churches and houses were built, soon causing the purpose of the underlying square to be forgotten. Stone and marble from the old monuments was used for the new buildings, or pulverised to make quicklime.

However, by the early years of the 1500s, people had become aware of the immense devastation being wreaked and in 1519 the famous man of letters Baldassar Castiglione, perhaps in collaboration with Raphael, wrote a letter to Pope Leo X (Giovanni de' Medici 1513-1521) inviting him to protect the ruins and prevent splendid marble monuments being reduced to quicklime. Nonetheless, ten years later, Pope Paul III authorised excavations in the Forum to quarry marble for the new basilica of St. Peter's. And the same thing happened during the 1600s, when many Roman palazzos were built using ancient stones taken from the Forum and the Coliseum.

Only at the end of the 18C, in the context of the reappraisal of antiquity by neo-classical culture, did the first excavations take place in what was then still known as the *Campo Vaccino* (pastureland for grazing cattle) so well illustrated in the engravings of Giovanni Battista Piranesi.

Further important work was undertaken in the Forum during the brief period of French occupation (1809-1814), then started up again in 1827 under the direction of Carlo Fea and Antonio Nibby.

Other excavation campaigns were carried out immediately after the unification of Italy from 1870 to 1886, headed by the famous archaeologist Rodolfo Lanciani, and again in the first decades of the 20C under the guidance of Giacomo Boni. The latter, using the stratigraphical method of excavation, unearthed among other things the *Lapis Niger*, an ancient black stone dating from the time of the Republic, or even perhaps of the kings, and marking, near the Senate House, the most sacred place in the city.

VIA SACRA Entering the Forum from via dei Fori Imperiali a short sloping path leads directly down into the via Sacra, the road that linked the Palatine Hill to the Capitol, site of the temple of Capitoline Jupiter, the most important in the city.

The original paving on the via Sacra dates back to the time of the kings; that visible today, with stones of basalt, is from the age of Augustus, the first emperor of Rome (27 BC-14 AD). Along here victorious armies would pass in triumphant cortege after their military campaigns, carrying with them the spoils of war and chained prisoners reduced to slavery.

Turning right along the via Sacra leads the visitor to the area at the foot of the Capitoline Hill.

BASILICA AEMILIA Immediately to the right of the access ramp is a stone tablet with an inscription in large letters dedicated to the son of the emperor Augustus, Lucius Caesar (grandson of the great Julius). Behind are the remains of the Basilica Aemilia, a rectangular building, perhaps used for civic purposes, as a kind of stock exchange or for the administration of justice. The entrance was on the side facing the Forum, which also had a series of *tabernae* (shops). The interior had four naves, of which the central one was much wider and higher than the others.

Built in 179 BC by the magistrate Marco Aemilius Lepidus, whence it gets its name, it was restored at the beginning of 1C BC and again at the beginning of the 5C AD, following a fire perhaps due to the sack of Rome by the Goths in 410. Today's ruins are the remains of the 5C interventions.

Basilica Aemilia

SHRINE OF VENUS CLOACINA Outside the basilica on the left, the traces of a round building are visible. This was the so-called shrine of Venus Cloacina, a small circular temple that indicated the entrance to the drain from the Forum.

Basilica Aemilia, inscription dedicated to Lucius Caesar

CLOACA MAXIMA On the left of the basilica, with one's back to the Forum, an excavation has brought to light certain structures of the *Cloaca Maxima*, the great sewer built during the period of Etruscan domination of Rome in the 6C BC in order to drain the valley of the Forum. An arch protected it from the buildings above.

COMITIUM This is an area in front of the Senate building, where the people used to gather, the heart of the political life of Rome during the Republican era.

CURIA It is a majestic building 21 metres high, the ancient seat of the Roman Senate. Rebuilt on a number of occasions, the current edifice dates from the era of Diocletian (circa 284 AD), but recent excavations have brought to light structures from the time of Julius Caesar and Augustus (1C BC) showing how the earlier building was oriented towards the Forum behind, in other words it faced the other way with respect to today. Transformed into a church under Pope Honorious I (625-638) with the name of Sant'Adriano, the Curia was again restructured during the Baroque and restored to its presumed "original" state during the 1930s.

Inside are two facing podia, one against either wall, and the 300 senators elected by the people would sit on one side or the other depending upon whether they voted for or against a motion. At the end is a porphyry statue found nearby and put here to replace a *Goddess of Victory*, now lost.

Along the sidewalls are the two great sculpted tablets known as the *Plutei of Trajan*. The architectural background images present an interesting view of the Roman Forum in antiquity. The scenes represented are, on the left, the emperor condoning certain Roman citizens from the payment of death duties, with the destruction of the registers in which such debts were recorded and, on the right, the distribution of economic aid to the poor.

Curia

LAPIS NIGER In front of the Curia is the famous *Lapis Niger* (the black stone) a small square area, perhaps covered in Caesar's time with black slabs, under which, according to tradition, is the grave of Romulus, the first king of Rome in the 8C BC. A more likely theory is that this is the place where Romulus, having grown too powerful, was killed.

Here too is the oldest Latin inscription (written from left to right on the top line and from right to left on the line beneath) perhaps dating back to the time of the kings. The text is difficult to decipher because some parts are missing, but probably indicates a sacred site and warns against profaning it.

Lapis Niger

Base of the Decennalia

BASE OF THE DECENNALIA A monument recalling the tenth anniversary of the Tetrarchate (division of the empire into four parts to facilitate its governance) ordered by Diocletian at the end of the 3C AD.

ARCH OF SEPTIMIUS SEVERUS It was erected by the emperor in 203 in order to commemorate his campaigns against the Parthians (a people inhabiting what today is Iran), a fact recalled in the inscription on the attic level over the cornice. It has three openings and is 21 metres high. The reliefs, showing scenes of battle and slaves being led away as prisoners, already show the loss of proportionality in the figures, with respect to the classical canons, that became a typical trait of late antiquity.

Arch of Septimius Severus

UMBILICUS URBIS Next to the left-hand opening is a small brick construction that marked the centre of the city. It is of the same age as the arch itself but its origins date back to Republican times.

TABULARIUM Against the background of the Capitoline Hill was the *Tabularium*, repository of the *tabulae* (tables of the Law), now incorporated into Palazzo Senatorio, headquarters of Rome's local authority. Built of great blocks of tufa (*opus quadratum*) the building had two tiers of arches between pilasters with Doric semi-columns on a high base. The constructions above are from the Middle Ages and the Renaissance.

TEMPLES AT THE FOOT OF THE CAPITOLINE HILL
Below the *Tabularium*, from right to left are:
- The temple of Concordia, built in 367 BC to celebrate a peace agreement between the patricians and the plebeians; reconstructed in the 1C AD over the remnants from the 4C BC. All that remains today is the outer wall.
- The temple of Vespasian, completed under Domitian (81-96 AD), with three columns still standing.
- The portico of the *Dei Consentes* (of the "gathering of the Gods") with splendid Corinthian capitals of the 1C AD, rebuilt in the 4C AD. Six rooms opened onto the corridor, which bends to form an oblique angle, and each room contained the statue of a divinity.
- The temple of Saturn, of which eight columns from the front portico remain, was built over an altar from the period of the kings and was reconstructed several times (the last being in the 4C AD). Here from 17 to 23 December every year, the feast of the *Saturnalia* was held, during which the Romans would wear masks and play all kinds of practical jokes, and slaves were allowed to sit at table with their masters and even to be served by them.

Capitoline Hill, from the left:
Temple of Saturn,
Column of Phocas,
Temple of Vespasian and Arch
of Septimius Severus

ROSTRA Back in the Forum, the political connotations of which are particularly evident in this area, are the *Rostra,* raised tribunes from which orators would address the crowds. Built at the end of the 1C BC the *Rostra* take their name from the "rostra" or iron beaks of enemy ships captured in battle in the 4C BC, with which they used to be decorated. The holes used to fix them in place are still visible on the base of the wall.

COLUMN OF PHOCAS This is the most recent monument in the Forum, erected in 608 by order of Phocas, emperor of the East, who reused a 2C AD column placing a statue of himself on top. To the left is a fenced-off area with a fig tree, an olive tree and a vine, recalling the ancient legend according to which a knight, in order to placate the anger of the gods of the underworld, hurled himself into a lake where, subsequently, these three plants sprang up. On the ground not far away is an inscription in bronze letters (restored) recalling the Roman magistrate Surdinus who in 14 AD restored the Forum following a disastrous fire.

BASILICA JULIA Almost symmetrically opposite the Basilica Aemelia, its construction was ordered by Julius Caesar in 54 BC, on the site of an earlier basilica called Sempronia, to close the south side of the Forum. It was completed by Augustus, rebuilt following a fire in 12 AD, and again restored in 284 by Diocletian. It had a rectangular layout, was slightly raised and had five naves, of which the central one was very wide. Still visible on the steps are engraved game boards, similar to our draughts. Still visible also are the remains of seven columns dating from the time of the emperor Diocletian, re-erected in the 1800s on high bases. At the top of each column was a statue, now lost.

ALTAR OF CAESAR Turning left out of the Basilica Julia is the so-called altar of Caesar, the remains of a temple ordered by the emperor Augustus in 29 BC to render homage to his predecessor. Here Caesar - killed in an attack organised by conspirators led by Brutus and Cassius outside the Curia of Pompey, near the modern Teatro Argentina - was cremated on the Ides (15th) of March 44 BC. Even today, Romans and tourists come to place flowers inside the monument as a sign of respect towards the great politician and solider.

TEMPLE OF CASTOR AND POLLUX To the right of Caesar's altar are the ruins of the temple of Castor and Pollux, or the Dioscuri, rebuilt over a pre-existing temple in the 2C AD. All that is left today are three great columns in the Corinthian style. The monument was raised to recall the Battle of Lake Regillus, which took place on the Alban Hills near Rome in 499 BC and in which, according to tradition, the Romans were able to defeat the Latin peoples thanks to the help of the divine twins on horseback, and so begin their expansion into the Lazio region. Under the podium were two small rooms perhaps used as the office of weights and measures.

SANTA MARIA ANTIQUA AND THE FOUNTAIN OF JUTURNA Behind the temple of Castor and Pollux, in the direction of the slopes of the Palatine Hill, are certain imposing buildings from the time of Domitian. These include a great hall with semicircular niches in the walls (considered by some scholars to be a school founded by Augustus) and, behind that, the so-called *Horrea* (storehouses) of Agrippa, dating from the 1C BC. Within this complex of buildings just under the lee of the Palatine Hill is the small church Santa Maria Antiqua which, founded in the 4C, provides evidence of the continuity of life in the Forum even in the early Middle Ages. Inside the church, which can be visited only with special permission, are some of the oldest frescoes in Rome, including a *Crucifixion* from the 8C in which Christ is shown wearing a tunic, a trait typical of Byzantine iconography. It is likely that the painting was done by an artist from the East.

Near the church is the so-called *Lacus Iuturnae*, a fountain dedicated to Juturna, an ancient Latin divinity associated with the presence of water. Nearby is a well-proportioned classical aedicule with Corinthian capitals, rebuilt at the beginning of the 2C AD under the emperor Trajan.

Going back towards the altar of Caesar is a triple arch dedicated to Augustus' victory over Cleopatra, queen of Egypt. Built in 29 AD, a few remains of the foundations are still visible.

TEMPLE OF VESTA Passing the remains of the Arch of Augustus, on the left are traces of the old Regia, the residence of the kings in ancient times, restored at the end of the 1C BC. To the right are the remains of the temple of Vesta, reconstructed by Septimius Severus

Temple of Vesta

(193-211) over a pre-existing building. It is a circular structure with Corinthian columns. It was rebuilt and restored around 1930.

ATRIUM VESTAE

To the left is the famous House of the Vestals, the priestesses whose job it was to guard the sacred flame in the temple of Vesta. The house was rebuilt under the emperor Hadrian (117-138). Around a rectangular atrium, with an octagonal flowerbed dating from the 4C, were the rooms of the Vestals, girls from the noble families of Rome. Six in number, they remained in office for 30 years during which time they made vows of absolute chastity. If they broke the vow they were condemned to be buried alive! For the first ten years the girls received instruction, for the following ten they acted as priestesses, for the final ten they instructed novices.

TEMPLE OF ANTONINUS AND FAUSTINA

Facing onto the via Sacra, it was ordered by the emperor Antoninus Pius (138-161) to commemorate his wife Faustina who died in 148. After his death the Roman Senate extended the dedication to include Antoninus. It has splendid columns in grey marble, with Corinthian capitals unfortunately much deteriorated. The front of the temple has been well conserved because in the 11C it was transformed into a church (San Lorenzo in Miranda), this however was dismantled in 1536. In 1602 it was again turned into a church, still dedicated to San Lorenzo in Miranda, leaving the old pronaos intact.

To the right of the temple are the ruins of an archaic burial ground. Excavations carried out in the 1950s by the archaeologist Giacomo Boni brought to light around 40 plots for both buried and cremated remains dating back to the 10-7C BC, confirming the fact that the Forum once served as a cemetery. Part of the finds are today on display in the *Antiquarium*.

House of the Vestals

Temple of Antoninus and Faustina

Temple of Romulus

TEMPLE OF ROMULUS Next to the ancient necropolis is the building known as the temple of Romulus, so-called, perhaps, because dedicated to the emperor Maxentius' son Romulus who died young in 309 AD. It has an entrance characterised by a concave wall and a round hall, mutually reinforcing curves typical of a 4C AD style known as the "Baroque of late antiquity" because it anticipated by some twelve centuries the 17C architecture of Bernini and Borromini. From the 4C, the temple was transformed into the basilica of Santi Cosma e Damiano.

BASILICA OF MAXENTIUS Further along the via Sacra, past a small mediaeval portico on the left, and the ruins of a temple dedicated to the god Bacchus on the right, are the imposing remains of the basilica of Maxentius and Constantine. The building, of enormous proportions and with three naves, was built by order of the emperor Maxentius (306-312). The entrance, unlike most basilicas of antiquity, was on the shortest side. At the end was an apse.

The central nave was covered with cross vaults, and the aisles with barrel vaults embellished with octagonal coffers. The emperor Constantine (306-337) completed the building, moving the entrance from the shortest side to the longest and constructing a new apse.

In that apse was a colossal statue of the emperor, 12 metres high, the remains of which may be seen in Palazzo dei Conservatori on the Capitoline Hill. A column from the basilica stands today in the middle of the square of St. Mary Major.

Unfortunately, all that remains of this magnificent building are the barrel vaults of the side aisles and the buttresses of the cross vaults, however we can imagine the magnificent interior, perhaps reaching as much as 35 metres in height.

Here the Romans' engineering skills touched a high point of technical proficiency.

Returning to the via Sacra, in a recently excavated area on the

Basilica of Maxentius

Arch of Titus

right are the *Horrea* (storehouses) of Vespasian and, in a corner near the Arch of Titus, the remains of a private *domus* (house).
A little further along on the left is the *Antiquarium* of the Forum, located inside the mediaeval monastery of Santa Francesca Romana with its beautiful 15C cloister. On display there, under old and bare glass cases, are many exhibits, mostly from the archaic period.

ARCH OF TITUS This arch, with a single opening, is the work of the emperor Domitian. He ordered it to be built, as the inscription on the attic level recalls, to commemorate the deeds of his brother Titus in Palestine, who conquered Jerusalem bringing its treasure and a multitude of slaves to Rome.
The reliefs on the interior walls, illustrating the moment of Titus' triumphal march, are of particular importance, beautiful sculptures that suggest the Romans had a knowledge of perspective. Composite capitals (Ionic and Corinthian) are used here for the first time.
In the Middle Ages, the arch was incorporated into the fortress of the Frangipane family. Like the Coliseum, it was restored in the early 19C, first by the architect Raffaele Stern and then by Giuseppe Valadier, who rebuilt the missing parts with "simplified" forms using travertine rather than the marble of the original. This restoration has been the subject of much discussion, considered by some scholars as groundbreakingly modern because it managed to recompose the original outline while differentiating the old from the new, and by others as a mediocre effort, dictated only by the need to use materials less costly than marble. Among the critics was the great novelist Stendhal, who considered the restoration "a true calamity of modern times".

Temple of Venus

TEMPLE OF VENUS Built during the reign of Hadrian (117-138), but restored at the beginning of the 4C, it was one of the largest temples of antiquity. It had two cellae and two apses positioned back-to-back, of which one is now incorporated into the *Antiquarium*. All that remains standing are a number of Egyptian columns of grey granite. The foundation wall of the terrace on which the temple stands is visible from the square in front of the Coliseum, and from via dei Fori Imperiali.

PALATINE

The Palatine (the name probably derives from *palatium*, palace) was, together with the Capitoline, the most important hill in ancient Rome because, according to tradition, it was here that the city had its origins. Inhabited from the period of prehistory, it initially had three summits: the *Germalus* facing towards the Capitoline, the *Palatium* overlooking the Circus Maximus, and the *Velia* towards the Coliseum. The hill's fame, however, is due to Romulus the mythical first king of Rome who, according to tradition, having been raised in a cave overlooking the *Velabrum* or the Circus Maximus, traced the outline of the ancient city in the 8C BC. In the last two centuries of the Republic, the Palatine became the site of important temples to such divinities as Magna Mater and Apollo, and dwelling place of famous politicians like Cicero, Hortensius, Agrippa and Mark Antony. From the time of Augustus (27 BC-14 AD) onwards, patrician families and emperors chose it as their place of residence, sometimes modifying existing buildings. Tiberius (14-37), Caligula (37-41), Claudius (41-54), Nero (54-68) - who after the fire of 64 extended his palace to cover the Oppian and the Esquiline and Caelian Hills - Domitian and, finally, Spetimius Severus (193-211) all built huge and imposing places, creating a complex stratification still visible today though sometimes difficult to decipher.
Following the emperor Heliogabalus (218-222), who built the terrace overlooking the Coliseum, the Palatine went through a period of abandonment. The emperor Diocletian (284-305) chose not to live there, building his palace at Spalato in Dalmatia, and in the year

330 Constantine transferred the capital from Rome to Byzantium (Constantinople), a city he completely restructured. The barbarian kings Odoacer and Theodoric (5-6C) did install themselves on the hill, but once Ravenna became the capital of the Roman empire of the West in 402, a sharper and more rapid decline set in. During the Middle Ages, churches such as Santa Maria Antiqua and San Sebastiano sprang up at the edge of the hill, and convents were built over earlier ruins. In the 11C and 12C it was occupied by the Frangipane family and during the Renaissance it was used as a marble quarry. At the end of the 16C, the Farnese family established their dwelling on the Palatine, building a magnificent villa with splendid gardens and terraces, the so-called *Orti Farnesiani* or Farnese Gardens of which the few remains still visible today are on the side of the hill facing the Forum. These include a nymphaeum known as *della pioggia* (of the rain) and the Aviary, which lacks, however, its original covering. The original entrance to the gardens has been moved to via di San Gregorio.

The first archaeological excavations, aiming to uncover the original Roman layout of the area, began in the early 1700s and continued throughout the 1800s, especially after Rome was annexed to the Kingdom of Italy in 1870. Further important excavations took place in the 1950s, which led to the discovery of the so-called House of Romulus, apparently confirming the truth of the tradition concerning the foundation of the city.

House of Romulus

HOUSE OF ROMULUS To visit the Palatine Hill as far as possible in chronological order, the first thing to see is the so called House of Romulus. The "house" is, in fact, the remains of three huts dating back to the 8C BC. They were brought to light by excavations in 1948 and confirm the existence of a village on this hill in archaic times. The finds, protected under tin roofs, consist of holes and channels dug into the tufa; the holes were used to fix wooden poles that held up the walls, most likely of mud, the channels to carry away the rainwater that fell around the little huts.

No trace has been found of the Lupercal, the cave in which, according to legend, Romulus and Remus were raised and which supposedly lies on the southwest slopes of the Palatine

Temple of Cybele

TEMPLE OF CYBELE Near the House of Romulus are the remains of the temple of Cybele, a goddess of Asia Minor and patroness of fertility. In the Roman world she was also known as Magna Mater. Her cult was introduced to Rome during the Second Punic War. According to tradition, a ship brought a black stone containing an image of the goddess from Asia Minor to Rome. The temple, on a podium with a cella and six columns at the front, was completed in 191 BC. It was reconstructed on a number of occasions, the last being under Augustus in 3 AD. A statue discovered inside is now on display in the Palatine Museum.

HOUSE OF LIVIA Of particular interest is the so-called "House of Livia", made up of three rooms slightly below ground level because the hill here originally sloped away steeply. It has splendid frescoes depicting naturalistic scenes, now removed from the walls to protect them from damp.

The name of the house derives from the letters IVLIA AVG(usta), found engraved on a pipe in the central room. This led researchers to believe that the owner was the wife of Augustus, who lived here in what was a wing of the palace created by amalgamating earlier buildings.

House of Livia

DOMUS TIBERIANA In the direction of the Roman Forum are the few visible remains of the *Domus Tiberiana*, the residence of the emperor Tiberius, later extended by Caligula and Nero. All that remains today are the foundation walls but we must imagine it as an enormous palace towering over the Palatine Hill and facing out over the Forum. It

Domus Tiberiana

was on these ruins that, in the second half of the 16C, cardinal Alessandro Farnese ordered the building of his own sumptuous villa, entrusting the project to the architect Vignola. The gardens visible today were laid out in the mid 19C. Some architects believe that the *Domus Tiberiana* was part of the immense *Domus Aurea*, the famous residence of the emperor Nero, which according to the sources stretched from the Palatine Hill to the Oppian and perhaps even as far as the Esquiline, where the basilica of St. Mary Major stands today. Of particular interest is the Cryptopoticus, the long barrel-vaulted corridor that linked the various wings of the building.

PALACE OF DOMITIAN: DOMUS FLAVIA, DOMUS

AUGUSTANA AND THE STADIUM In the middle of the Palatine Hill is the great palace built by the emperor Domitian, which filled what had previously been a fairly deep valley between the two summits of the *Germalus* and the *Palatium*. The building was divided into a public area, the *Domus Flavia*, and a private area, the *Domus Augustana*, and had a number of courtyards, including one with an octagonal fountain (now largely rebuilt) and another with a basin. There is also a splendid elliptical nymphaeum with niches that once contained statues. The same emperor also built the stadium, 160 metres long and 50 wide of which the semicircular tribune is still visible on the far wall. The traces of an oval wall inside the stadium are

Domus Flavia

all that remains of an enclosure built by order of the emperor Theodoric in the early 6C.

Looking towards the Circus Maximus, to the right of Domitian's Palace, are a number of constructions known as the *Paedagogium* (perhaps a school for servants of the imperial court) and the *Schola Praeconum* (headquarters of the corps of heralds). To the left is the extension built by Septimius Severus on the *Domus Augustana*, and the baths of Septimius and of Maxentius. The arched foundation walls of the *Domus Augustana* are what characterise the extraordinary view of the Palatine Hill as seen from the Circus Maximus. Finally, on a site near what today is the intersection of via di San Gregorio and via dei Cerchi was a monumental fountain, the *Septizonium* or *Septizodium* built by order of Septimius Severus. Its remains, still visible on old engravings, were finally removed by order of Pope Sixtus V. Today a line of cypress trees marks the exact location.

Domus Augustana, courtyard

AULA OF ISIS In the north corner of the *Domus Flavia*, bereath the so-called basilica, is the Aula of Isis which has recently been reopened to the public. It is a small room with an apse dating back to the early years of the reign of Augustus (circa 20 BC). Originally covered in frescoes in the "second style" of Pompeian painting (i.e., with architectural elements shown in perspective), these have now been detached and are on display in the *Loggetta Mattei*. They depict episodes connected with the Egyptian divinity Isis, whose cult became widespread in Rome following the conquest of Egypt in 31 BC. The Aula of Isis was first discovered in 1724 but then reinterred, to be unearthed again in 1912.

HOUSE OF THE GRIFFINS Located under the so-called Lararium (the altar dedicated to the divinities that protected the home) of the *Domus Flavia*, the House of the Griffins is a small building from the Republican age over which the Palace of Domitian was later built. It has splendid frescoes - now detached, also in the "second style" and dating from the late 1C BC - depicting *griffins*, mythological winged beasts with goats' heads and lions' bodies.

PALATINE MUSEUM The Palatine Museum is located in the former convent of the Visitation, which was restructured to accommodate the museum in 1937. It contains exhibits covering the period from prehistory to the 4C AD, with many fragments of Greek originals as well as Roman copies of the works of Skopas and Praxiteles. The ground floor - where ruins from Domitian's imperial palace, over which the convent was built, are still visible - has exhibits of different periods: from the Palaeolithic (40,000 BC, proof of just how long the Palatine Hill has been inhabited) to the Republican age (late 1C BC). Of particular interest, in Room 2, are the porcelain and funerary urns from the Iron Age (9-8C BC), and the reconstruction of ancient huts from the earliest period of Rome. Room 4 contains painted terracotta masks from the Republican period. On the first floor, Room 5 has artefacts from the age of Augustus (late 1C BC to early 1C AD), including a splendid Corinthian capital and three *hermae* of female figures in black Egyptian marble taken, in all probability, from the temple of Apollo Palatino (*hermae* were stone pillars normally positioned at crossroads to protect wayfarers). Room 6 has fragments removed from the *Domus Transitoria*, and beautifully made panels of marble intarsia with figurative and stylised motifs. Finally, Room 9 contains monumental sculptures from the imperial *Domus*. Coming out of the museum, to the left is a small building from the 16C known as the *Casino Farnese*.

Palatine Museum

Loggetta
Mattei

LOGGETTA MATTEI The *Loggetta* was once part of a large villa built by a noble family around the year 1520 over the remains of Domitian's private residence, the *Domus Augustana*. It was subsequently modified by Paolo Mattei, who bought the property in 1561, and by his heirs. Having changed hands many times, in the mid 19C the villa became part of a convent of nuns, and in 1906 it passed to the Italian State. The frescoes, some of which have been detached and now belong to the Metropolitan Museum of New York which has returned them on loan, are by Baldassarre Peruzzi, a sophisticated painter and architect from Siena, and his pupils. The *loggetta* also contains paintings from the Aula of Isis.

AQUA CLAUDIA The majestic arches in via di San Gregorio are the final stage of an extension ordered by the emperor Domitian to connect his palace to the Aqua Claudia, an aqueduct built by Claudius in the mid 1C AD.

Aqua Claudia

BATHS OF HELIOGABALUS Commissioned by the emperor Heliogabalus (218-222) not far from the great temple of the Sun, the baths are on the side of the hill overlooking the Coliseum, along the last stage of the via Sacra.

PORTAL OF THE FARNESE GARDENS This portal, by the 16C architect Vignola, was reassembled here in 1955. Originally, it constituted the monumental entrance, on the Forum side, to the so-called Farnese Gardens, the magnificent villa built in the mid 16C by cardinal Alessandro Farnese, nephew of Pope Paul III. The lower part, which includes pilasters and columns, is of ashlar blocks, while the upper has an arched opening flanked by two *hermae* (pilasters with a sculpted half-bust female figure); the lily, symbol of the Farnese family, is much in evidence.

Portal of the Farnese Gardens

SAN SEBASTIANO AND SAN BONAVENTURA Outside the enclosure of the Palatine excavations, along via di San Bonaventura, are two small churches.
The first, San Sebastiano, near the great temple to the Egyptian Sun god built by the emperor Heliogabalus, dates from the 10C but was restored in the 1600s; the second is the church of San Bonaventura, from the late 17C.

CIRCUS MAXIMUS

The biggest stadium in Rome, whence its name, the Circus Maximus was used to stage chariot races. Currently it is an open field, and part of it has yet to be excavated. According to tradition it was built at the time of the Etruscan kings (7C BC), but was reconstructed and restored on numerous occasions, during both the Republican and Imperial periods. It reached its largest dimensions under the emperor Trajan at the beginning of the 2C when it was more than 600 metres long, almost 200 wide and had space to accommodate an estimated 300,000 spectators. The central *spina* around which the chariots raced is 340 metres long and was adorned with statues, aedicules and little shrines. In 10 AD Augustus ordered an Egyptian obelisk taken from Heliopolis to be placed there, and in the 4C the emperor Constantius II ordered the erection of another obelisk from Thebes. Both were removed by order of Pope Sixtus V in 1587 and positioned, respectively, in piazza del

Popolo and in the square of St. John Lateran.

The two long straight sides were very much as they still appear today, while only one of the ends, the one facing piazza di Porta Capena, was curved. The imperial box was on the Palatine side and at the non-curved end were the *carceres* (gates), which opened to let the chariots in.

Externally, the façade had three tiers of arches. At the curved end is a mediaeval building that was once part of the fortress built by the Frangipane family. In piazzale Ugo La Malfa is the 1949 *monument to Giuseppe Mazzini*, one of the most important figures of the *Risorgimento*, the period of Italian unification. This square affords a magnificent view over the Circus Maximus and the Palatine Hill, with the ruins of the *Domus Augustana* in the centre, and the palace of Septimius Severus to the right. The Baroque façade visible on the lower left covers part of the church of Sant'Anastasia.

COLISEUM

The biggest and most famous amphitheatre of the Roman world. Its name comes from a colossal gilded-bronze statue of the emperor Nero, some 32 metres high, which occupied the site today marked by the small garden with trees in front of the entrance to the underground railway.

Construction work began in the year 72 AD under the emperor Vespasian who, according to tradition, wanted to build a great arena to stage games in the place where his predecessor Nero (despised by the Romans for having caused the great fire of the city in 64) had created an artificial lake to ornament his imperial palace, the *Domus Aurea*. Building work was completed under the emperor Titus, and the Coliseum was opened to the public in the year 80 AD. Titus' successor, Domitian, put on the final touches, positioning bronze shields around the top and, perhaps, adding the underground vaults.

The Coliseum is an oval with a maximum diameter of 188 metres, a minimum diameter of 156 metres, and a circumference 527 metres. Its outer walls reach a height of 50 metres, and it has been calculated that the building could hold up to 50,000 spectators. The outer ring-wall of travertine from Tivoli encloses a raised cavea supported on pillars and arches. The surface of the arena must have been made

of wood, now lost. The underground passageways were fitted with a system of pulleys and narrow cages to enclose gladiators and wild beasts and raise them into the arena. Originally, the Coliseum had 80 arches containing statues, overlaid in three tiers and separated by cornices. The numerous irregular holes visible in the travertine are due to the removal, during the Middle Ages and the Renaissance, of the lead and iron that held the various blocks together. The arches, resting on pillars with corbels, are flanked by semi-columns of the Tuscan Order on the first level, the Ionic Order on the second, and the Corinthian Order on the third. Above the third level, Corinthian pilaster strips adorn a closed attic storey, with windows at intervals. It is probable that the sections of wall without windows were hung with bronze shields ordered to be put there, tradition holds, by Domititan. About two thirds of the way up the wall of the attic storey is a series of projecting corbels, most of them still in place, upon which rested the posts used to support the *velarium* (a vast segmented awning of silk or linen that covered the seats, manoeuvred by a team of 100 sailors from the port of Misenum near Pozzuoli). The support posts were held in place by passing through holes in a high cornice surrounding top of the building.

The cavea was divided into five horizontal sections. The first four had marble steps upon which the male spectators would sit in an order reflecting their social rank (the lowest section for senators, the next for the *equites* (knights), etc., the plebeians at the top). The fifth order, of wood under a portico, was for the women. The numbered accessways, known as *vomitoria*, enabled spectators to enter and leave the building rapidly. The galleries and corridors, covered with cross vaults, were decorated with stuccowork and frescoes. Entrance to see the spectacles was free, and the games were offered by the emperors until the 5C AD. As for the *naumachiae* (naval battles), which according to some sources were already being held in the Coliseum during the time of Vespasian and Domitian, no trace of the structures necessary for such events has been found.

RECONSTRUCTION

1 Outer ring in travertine
2 Entrance
3 Imperial entrance
4 Semi-columns of the Tuscan Order
5 Semi-columns of the Ionic Order
6 Semi-columns of the Corinthian Order
7 Corinthian pilaster strips
8 Shields hung by order of the emperor Domitian
9 Vomitorium
10 Velarium

Drawing by Piero Renzulli

10

3

Coliseum, interior

Coliseum, detail of Stern's restoration

The transformation of the Coliseum began in 438 when games with gladiators were banned. Finally, in 523, under Theodoric, all the games came to an end and the building began to decline. In the 11C, it was incorporated into the fortress of the Frangipane family, and in the mid 13C became the property of the Church.

In 1349, an earthquake caused the collapse of the side facing the Caelian Hill. The amphitheatre then became a marble quarry, stone from which was used to construct many Renaissance and Baroque buildings in Rome such as Palazzo Farnese, Palazzo Barberini, and Palazzo della Cancelleria.

Sixtus V (1585-1590) planned to use it as a wool factory, and Pope Benedict XIV (1740-1758) consecrated it to the memory of Christian martyrs, none of whom however were ever killed there.

Following a great earthquake in 1806, Pope Pius VII (1800-1823) ordered the building be restored. The project was undertaken by the architect Raffaele Stern who planned and built the great buttress on the eastern side and the brick walls to support the unstable arches, almost an attempt to stop time. It is not known whether the use of brick, in contrast with the original travertine, was to differentiate the original from the restoration, or simply to save on building costs.

Work continued under Pope Leo XII (1823-1829), supervised by Giuseppe Valadier who built the famous buttress of the other side, facing via dei Fori Imperiali. He used the same system as his predecessor, but the fame of his intervention quite obscured that of Stern. He used brick arches, that decrease in number with height. The work was completed in 1826, when the inscription stone with the date was fixed in place.

The restoration of the Coliseum was completed under Pope Pius IX (Giovanni Maria Mastai Ferretti 1846-1878), between 1846 and 1852, when the architect Canina completed the internal ring of arches on the west side.

Meta Sudans

META SUDANS The name derives from the Latin (*meta*, a conical form and *sudans*, gushing). It was a large Roman fountain from the late 1C BC in the form of a flat-topped cone, 18 metres high and 16 metres wide at the base, located between the Coliseum and the Arch of Constantine. It appears in old photographs, and was demolished in 1936 in order to pave the area linking via dei Fori Imperiali with the *Passeggiata Archeologica*.

Recent excavations by the *Soprintendenza* have uncovered the base of the fountain.

ARCH OF CONSTANTINE The arch was on the via Triumpha-
lis, along which victorious armies would march in parade. It has three
openings and is about 25 metres high. According to tradition, it was
ordered by the emperor Constantine to celebrate his victory over Maxentius at the Battle of the Milvian Bridge in 312 following which, with
the Edict of Milan in 313, he granted freedom of worship to Christians.
However, recent painstaking studies undertaken by the *Soprintendenza
Archeologica di Roma* have revealed the existence of an earlier structure extending from the base to the cornice, built at the time of Trajan
(98-117) or Hadrian (117-138), and that Constantine simply reused,
adding the attic storey with the inscription, as well as the reliefs, which
were taken from 2C monuments.

Stylistically speaking, the sculptures from the time of Trajan and Hadrian
(especially the medallions), are elegant, well proportioned and in harmo-
ny with the surroundings; those from the time of Antoninus Pius (138-
161) and of Marcus Aurelius (161-180) are characterised by a gradual
adjustment of the depth, with figures tending to occupy all the space
available; however, by Constantine's day the depictions are completely
out of proportion, the figures have large heads and the architectural
elements are out of scale. This is particularly noticeable on the panel
in which the emperor appears seated in the centre, raised above his
subjects and with the dignitaries of his court grouped together in an
enclosure. The deformation of the image had become a fait accompli
and it was not until the 13C that it reacquired volume and form.

Arch of Constantine

IMPERIAL FORA

The Imperial Fora of ancient Rome were a constellation of great squares, temples and commemorative monuments. It was in the Imperial Fora, and in the older Roman Forum, that the main political, judicial, religious and civil functions of the city were located throughout the Imperial age.

The Fora were built by Julius Caesar and by the emperors who came after him, from 46 BC to the beginning of the 2C AD, one perpendicular to the other so as to form a unitary whole. Today, unfortunately, it is no longer possible to get an overall picture because via dei Fori Imperiali has interrupted the continuity of the original layout.

VIA DEI FORI IMPERIALI After having been abandoned for centuries, the Republican and Imperial Fora began to be rediscovered and ex-

cavated, particularly in the middle and at the end of the 1800s. However, it was only at the beginning of last century that many of the ruins visible today were finally brought to light. Via dei Fori Imperiali (originally called via dell'Impero), designed in 1925 at the direct request of Mussolini, was inaugurated in 1932.

Eight hundred and fifty metres long, the road was conceived to meet the anti-historical requirement of creating a monumental and imposing back-drop for parades, and buried under a thick layer of tar the remains of an entire neighbourhood that had risen up during the Middle Ages and the Renaissance. However, more than anything else, it broke what remained of the ancient unity of the Fora.

A number of town planners have been seeking to reunite the Fora, thus restoring their lost unity and creating the world's largest archaeological park, stretching from piazza Venezia to the via Appia. But this fascinating

Forum of Caesar

project, if realised, would require a great deal of time because it would be necessary to divert the huge amount of traffic that uses via dei Fori Imperiali today.

FORUM OF JULIUS CAESAR The first of the monumental Fora, its construction was ordered by the conqueror of the Gauls in order to increase the amount of public space available, evidently insufficient for a city population that had already reached one million. Inaugurated in 46 BC, it was composed of a rectangular square surrounded by a portico. At one end was a temple of archetypal form (raised on a podium with a stairway leading to the front entrance, pronaos and a single cella), dedicated to the goddess Venus from whom, by her son Aeneas, Caesar claimed to descend. All that remains of the square is the lefthand corner with two-storey *tabernae* (shops) and part of the base of the temple with three raised columns. The part in brickwork is, of course, a restoration, while the bronze statue of the emperor is a copy.

Forum of Augustus

FORUM OF AUGUSTUS Built by the first emperor of Rome (27 BC - 14 AD), according to the ancient sources it was inaugurated in 2 AD. What remains today is on the right of via dei Fori Imperiali as one looks towards piazza Venezia. It was positioned perpendicularly with respect to Caesar's Forum and also had a rectangular square with a portico and a temple at one end. This temple, larger than Caesar's but with the same characteristics, was dedicated to Mars Ultor (the avenger) whom Augustus wished to thank for his victory over Caesar's assassins, and to Venus, considered by the emperor as his progenitrix.

On each side of the square was a semicircular niche with statues of *Aeneas* in one and *Romulus* in the other, founders of the Roman race. A wall of blocks of tufa behind the temple (note the outline of the roof) divided the Forum from the Suburra, the famous popular neighbourhood of ancient Rome consisting mostly of wooden houses and which, for this reason, often went up in flames. In front of the temple was a four-horse chariot with a statue of *Augustus*.

FORUM OF VESPASIAN The next Forum along, after that of Augustus, is due to Vespasian (69-79). Almost completely buried under via dei Fori Imperiali and via Cavour, it has recently been the subject of research and investigations to examine its original structure. It had a great temple known as the temple of Peace containing spoils from the war prosecuted by Vespasian's son Titus (79-81) against the Jews in Palestine.

In this Forum, closed at one end by a wall that is today part of the basilica of Santi Cosma e Damiano (to the right of the entrance), was the *Forma Urbis*, an extraordinary marble "map" of Rome dating from the early years of the 3C AD (under the Severan dynasty), of which some fragments have been recomposed inside the Capitoline Museums.

FORUM OF NERVA Little remains of this Forum, ordered by Domitian (81-96) and completed by Nerva (96-98). It had the form of a very elongated rectangle and served to link together the three Fora mentioned above; for this reason it was also known as the Transitional Forum.

A street called the *Argiletum* crossed the Forum of Nerva, linking it to the Republican Forum and to the Suburra. It was dominated by a temple dedicated to Minerva, still partly visible in Renaissance drawings. All that remains today are two columns from the side enclosure, known by Romans as the *colonnacce*, surmounted by a frieze showing female labours and at the top the goddess Minerva, protectress of craftsmen.

When the Fora were excavated and restructured, it proved possible to create a pedestrian link between the two parts separated by via dei Fori Imperiali, by using the famous *chiavicone*, a large drainage pipe from the late 16C, which had been built over the old Roman and mediaeval remains.

FORUM OF TRAJAN The last and most complex of the Imperial Fora is that of Trajan (98-117), access to which is through the Markets of Trajan. It was probably the work of Apollodorus of Damascus, one of the greatest architects of the age, and was made up of a series of adjacent buildings and spaces divided as follows: a large porticoed square with exedrae on two sides and a large equestrian monument of Trajan in the middle, now lost; a basilica known as Ulpia (from Ulpius, one of the emperor's names), of which the outline with five naves and two side apses is still visible; two libraries, according to sources

Forum of Trajan and Trajan's Column

one Greek and one Latin, enclosing a small space in the centre of which was Trajan's Column. The column has an internal staircase and its spiral frieze depicts the emperor's wars in Dacia, modern-day Romania. The Forum of Trajan also contained an enclosure beyond which there was, perhaps, a temple dedicated to the deified emperor built by his successor Hadrian (117-138); however, recent studies tend to place this temple on the other side of the forum, towards the porticoed square and adjoining the Forum of Augustus. Above, on the slopes of the Quirinal Hill, are the Markets of Trajan which complete the magnificent panorama.

Trajan's Column, detail

Trajan's Column, extremely well preserved, evokes the form of a Roman *volumen* (a length of parchment rolled around a rod) and was perhaps positioned between the two libraries to facilitate its being "read". Resting on a base that contained the funerary urns of the emperor and his wife, the column is made up of blocks of marble laid one over the other without cement. It is 100 Roman feet (29.78 metres) high, from the base up to and including the Doric capital. At the top was a statue of *Trajan* replaced in 1585, by order of Pope Sixtus V, with of *St. Peter* who, keys in hand, looks towards the basilica that bears his name, then still under construction. It was part of the spirit of that age to "Christianise" pagan buildings.

The frieze gets higher as it winds upwards to facilitate its being viewed, and depicts, with more than 2500 figures, the two wars undertaken by Trajan in Dacia (the first from 101 to 102, the second from 105 to 107). The two cycles are interrupted at the 12th level on the side facing the churches by a famous *winged victory* (much reproduced in mediaeval and Renaissance works).

Some scholars have advanced the extremely plausible suggestion that in antiquity the column was painted. It is certain that it was covered in a layer of limewash, which has helped preserve it over time.

MARKETS OF TRAJAN Overlooking the forum are the famous Markets of Trajan, an extraordinary structure built in the lee of the Quirinal Hill. It had six levels of streets, one over the other and lined with *tabernae*, i.e., shops and storehouses. It is not known when construction began but the work is generally attributed to Trajan although it may have begun under Domitian. The architect was probably Apollodorus of Damascus, the same who built the Forum of Trajan. Nor is it known what exact purpose the market served, but it is nonetheless a striking fragment of Imperial Rome in which the excellent state of preservation of

Markets of Trajan

the urban fabric, despite restorations and missing portions, enables one to imagine a complex and intricate city, strangely "modern" and up-to-date.

The complex was discovered and first restored by the archaeologist Corrado Ricci (1926-1934).

In the Middle Ages, the Torre delle Milizie was built over the ruins of the market and, in the 15C, the House of the Knights of Rhodes.

SANTA FRANCESCA ROMANA In via dei Fori Imperiali, next

to the splendid walls perforated with what remains of the windows of the great basilica of Maxentius, are two churches built over ancient remains: Santa Francesca Romana and Santi Cosma e Damiano.

Santa Francesca Romana occupies part of the temple of Venus (2C AD). A church already existed on this site in the early Middle Ages, rebuilt in the 10C with the name of Santa Maria Nova, then restored in the 12C when the bell tower was erected, and altered again in the 13C. In 1440, with the burial in the crypt of Santa Francesca, a Roman widow and foundress of the Order of Oblates, the church took on its present name. It was restructured again during the Baroque with the addition of a white travertine façade completed in 1615.

Santa Francesca Romana

In the apse and over the altar are images of the Virgin Mary from the 12C, while the sacristy contains a rare example of painting on wood dating from the 6 or 7C.

On 9 May every year, many faithful drive to the church in order to have their cars blessed, as Santa Francesca is the patron saint of motorists.

SANTI COSMA E DAMIANO This church is dedicated to two

Syrian brothers, medical doctors and martyrs who perhaps died during the reign of Diocletian (284-305).

Built in 527 under Pope Felix IV (526-530) in part of the Forum of Vespasian, this church was also restructured with Baroque additions

Santi Cosma e Damiano

during the first half of the 1600s. It contains numerous examples of mediaeval art, very rare in Rome, such as the mosaic decorations from the 6C on the triumphal arch and the famous mosaic in the apse, dating from the 7C but much altered during the Baroque restorations. The apse mosaic shows Christ at the centre over a stream of red clouds (colour of fire and hence of hell) and blue clouds (colour of air and hence of Eden); around him are Sts. Peter, Paul Cosmas, Damian and Theodore, and Pope Felix IV (whose image was completely restored in 1660) holding a model of the church in his hand. At the bottom, beyond the Jordan River, are twelve sheep representing the Apostles, all facing towards Christ.

In the chapel facing the entrance is a fresco from the 8C showing the crucified Christ, clothed in the Byzantine style.

Another thing not to be missed in this church is the Neapolitan nativity scene from the 1700s (access is from via dei Fori Imperiali).

itinerary

PANTHEON

PANTHEON

Dedicated to all the gods, the Pantheon was one of the greatest temples of ancient Rome. It has been perfectly preserved down to our own times thanks to the fact that in the year 609 it was donated to Pope Boniface IV (608-615) by the Byzantine emperor Phocas and transformed into a Christian church with the name of Sancta Maria ad Martyres (St. Mary and Martyrs), becoming the fulcrum of the city throughout the Middle Ages, the Renaissance and the Baroque.

The current edifice was constructed by Hadrian (117-138) who completely rebuilt a pre-existing structure perhaps damaged by a fire. Two earlier temples, having the same dedication but with the entrance of the opposite side, had been erected by Augustus (27 BC -14 AD), and by Domitian (81-96), and it is precisely to the former of these two that the inscription on the architrave seems to refer: M. AGRIPPA L. F. COS. TERTIUM FECIT (Marcus Agrippa,

son of Lucius, consul for the third time, built this). The inscription was put in place by Hadrian to commemorate the original building The Pantheon has a deep pronaos with eight columns in the front rank, and a great circular hall commonly known as a "rotunda", covered with a dome. In Roman times, the area in front of the Pantheon was occupied by long and narrow rectangular square with porticoes, similar to the Forum of Nerva. The dome was not visible from the square, which was at least three metres lower than the current ground level, and access to the temple was via a stairway, now lost, that led into the pronaos. Thus, visitors of antiquity found themselves unexpectedly in the great circular hall, a "surprise effect" that later came to characterise Baroque architecture. Today it is the other way round, the square slopes slightly down towards the building and the circular wall of the rotunda is visible from the outside.

Pantheon, interior

Tomb of Raphael

Façade

The sixteen columns of the pronaos are all of Egyptian granite and are 12.5 metres high with a circumference of 4.5 metres. The front columns are grey, those behind pink. The Corinthian capitals are originals except for the outside three on the left side which were restored under Pope Urban VIII (Maffeo Barberini 1623-1644, note the bees, symbol of the Barberini family) and Pope Alexander VII (Fabio Chigi 1655-1667, his heraldic motif of six mounts and a star is also present). The façade was perhaps decorated with an eagle, the symbol of imperial power, while the holes are due to the removal of brackets that held sculptures to the wall. The ceiling of the pronaos had bronze decorations removed in 1623 to make Bernini's *baldachin* in St. Peter's. The great bronze door, probably original, was restored in the mid 16C.

The vast, majestic, rotunda is one of the finest masterpieces of Roman architecture. The perimeter wall, as much as six metres thick in places, has alternate rectangular and semicircular niches. In the 18C, the top section of the wall was decorated with false windows in stucco. The magnificent concrete dome reaches a height of 43.3 metres, a dimension equal to the diameter of the rotunda. The square coffers of diminishing size have both a decorative purpose (they were once adorned with bronze embellishments) and a functional one (they serve to reduce the mass of the cupola, diminishing its weight). The central eye, some nine metres wide, also serves to "eliminate" matter and lighten the dome; and it lets in not only the rainwater, which is carried away by the drain in the floor below, but also the light that illuminates the entire building. It is probable that this central opening helped to ensure the survival of the Pantheon because it was seen, as was typical during the Middle Ages, as the symbol of the divine presence descending to illuminate the faithful gathered below. The floor, in beautiful polychrome marble, is the original though much restored in the 19C.

Entering the Pantheon, the second chapel on the left contains the *tombs of Umberto I* (1878-1900), son of Victor Emanuel II, and *of Queen Margherita*, with the heraldic insignia of the House of Savoy. The third recess holds the *tomb of Raphael* (1483-1520) with the famous epitaph written by the humanist writer Pietro Bembo: ILLE

HIC EST RAPHAEL TIMVIT QVO SOSPITE VINCI RERVM MAGNA PARENS ET MORIENTE MORI (Here lies that Raphael who, living, great Nature feared he might outvie her works, and dying, fears herself may die).

In the first chapel on the right is a beautiful fresco of the *Annunciation* by Melozzo da Forlì. In the second is the *tomb of Victor Emanuel II*, first king of Italy and Father of the Country (1861-1878).

In the square in front of the Pantheon is a fountain, designed by Giacomo Della Porta (a pupil of Michelangelo) in 1578, surmounted by a small but well-proportioned obelisk 6.34 metres high. The obelisk comes from the ruins of the Temple of Isis that once stood on the site now occupied by the church of Santa Maria sopra Minerva, and was put here in 1711 by order of Clement XI (Giovanni Francesco Albani 1700-1721). The insignia are, of course, the pope's.

SANTA MARIA SOPRA MINERVA

The only Gothic-style church in Rome, though much altered over the centuries.

Building work began in 1280 to a design traditionally attributed to Fra Sisto Fiorentino and Fra Ristoro da Campi, both members of the Dominican Order and architects of the church of Santa Maria Novella in Florence. The building was erected over the remains of three Roman temples that were already being used as a church in the 8C. These were the temples of Minerva Calcidica (whence the name of the current church), and two other curious places of worship: the shrine of Isis and that of Serapis, oriental divinities of Egyptian origin that had an enthusiastic following in Rome. Remains from these two temples are on display in the Museum of Palazzo dei Conservatori at Campidoglio.

As was always the case with Gothic churches, building work lasted many years, also because the papacy abandoned Rome for Avignon, the so-called "Babylonian Captivity" of the Popes (1309-1377).

The façade dates from the 17C. It is similar to the mediaeval façade of Santa Maria in Aracoeli, and incorporates elegant 15C portals.

The interior was much restructured during the 17C and 18C, giving the church a Baroque appearance. However in the mid 19C it was decided to restore the Gothic original with a return to the mediaeval structures, except that the columns, vaults and walls were covered with new paintings in order to "enrich" the church and not leave it bare as it had been originally. The church has a nave and two side aisles, wide and slightly pointed ogee arches, and a transept and apse flanked by side chapels. In all, it expresses the ideology of the Dominican Order: that of creating a large unbroken space so as not to divide the faithful gathered in prayer with columns or pillars.

In a 15C structure under the main altar are the earthly remains of St. Catherine of Siena (died 1380), patron saint of Italy.

In the left-hand transept are: the *tomb of Fra Angelico* (1395-1655), the great painter and Domincian friar to whom the *Madonna and Child* in the adjoining Frangipane Chapel is attributed, and Michelangelo's *Risen Christ* (1521). In the right transept is the Carafa Chapel, decorated with frescoes by Filippino Lippi (1457-1504).

The choir dates from the mid 16C.

On the square in front of the church is a small obelisk, 4.5 metres high, from the temple of Isis. In 1667, during the papacy of Alexander VII (1655-1667), the obelisk was mounted on the back of a delightful little elephant. Affectionately known to Romans as *il*

Santa Maria sopra Minerva, central nave

Michelangelo, Risen Christ

Pulcino, the elephant was designed by the great Baroque architect and sculptor Gian Lorenzo Bernini, and crafted by Ercole Ferrata.

CHIESA DEL GESÙ

This church belongs to the Society of Jesus (Jesuits) founded in Rome in 1540 by St. Ignatius of Loyola, a Basque of noble origins who came to the eternal city in 1537. The start of building was beset with difficulties due to legal problems over the land, and the ceremony for laying the first stone had to be repeated three times: in 1551, in 1554, and again in 1568 twelve years after the death of the founder of the Order. The definitive design was by Jacopo Barozzi, known as Vignola from the name of his home town in the Emilia region, the trusted architect of cardinal Alessandro Farnese who funded the construction. The church Vignola designed has a single nave in order to give the faithful a greater sensation of being "gathered", three chapels to either side, a transept that protrudes only very slightly, and an apse. In 1571 he withdrew and the project was entrusted to architects of the Order, among them Giacomo Della Porta, a pupil of Michelangelo and of Vignola himself. To him is due the cupola on its octagonal drum and the façade of two orders enclosed within elegant volutes and a pediment. The church was consecrated in 1584. The interior decorations are remarkable, with the famous ceiling of 1679 by the Genovese painter Giovanni Battista Gaulli known as Baciccia, a masterpiece of Roman Baroque art depicting the *Triumph of the Name of Jesus*. The figures seem to be attracted upwards towards the heavens where a blinding light appears to cancel the materiality of the vault. The surrounding stucco statues are by Ercole Antonio Raggi and Leonardo Retti to designs by Gaulli himself. The decorations of the cupola, of the spandrels and of the apse are also by Gaulli. The magnificent chapel of St. Ignatius of Loyola in the left-hand transept was painted by Andrea Pozzo between 1696 and 1700.

Piazza della Minerva,
Ercole Ferrata, Pulcino

Chiesa del Gesù, façade

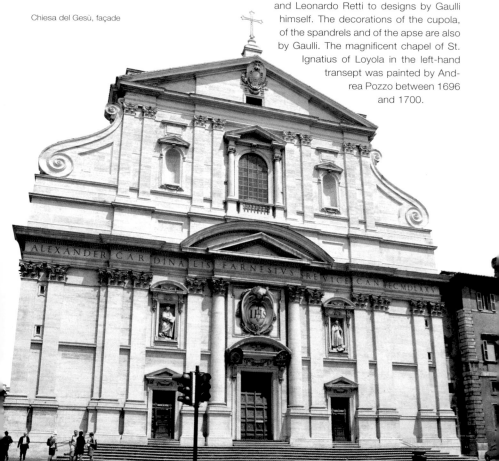

GALLERIA DORIA-PAMPHILJ This gallery is located in the palazzo of the same name, the entrance to which is in piazza del Collegio Romano.

Like Galleria Corsini, the interest of this museum, apart from the presence of a large number of valuable works of art, lies in the fact that the statues and paintings are arranged in a building designed by its original proprietors around the collections it was to contain, and thus furnished it with frescoes, sculptures and tapestries.

The collection, formed mostly in the mid 1600s by Camillo Pamphilj - the nephew of Pope Innocent X (1644-1655) - and by his wife Olimpia Aldobrandini, was arranged in its current form in the 18C. The frescoes on the ceiling of the Galleria degli Specchi, with the *Fall of the Giants* and the *Stories of Hercules* by the Bolognese painter Aureliano Milani, were completed in 1734, while the Sala Aldobrandini was restored with a modern roof and floor after 1956.

Galleria Doria-Pamphilj, Galleria degli Specchi

Among the many masterpieces it contains, mention must be made of works by: Raphael (*Double portrait*), Titian (*Salome with the head of John the Baptist*), Caravaggio (*Rest on the flight into Egypt*), Annibale Carracci (*Landscape with the flight into Egypt*), Velázquez (*Portrait of Innocent X*), Claude Lorrain (*Landscape with figures dancing*), and busts by Alessandro Algardi (*Benedetto Pamphilj*) and Gian Lorenzo Bernini (*Innocent X*).

Diego Rodriguez de Silva y Velázquez, portrait of Innocent X

Caravaggio, Rest on the flight into Egypt

Titian, Salome with the head of John the Baptist

Sant'Ignazio, façade

PIAZZA DI SANT'IGNAZIO This is one of the most beautiful squares in Rome, a typical late Baroque design of 1727-1728 by the architect Filippo Raguzzini, who counterpoised the pre-existing 17C façade of the church, cold and imposing, with buildings of rounded outlines, juxtaposing concave and convex curves, stuccowork and other graceful architectural features. The environment thus created is warm and intimate, almost a recreation of a theatrical stage in which the buildings are the wings, and in this way visitors' attention is naturally drawn into the complex and dynamic space. However, this solution did not find favour with the severe criticism of Neo-classicism, which established itself in Rome in the mid 18C and defined the buildings of Filippo Raguzzini as *canterani* (chests of drawers).

SANT'IGNAZIO This church, dedicated to the founder of the Society of Jesus (Jesuits) St. Ignatius who died in 1556, was planned by Orazio Grassi under the guidance of Carlo Maderno, the architect who designed the façade of St. Peter's. The building has a monumental classicist façade built between 1623 and 1650 and an interior layout typical of Jesuit churches: a single nave, three chapels to either side, transept and apse.

The ceiling over the nave is particularly interesting, a masterpiece of Roman Baroque art by the painter Andrea Pozzo, from the Trentino region of Italy. It is dated 1691-1694 and shows *St. Ignatius in Glory*, with allegories to the sides representing *Asia*, *Africa*, *Europe* and *America*, the continents on which the Jesuit Order was present. The painting creates the illusion of elongating the real architectural structures so as to create a very deep space inundated with light and populated by a myriad of figures that seem to be drawn upwards by an irresistible force. Imagination and technical ability in rendering perspective, typical Baroque traits, here touch their highpoint, and this work will remain an example of fine painting for many future generations of artists.

Also by Andrea Pozzo are the frescoes in the presbytery, in the apse and in the chapels facing the altar, as well as the false dome, which was painted first on canvas then applied to the ceiling.

PALAZZO AND PIAZZA DI MONTECITORIO The Palazzo di Montecitorio, since 1871 the seat of the Italian Chamber of Deputies, was designed in 1650 by Gian Lorenzo Bernini on the orders of Pope Innocent X (Giovanni Battista Pamphilj 1644-1655), but was only completed in 1694, by Carlo Fontana, after which it was used as a court of law (whence its 18C name of *Curia Innocenziana*). In 1870, when the capital of Italy was transferred from Florence to Rome, the palazzo was chosen to house the Chamber of Deputies. It was here that on 2 June 1946 the outcome was announced of the referendum that turned Italy from a monarchy to a republic.

At the centre of the square is one of Rome's thirteen Egyptian obelisks.

Palazzo di Montecitorio, façade

Entrance

About 22 metres high and made of red granite, it dates from the time of Psammetichus II (mid first millennium BC). It was brought to Rome by the emperor Augustus and turned into the gnomon (vertical pillar) of a sundial nearby, traces of which are still visible in excavations behind the church of San Lorenzo in Lucina. The obelisk was placed in front of Palazzo di Montecitorio in 1792, during the pontificate of Pope Pius VI (Angelo Braschi 1775-1799).

PIAZZA COLONNA The square is enclosed by Palazzo Wedekind (from the name of the banker who owned it in the late 19C) and, on the right, by the vast Palazzo Chigi, which was commissioned by the Aldobrandini family in 1562 to a design by Giacomo Della Porta. Completed in 1630, it became the property of the Chigi family in 1659 and in 1917 passed to the Italian State. Under Mussolini it became the seat of the Presidency of the Council of Ministers, a function it still has today. The fountain in the square is from 1570-1577 and was also built to a design by Della Porta.

At the centre of the square is the *Column of Marcus Aurelius* (161-180 AD), completed in 193 AD. On this column, as on Trajan's, the sculpted frieze winds upwards in 23 spirals, with reliefs recounting the emperor's wars against the Marcomanni (a Germanic people) and the Sarmatians (inhabitants of eastern Europe). Like *Trajan's Column* (early 2C AD), this one also remained standing throughout the Middle Ages, providing a stylistic model for mediaeval and Renaissance sculptors. It was restored by Domenico Fontana in 1588 under Pope Sixtus V who ordered a bronze statue of *St. Paul* be placed at the top to replace that of *Marcus Aurelius*, and at the base had a plaque affixed attributing the monument to the emperor Antoninus Pius (138-161). For this reason the column has often been confused with the *Colonna Antonina*, which was nearby but of which only the base remains, discovered in 1703 in via della Missione and kept today in the Vatican Museums.

The Y-shaped Galleria Alberto Sordi was built by the architect Marcello Piacentini between 1911 and 1922 to join two pre-existing buildings. The reference models used were the galleries of Milan and Naples. Recently restored, it has been dedicated to Alberto Sordi, the great Roman actor who died in 2003, star of such films as *Un Americano a Roma* and *Il Marchese del Grillo*.

Column of Marcus Aurelius, and aerial view of piazza Colonna

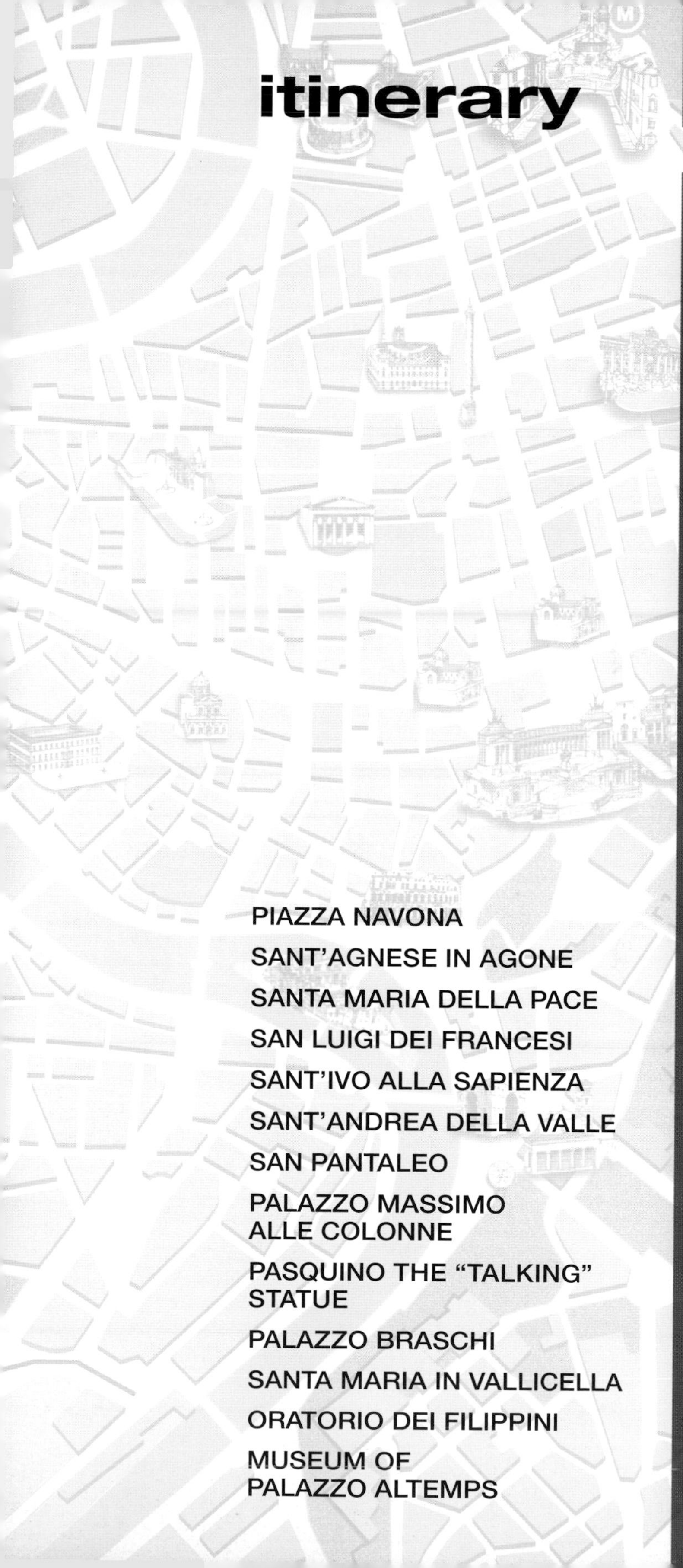

itinerary 4

PIAZZA NAVONA

- PIAZZA NAVONA
- SANT'AGNESE IN AGONE
- SANTA MARIA DELLA PACE
- SAN LUIGI DEI FRANCESI
- SANT'IVO ALLA SAPIENZA
- SANT'ANDREA DELLA VALLE
- SAN PANTALEO
- PALAZZO MASSIMO ALLE COLONNE
- PASQUINO THE "TALKING" STATUE
- PALAZZO BRASCHI
- SANTA MARIA IN VALLICELLA
- ORATORIO DEI FILIPPINI
- MUSEUM OF PALAZZO ALTEMPS

PIAZZA NAVONA

The buildings overlooking Piazza Navona, with the exception of the Baroque monuments and one or two earlier structures, largely date from the 19C. However the outline of the square, one of the most important in Rome, goes back to Roman times, being the perimeter of a stadium built by the emperor Domitian and inaugurated in 86 AD.

Excavations undertaken in various periods have shown that the buildings along the sides of the square were erected over two orders of sloped seating of an arena 240 metres long and almost 60 wide. Unlike the Circus Maximus, the stadium of Domititan did not have a central *spina* as it was not used for chariot races but for sporting events and games, *agones*, whence the Italian

word *agone*, meaning a struggle or contest, later corrupted into *navone* and then *navona*. Remains of the stadium unearthed in 1938 may still be seen in piazza di Tor Sanguigna. It is known that this structure, capable of holding 30,000 spectators, was still functioning in the 4C, and that it was destroyed in the 5C following the Barbarian invasions and the Gothic Wars. However, in the 11C it was again being used to stage sporting contests, and it came to be known as *Campus Agonis*.

According to tradition, it was here that Agnes, a young Roman Christian girl, suffered martyrdom in the 4C. An oratory was built on the site in the 8C, extended in 1123 by Pope Callistus II and later replaced, about the year 1650, with a great Baroque church.

Fontana del Nettuno

Fontana del Moro

Fontana del Moro,
detail

After centuries of partial abandonment, between the 13C and 14C, various noble families built their tower-residences in and around the square, such as the Torre Millina which still exists today. From the beginning of the 15C onwards, other buildings were constructed that absorbed the earlier ones.

The church of San Giacomo, once the Spanish national church in Rome, was built about the year 1450. Now called Nostra Signora del Sacro Cuore, it used to face towards the current corso del Rinascimento, but in the early 16C a new façade was built facing over piazza Navona. This façade was much altered at the end of the 19C. Unfortunately, the "clearance" of corso del Rinascimento in 1938 also destroyed the apse end of the building and the new façade, dating from the early 1940s, is very cold, hardly enlivened by a 16C portal that was once in piazza Navona itself.

In September 1477 the city market was moved from Campidoglio to piazza Navona, where fruit and vegetables were on sale daily and, on Wednesdays, other objects too (books, old clothes, silverware, shoes). The stalls at the north end of the square belonged to Jewish traders, those at the south end to Catholics. In 1485, under Pope Innocent VIII (Giovanni Battista Cybo 1484-1492), the area was resurfaced.

One of the most important buildings on piazza Navona lies at the south-east end. It was commissioned by Innocent X (Giovanni Battista Pamphilj 1644-1655) for his sister-in-law Olimpia Maidalchini, and since 1960 has housed the Brazilian embassy. It is said that the "talking" statue *Pasquino* commented the construction with the words: *Olimpia, nunc impia* (*Olim pia, nunc impia*, once pious, now impious).

Over the following centuries, piazza Navona was always one of the liveliest places in the city, a site for pageants and spectacles. Contrary to some suggestions mock naval battles were never held here, however from the 17C to the mid 19C on weekends in August the end of the square, then slightly curved, would be flooded to a depth of about 40 centimetres, enabling refreshing water games to take place, in which people participated with great enthusiasm.

In 1869 the market was moved to Campo de' Fiori, but every year between Christmas and Epiphany, the stalls return to piazza Navona for the sale of toys, sweets and figures for nativity scenes.

Fontana dei Fiumi,
detail of the Ganges

FONTANA DEL MORO The central basin and the marine figures were done in 1574 to a design of Giacomo Della Porta. The heraldic symbols are those of the client who commissioned the work, Pope Gregory XIII (Ugo Boncompagni 1572-1585).
Later Bernini, by order of Innocent X, added another basin and, in 1655, designed the central statue, known to Romans as *il Moro* (the Moor) but in fact a *Triton* holding a *dolphin*. The statue was executed by the sculptor Giovanni Antonio Mari. In 1708 Bernini's basin was replaced and in 1874 the marine creatures were also substituted with copies.

FONTANA DEL NETTUNO It was built in 1574, also to a design by Giacomo Della Porta. Later, like the preceding fountain, it was modified by Bernini who designed the basin. The figures of *Neptune* and the *sea horses* date from 1878.

FONTANA DEI FIUMI Pope Innocent X originally commissioned the work from Francesco Borromini. However Borromini's rival, Gian Lorenzo Bernini, managed to get the commission transferred to him by giving a silver model of his own design to the pope's sister in law, the famous Donna Olimpia Maidalchini. He completed the fountain in 1651. The daring construction seems to defy the laws of stability as an obelisk rests on a hollow rock from which *horses* and *marine figures* emerge. Four imposing figures, sculpted by Bernini's pupils, rest against the central block. They represent the main rivers of the earth and, hence, the four parts of the world: Asia, Africa, Europe and America. The *Ganges* is shown as a boat aground on the rocks; the head of the *Nile* is covered because at the time the sources of the river were unknown; then come the *Danube* and the *River Plate*. The latter seems to be hiding its face from the sight of

Fontana dei Fiumi

Borromini's church of Sant'Agnese, but the truth is that work on the church began only the year after the fountain was completed. Nonetheless, the popular rumour spread that the statue was seeking to protect itself from an imminent collapse of the church.

The granite obelisk, 16.5 metres high, dates from Roman times and comes from the temple dedicated to Isis in Campo Marzio. Domitian (81-96 AD) had the hieroglyphics added, and at the beginning of the 4C the emperor Maxentius ordered the obelisk be transported to his circus on the Appian Way. Innocent X had it moved from there to piazza Navona. The coat-of-arms with a dove bearing an olive stem in its beak is that of the pope's own family.

SANT'AGNESE IN AGONE The church stands on a site once occupied by a mediaeval chapel. According to tradition, it was here that the martyred body of St. Agnes was exposed. Legend has it that her hair miraculously grew to cover the nudity she was forced to display before the public. In 1652, on commission from Pope Innocent X who owned the great building to the left, the architects Girolamo and

Sant'Agnese in Agone with the fontana del Nettuno in the foreground

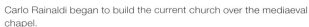

Carlo Rainaldi began to build the current church over the mediaeval chapel.

Borromini took over the following year. The project he inherited had the form of a Greek cross, but by introducing rounded corners and side niches he rendered it almost elliptical, placing the entrance perpendicular to the main axis.

The interior, decorated with gold and marble, contains frescoes by Ciro Ferri (*Glory of Heaven*, on the ceiling of the dome) and by Bacciccia (*Cardinal virtues*, on the spandrels). Over the entrance is the *funerary monument of Innocent X*, buried in the church together with members of his family, by Giovanni Battista Maini.

Santa Maria della Pace,
façade

SANTA MARIA DELLA PACE
Built in the second half of the 15C under Pope Sixtus IV (Francesco della Rovere 1471-1484),

probably to a design of the Florentine architect Baccio Pontelli, the church was dedicated to Santa Maria della Pace (St. Mary of Peace) perhaps to celebrate the end of conflict between Rome and Florence. It contains important frescoes by Raphael (the famous *Sibyls*) and by Baldassarre Peruzzi, completed between 1510 and 1516.

The cloister (1500-1505) is Bramante's first work in Rome, while the Baroque façade (1656) with its semicircular pronaos is by Pietro da Cortona.

Santa Maria della Pace,
cloister

San Luigi dei Francesi,
central nave

SAN LUIGI DEI FRANCESI
The church was consecrated in 1589, but building work had begun in 1518 to plans by Jean de Chenevières on commission from the French community in Rome.

In 1527 operations were suspended following the Sack of Rome, when the invasion of the Landsknechts left the city completely devastated. From 1580 on, the building was completed by Domenico Fontana. The façade is attributed to Giacomo Della Porta.

Inside is the famous Contarelli Chapel, which contains a cycle of three canvases depicting *Stories of St. Matthew*, painted between 1597 and 1601 by Michelangelo Merisi, known as Caravaggio from the name of his home town, the greatest Italian painter of the 1600s.

In *St. Matthew and the Angel* (centre), the *Calling of St. Matthew* (left) and the *Martyrdom of St. Matthew* (right), the artist depicts his ideal of a purer former of religiosity, one closer to everyday life with Gospel figures interpreted by ordinary men, and none of the artificial idealisation imposed by the artistic canons of the time. This extreme realism, expression of an emancipated spirituality quite contrary to the morals of the

Caravaggio,
Calling of St. Matthew

age, brought the artist a certain degree of isolation from official circles. However, modern historiography has re-evaluated the tradition of the "cursed painter", tending rather to underline the great influence he had on ecclesiastical circles. In 1606, Caravaggio was forced to flee to Malta after having committed a crime. He later returned secretly to Italy where he died, alone and in despair, on the beach at Porto Ercole on 18 July 1610. According to tradition, the papal pardon arrived the following day.

SANT'IVO ALLA SAPIENZA
The buildings adjoining this church were, from the year 1303, the site of the first university in Rome. They were restructured on a number of occasions and finally completely rebuilt at the end of the 16C by Pirro Ligorio (the architect of Villa d'Este at Tivoli), and by Giacomo Della Porta, who built the façade facing corso del Rinascimento and the concave façade of the interior courtyard.

In 1632 the commission for the construction of the church was given to Francesco Borromini, an architect of great renown. The building has a hexagonal plan with a mixtilinear perimeter of broad concavities and narrow convexities. The pilasters and entablature emphasise its complex outline. The cupola is composed of concave segments decorated with the coats-of-arms of Borromini's patrons: a dove with an olive stem in its beak, the symbol of the Pamphilj family of Pope Innocent X, and six mounts and a star, the heraldic symbol of Pope Alexander VII (Fabio Chigi 1655-1667). The outside of the dome is also extraordinarily original, with an arrangement of concave and convex elements culminating in a spiral over the lantern, probably inspired by oriental architecture.

Sant'Ivo alla Sapienza
and detail of the dome

Sant'Andrea della Valle

Pasquino, the
"talking" statue

SANT'ANDREA DELLA VALLE

Begun by the architect Giacomo Della Porta in 1591, the interior and the dome were completed by Carlo Maderno between 1608 and 1623. The façade, made entirely of travertine, is by Carlo Rainaldi (1665). It has two levels separated by a broad horizontal band, with columns of the Corinthian Order on both levels flanking windows and doors with triangular and curved pediments. Above the entrance are the statues of *Hope* and *Prudence*, while over the pediment at the very top are two *angels* bearing a coat-of arms. The original plans included a further two angels to unite the lower and upper levels of the façade, but only one (on the left) was made, the work of the sculptor Ercole Ferrata.

As in the chiesa del Gesù, the interior has a single aisleless nave, side chapels, transept and apse. The pilaster strips on the walls accentuate the vertical rise of the church, giving it a monumental quality. Among the more important works it contains are the frescoes on the dome, the work of Giovanni Lanfranco (1621-1625); the *Evangelists* on the spandrels, the frescoes in the apse and those in the arch of the presbytery, all by Domenichino (1628); and the frescoes on the walls, by Mattia Preti (1613-1699). Among the people buried in the church are Pope Pius II (Enea Silvio Piccolomini 1458-1464) the great humanist, man of letters and poet, and Monsignor della Casa, author of the famous *Galateo*, a treatise on etiquette published in Venice in 1558.

SAN PANTALEO

Built over a pre-existing medieval structure dating from the 13C, this church was completely reconstructed at the end on the 1600s. It is famous above all for its neo-classical façade by Giuseppe Valadier (1806), with a stucco frieze by the sculptor Pietro Aurelj.

PALAZZO MASSIMO ALLE COLONNE

It was built in 1532 over the remains of a small 1C musical theatre (the Odeon of Domitian), and the curved façade follows the outline of the cavea of the theatre. It is the work of the Sienese architect Baldassarre Peruzzi, who also built Villa Farnesina. The central portal with six columns of the Doric Order and the small internal courtyard are particularly graceful. The interior, to which it is difficult to gain admission, is decorated with fine frescoes from the Roman school of the 16C.

PASQUINO, THE "TALKING" STATUE

Behind Palazzo Braschi, in a little square known as piazza di Pasquino, is the statue of that name, the most famous of Rome's "talking" statues. Anonymous authors, under cover of darkness, would come here and append satirical verses and irreverent comments, an expression of popular opinion on current events and a means of criticising those in power.

The name of sculptor and the period of the statue, which was much admired by Michelangelo, are unknown. It has no legs or arms and its face is disfigured. Perhaps it is a Roman copy of a Greek original from the 3C BC. All that is known for sure is that its various parts were recomposed, as the inscription below the statue states, by cardinal Oliviero Carafa in 1501. Nor is it certain where the statue's name comes from, perhaps derived from that of a tailor who worked nearby, or maybe an innkeeper or barber. The satirical poems, or pasquinades, in vogue from 1500 onwards, were extremely scathing and, in a time when the Church exercised complete temporal power, targeted above all popes and cardinals.

Frequently dialogues would take place with the other "talking" statues: *Marforio*, on the Capitoline Hill, *Madama Lucrezia* in piazza di San Marco near piazza Venezia, *Abate Luigi* near Sant'Andrea della Valle, *Facchino* near the church of Santa Maria in via Lata on via del Corso, and *Babuino* in front of the church of Sant'Atanasio dei Greci on via del Babuino.

PALAZZO BRASCHI Construction began in 1792 under the direction of Cosimo Morelli on commission from Pope Pius VI (Giovanni Angelo Braschi 1775-1799). It currently houses the civic museum of Rome, a collection of paintings, sculptures and other objects, and also hosts important temporary exhibitions, dedicated especially to the history of the city.

SANTA MARIA IN VALLICELLA (CHIESA NUOVA) Building work started in 1575 by order of St. Philip Neri (1515-1595), founder of the Congregation of the Oratory, an order dedicated to charity and assistance (it was St. Philip Neri who popularised the practice of visiting, over two days, the seven major basilicas of Rome: St. Peter's, St. Paul's Outside-the-Walls, St. Sebastian, St. John Lateran, Holy Cross of Jerusalem, St. Lawrence Outside-the-Walls, and St. Mary Major). The façade of the Chiesa Nuova, rather flat and classical, dates from 1605. Inside are two canvases from 1608 by Pieter Paul Rubens, at the sides of the apse, and a large fresco from 1665 by Pietro da Cortona, on the ceiling of the central nave.

Santa Maria in Vallicella, interior

ORATORIO DEI FILIPPINI Built between 1637 and 1642, it is one of the most important works of Francesco Borromini (1599-1667). It too was built for the Congregation of the Oratory and is part of a larger complex that also includes a building with an oval staircase. The great hall is particularly noteworthy; here were performed those vocal compositions that gave rise to the genre of Baroque music known as the oratorio.

The façade is concave and has two levels separated by a high stringcourse; the tympanum is no longer classically triangular, but mixtilinear as favoured by the architects of the Baroque. Indeed, much licence is taken in contradicting the rules of classical art on the basis of which artists still worked. The pilaster strips, simple or double, are cleverly positioned so as to create effects of chiaroscuro at different hours of the day. The capitals of the lower level have volutes that point upwards, the windows are different on each floor and the convex balcony counterpoises the concavity of the space over the central window creating a strong concave-convex contrast, typical of the Baroque.

The building is occupied by the Vallicelliana Library, a vital source for the history of Rome, the Capitoline Historical Archive, the *Società Romana di Storia Patria* and the *Istituto Storico Italiano per il Medioevo*.

Oratorio dei Filippini

Palazzo Altemps

MUSEUM OF PALAZZO ALTEMPS The Museo Nazionale Romano in Palazzo Altemps was inaugurated in December 1997 following years of restoration and modernisation work. The palazzo is an old private house that, over the course of three centuries, cardinals and noble families continually embellished with splendid works of art.

The original nucleus of the building (distinguishable from the outside, towards via dei Soldati, by its light-coloured plaster) dates from 1477, the year in which Count Girolamo Riario ordered it be built for the occasion of his marriage to Caterina Sforza, daughter of Gian Galeazzo, the powerful duke of Milan. The fresco in the Sala della Piattaia on the first floor dates from this period. The work, a highly realistic depiction of the gifts received by the newlyweds, is attributed to Melozzo da Forlì, an important 15C painter from the Romagna region of Italy. After being sold to cardinal Francesco Soderini in 1511, the building was transformed and extended to incorporate pre-existing structures. It went through another period of splendour after 1568 when, following further changes of ownership, it was bought by a cardinal of Austrian origin, Marco Sittico Altemps, nephew of Pope Pius IV (Giovanni Angelo Medici 1559-1565), who had it further extended and decorated. The chapel of Sant'Aniceto, an integral part of the building dedicated to that saint and to the Virgin of Clemency, contains an interesting painting of the *Decapitation of St. Anicetus*, one of the first popes of Christianity, by Antonio Circignani known as Pomarancio. The work was commissioned by Giovanni Angelo Altemps to recall the sad fate of his father, Roberto, also decapitated, by order of Pope Sixtus V (1585-1590) as punishment for his adultery.

In the 1600s, Palazzo Altemps was adorned with further works of art, mostly sculptures "restored" with additions by important artists such as Gian Lorenzo Bernini and Alessandro Algardi.

In the 18C, the Altemps family moved to the town of Gallese and the building was leased. At the end of that century it became one of the sites favoured by neo-classical artists. Winckelmann in particular

Painted loggia

Museum of Palazzo Altemps,
the Ludovisi Ares and Thetis

Gaul committing
suicide with his wife

dedicated much study to its ancient statues, but it also drew the attention of the poet Metastasio and of the composer Mozart. In the early years of the 19C, Goethe and Stendhal also visited the palazzo and were enchanted.

At the end of the 19C, Palazzo Altemps was ceded by the Vatican to a congregation of Spanish nuns who had the building restructured, despite its artistic value, creating small cells with bathrooms and whitewashing over all the frescoes. In 1982 it was acquired by the Italian State which has used it to house the items of the Ludovisi collection, a property-owning family with lands in the area now occupied by via Veneto.

The courtyard, built over various phases during the course of the 16C, has openings on three levels with the heraldic insignia of the various families that owned the building, including the steinbock and the bridge struck by lightning of the Altemps. The statues date from the Roman age.

The fifteen rooms on the ground floor hold part of the Boncompagni-Ludovisi collection. Among the most important works are the *Aphrodite of Knidos*, the *Athena Parthenos* and the *sarcophagus with the Labours of Hercules*.

On the first floor are well-known statues from the Del Drago and Brancaccio collections, as well as the most famous sculptures of the Ludovisi collection, such as the so-called *Ludovisi Throne* (the authenticity of which has been questioned by the art critic Federico Zeri), the group of the *Gaul committing suicide with his wife* and a splendid monumental *sarcophagus with a Battle between Romans and Barbarians*.

On the outside of the building is the beautiful *altana* (covered roof-terrace), the work of Martino Longhi the Elder (late 16C), which gave rise to the widespread use of this element in Roman architecture.

Sarcophagus with
a Battle between
Romans and Barbarians

5

CAMPO DE' FIORI

itinerary

CAMPO DE' FIORI
PALAZZO SPADA
PALAZZO FARNESE
VIA GIULIA
PALAZZO DELLA CANCELLERIA
PICCOLA FARNESINA
LARGO DI TORRE ARGENTINA
AREA SACRA DELL'ARGENTINA
TEATRO ARGENTINA
CRYPTA BALBI
ISOLA TIBERINA
JEWISH QUARTER OF ROME
PORTICO D'OTTAVIA
SYNAGOGUE
JEWISH MUSEUM

CAMPO DE' FIORI

This square is one of the liveliest in the city, where every weekday morning a picturesque fruit and vegetable market is held. Its name probably derives from the fact that in the Middle Ages it was a great field (in Latin *campus*, a flat area or meadow) that stretched down to the Tiber. In Roman times, however, the area was densely populated. Here were the ruins of the theatre of Pompey, occupied in 1150 by the Orsini family and transformed into a residence-fortress. Beginning in the 15C, another Roman family, the Anguillara, sought to dominate the area.

According to some studies, the square was first paved under Pope Eugenius IV (1431-1447),

according to others, under Nicholas V (1447-1455). After the market of Campdoglio was moved to the nearby piazza Navona in 1478, there is a record of further work on the square ordered by Popes Sixtus IV (1471-1484) and Alexander VI (1492-1503) in order to facilitate the passage of religious processions from the old basilica of St. Peter's to St. John Lateran and to St. Mary Major. During the 16C and 17C, Campo de' Fiori retained its vital importance as a central hub and meeting point for the people, with many hotels and public houses. It was also used for public executions, which were extremely frequent in the late 1500s. It was here that the philosopher and man of letters Giordano Bruno was burnt alive on the accusation of a heresy on 17 February 1600. The statue at the centre of the piazza was raised in his memory in the 19C.

Also worthy of note is the white marble fountain, the *Fontana della Terrina*, so-called in memory of another fountain that used to be in the centre of the piazza but was moved in 1899 to the square in front of Chiesa Nuova to make way for the monument to Giordano Bruno.

The names of many of the surrounding streets recall the trades of the craftsmen who once worked there: *i baullari* (trunk makers), *i cestari* (basket weavers), *i chiavari* (key makers), *i sediari* (chair makers), *i cappellari* (hatters), etc.

Palazzo Spada

Palazzo Spada, Guido Reni,
portrait of cardinal
Bernardino Spada

PALAZZO SPADA It was constructed over an ancient building between 1548 and 1550 by cardinal Girolamo Capodiferro, treasurer of the Apostolic Camera and a personal friend of the recently-elected Pope Julius III (Giovanni Maria de' Ciocchi del Monte 1550-1555). The architect was probably Giulio Merisi da Caravaggio, a pupil of the Sangallo brothers. Its structure is typical of Italian Renaissance palaces, being divided into three horizontal bands, heavier at the bottom and lighter at the top. The building is covered in extraordinary stucco decorations including niches, festoons and medallions, the work of the decorator Giulio Mazzoni (1556-1560). The statues on the façade represent the figures of outstanding Romans from *Romulus* to *Trajan*, whose lives are recalled in the framed inscriptions at the top. The circular medallions contain symbolic motifs associated with the Capodiferro family, whose coat-of-arms is at the centre flanked by two Virtues. From the library window it is possible to admire Borromini's famous gallery with its trompe l'oeil perspective commissioned by the new proprietor, cardinal Bernardino Spada, who bought the building in 1632. The corridor, in reality only nine metres long, appears to the eye to measure more than 35 metres. This effect is achieved by diminishing the height of the columns (the first are 5.7 metres high, the last around 2.5 metres), raising the level of the ground and narrowing the width of the portico from about three metres to just one: The statue at the end is just 80 centimetres high.

PALAZZO FARNESE In piazza Farnese, with its dignified tranquillity and reserve that distinguishes it so sharply from the popular bustle of the adjacent Campo de' Fiori, is one of the most important palazzos of Rome. Fifty-seven metres wide and 27 high, it is known to Romans, because of its form, as *il dado*. It was designed in 1514 by Antonio da Sangallo the Younger on commission from cardinal Alexander Farnese who, having become pope with the name of Paul III (1534-1549), had it further enlarged to reflect his new function.

Palazzo Farnese

The façade is divided horizontally into three levels, and the windows on the top two floors are flanked by small columns with alternate curved and triangular pediments. When the architect died in 1546, supervision of the project passed to Michelangelo. He increased the height of the top floor and added the cornice, which is 2.6 metres high but rendered less visibly imposing by the protruding dado and the decorations with the Farnese lilies. He also modified the central window of the first floor, to which the balcony was added in 1861. Michelangelo had also planed a bridge, never in fact built, to link the palazzo to Villa Farnesina on the other side of the river. On the first floor is the great gallery, with early 17C frescos by Annibale and Agostino Carracci, and Domenichino; and the Salone and Sala dei Fasti Farnesiani with paintings by Taddeo Zuccari. In 1731, when the Farnese dynasty died out, the palazzo passed to the Bourbons of Naples but they lived there for just ten years, from 1864 to

1874, the year in which the building became the seat of the French embassy. Recent restoration work, undertaken in agreement with the *Soprintendenza ai Monumenti di Roma*, restored the façade to is presumed original state, although not without controversy for the removal of a layer of grey plaster that covered the building like a "skin".
Symmetrically placed to the sides of the piazza are twin fountains with basins in Egyptian granite taken from the baths of Caracalla. They were modified and had the Farnese lilies added in 1626.

VIA GIULIA This arterial road, ordered by Pope Julius II (1503-1513), was intended to be longer than its actual 1050 metres. It was planned, in fact, to link the Vatican to the Campidoglio. The course it was to have taken is not known, especially beyond the Tiber towards the basilica of St. Peter's, which had just begun to be rebuilt. During the 16C, and in particular under Pope Leo X (Giovanni de' Medici 1513-1521), numerous churches were built along via Giulia: San Giovanni dei Fiorentini, the interior of which was completed by Carlo Maderno in the early 1600s, and with an 18C façade by Alessandro Galilei; Sant'Eligio degli Orefici, built to a design by Raphael, with a façade by the Mannerist architect Flaminio Ponzio; Santa Caterina da Siena and, in the parallel via del Monserrato, Santa Maria in Monserrato. Apart from the churches, splendid residences for Rome's patrician families were also erected: Palazzo Medici Clarelli, Palazzo Sacchetti and Palazzo Falconieri.

The church of Santa Maria dell'Orazione e Morte, just behind Palazzo Farnese, was built in 1737 to plans by Ferdinando Fuga, for a religious order dedicated, as the inscription recalls, to ensuring a serene death for the poor.

Via Giulia,
fontana del Mascherone

PALAZZO DELLA CANCELLERIA Overlooking piazza della Cancelleria is this large and splendid Renaissance palace, which incorporates in its interior the ancient church of San Lorenzo in Damaso.

Work on the building began in 1485. Tradition has it that it was designed by Bramante, but he arrived in Rome only after 1499, although he had spent a brief period there in 1493. It is more likely the work of Antonio da Montecavallo who undertook the project for cardinal Raffaele Riario, the nephew of Pope Sixtus IV. The building later became a model for other Roman palazzos. For centuries it was the headquarters of the Apostolic Chancellery, the office that wrote papal Bulls, abolished in 1973. Today it is still the property of the Vatican and has the status of extraterritoriality.

The long inscription along the stringcourse, which refers to the foundation of the palazzo, recalls the cardinal who ordered it and the date (1495) the façade was completed. The internal courtyard, in which it is more likely that Bramante was involved, is particularly elegant. It has three graceful levels, the first two with Doric and Ionic columns supporting round arches, the third closed and with composite pilaster strips alternating with elegant architraved windows.

Palazzo della Cancelleria

Inside are frescoes by Mannerist painters such as Giorgio Vasari and Perin del Vaga.

The church inside the palace was originally built by Pope Damasus (366-384). Restructured for a first time in the 8C, it was altered again at the end of the 1400s when cardinal Riario had it incorporated into his new palazzo. In 1798, during the Napoleonic occupation, the church was transformed into a stable for the French troops.

PICCOLA FARNESINA The building (originally known as *ai Baullari*) was so-called because the lilies on the stringcourse were erroneously thought to belong to the Farnese family. In fact they were part of the coat-of-arms of the French prelate Thomas Le Roy who, in 1523, had this graceful Renaissance palace built, probably by Antonio da Sangallo the Younger. The original façade gives over vicolo dell'Aquila, while the façade over corso Vittorio Emanuele II is an imitation built in 1898-1901.

The palazzo houses the Museo Barracco, made up of Egyptian and oriental art, and copies of Greek art, given to the city of Rome by baron Giovanni Barracco and placed here in 1947.

LARGO DI TORRE ARGENTINA

The name comes from the tower and house - still to be seen in via del Sudario near the square - of Burchard, master of pontifical ceremonies in 1500, who was from *Argentoratum*, modern-day Strasbourg. At the centre of the square is an important archaeological site, and on the west side one of the capital's most famous theatres.

AREA SACRA DELL'ARGENTINA Discovered by chance during construction work in the 1920s, it contains some of the oldest remains in Rome, dating back to the Republican age. The main buildings identified are four temples, all facing east. It being unclear to which deities the temples were dedicated, they have been called with the first four letters of the alphabet. The first, A, towards the centre of the square, dates from the mid 3C BC. In the Middle Ages it was transformed into a church as is clear from wall fragments of the two apses and the traces of frescoes. The second, B, was circular and dedicated to a female deity whose statue was unearthed and is now in the Capitoline Museums. The third, C, has been dated to the 3C BC, and it would appear that the fourth, D, dates from the 2C BC. To the side of temple A, a number of columns are visible, all that remains of a great portico from the 1C BC which, according to the sources, had 100 columns and surrounded the entire area. Behind temples B and C are the ruins of a podium from the time of Pompey (second half of the 1C BC).

The tower at one end of the area is mediaeval and the small portico next to it a reconstruction from 1932.

Area sacra dell'Argentina, from the left: temple B, two buildings in opus reticolatum and temple A

TEATRO ARGENTINA Teatro Argentina, recently restored, dates from the mid 1700s, the only one of the famous Roman theatres of that period to survive almost intact. The façade, however, is from 1826. It was here that, on 20 February 1816, the first performance of *The Barber of Seville* by Gioacchino Rossini (1792-1868), was staged; a "comic opera" that aroused clamorous protests on the first night, but a standing ovation on the second.

CRYPTA BALBI Excavations begun in 1981 brought to light an entire city block, highlighting its various transformations from Roman times to the Middle Ages, from the Renaissance to the Baroque. The archaeological site takes its name from the theatre (under the adjoining Palazzo Mattei) with attached windowless portico, later much modified, built in 14 BC by Lucius Cornelius Balbus, a Roman general and consul who had participated in the military campaigns of Caesar and Octavian. In its current layout the museum (the early mediaeval section of the Museo Nazionale Romano) contains, on the ground floor, remains of Roman masonry and a small but interesting exhibition on the complex transformations of the area from the late Republican to the Imperial age. On the top floor is a permanent exhibition, laid out in a modern and elegant style, illustrating the evolution of Rome from the 5C to the 10C, with oriental vases, fragments of paintings and models reconstructing the reuse of Roman buildings that had fallen into ruins. Plans are afoot to extend the museum to illustrate the changes of the city from the 10C to the 14C.

ISOLA TIBERINA

Two of the principal legends concerning the origins of the Isola
Tiberina share the hypothesis that it was formed naturally by the
accumulation of mud and debris around an obstacle in the middle
of the river.

According to the first of these legends, the island was created in
509 BC when the Romans, having driven from the city their last
king, Tarquinius Superbus, threw into the river a huge quantity of
grain harvested from his fields in the Campo Marzio. The second
legend holds that the island's origins go back to a great ship that
ran aground in the centre of the Tiber.

The truth is that the island is of volcanic origins, just like the hills
upon which Rome was founded and grew. It is much older than
any of the traditional sources claim; indeed, its very existence was
fundamental to the birth of Rome because it made it easy to ford
the river, facilitating trade between the two banks.

Another legend explains why the island later became a sacred
place. In the 3C BC, a terrible plague struck the city of Rome
and an embassy was sent to Greece, to the shrine of Epidaurus,
dedicated to Aesculapius the god of medicine. On the return
of the ambassadors, a serpent, the symbol of the god, slid
overboard from their vessel and swam away in the direction of
the island. A temple was built on that spot and immediately the
pestilence ended. Later, next to the temple, a building was erected
to house the sick.

In the Classical age, the island was encircled with travertine blocks
to accentuate its naturally ship-like outline. All that remains today
are a few stones on the downstream end of the island facing the
right bank.

Over the remains of the 3C temple of Aesculapius was erected
the church of San Bartolomeo all'Isola. It was first founded in the
10C and the interior still contains about ten ancient columns. The
Romanesque campanile with its three-light windows has survived
intact since being built in the 1100s, while
the façade, with two levels and a portico, is

a Baroque work from 1624. In front of the church is a small "spire" from the second half of the 19C marking the spot occupied, in Roman times, by a pink Egyptian obelisk which, on the island-ship, indicated the main mast. The Torre Caetani was constructed in the Middle Ages by one of the most important families of the time. It was part of a larger fortification built before the year 1000.

As if to confirm the extraordinary persistence of certain vocations, the site occupied by the Roman building for the care of the sick has ever since been dedicated to healthcare and healing. It is currently occupied by a religious hospital, one of the most important in the city, which dates from the year 1548 and is run by the Order of Fatebenefratelli.

The island is linked to the city by two bridges:

- The first of these, on the side facing the Jewish quarter, is Ponte Fabricio which, after Ponte Milvio of the 2C BC, is the oldest in Rome, having been built in 62 BC. It has two slightly flattened curved arches, with an opening in the central pillar to facilitate the passage of water when the river is in flood. Pope Innocent X (Giovanni Battista Pamphilj 1644-1655) had the bridge restored and covered with brick. An inscription recalls the name of the Roman architect who built it, one Lucius Fabricius.

- The second, facing towards the area of Trastevere, is Ponte Cestio. Originally it too was from the 1C BC, but it was restored in 370 and then rebuilt at the end of the 1800s, though using ancient materials. Finally, particular mention must be made of the remains of Ponte Emilio, known to Romans as *Ponte Rotto*. Dating from the 2C BC, it was rebuilt for the Jubilee Year 1575 by Pope Gregory XIII (1572-1585), whose heraldic symbol of a dragon is still to be seen. It collapsed during a flood in 1598, leaving just one of the central arches standing, still visible today.

JEWISH QUARTER OF ROME

In Rome, the Jewish quarter, known as the *Ghetto* (*ghèto* was the name of an area of Venice inhabited by Jews, whence the term spread throughout Europe to indicate the neighbourhoods in which they lived, usually forcedly), is on the left bank of the Tiber facing the Isola Tiberina. The outline of the synagogue, inaugurated in 1904, provides a striking visual point of reference. The history of the Jews in Rome stretches far back into antiquity, beginning in the 2C BC when merchants began to migrate out of Palestine in search of fortune towards Egypt, Asia Minor, Greece and Italy. Jews were also brought to Italy by force, as in 63 BC when the Roman troops under Pompey conquered Jerusalem and reduced many people to slavery.

The Jewish population underwent further increases under sad circumstances occasioned by Vespasian (69-79) and Titus (79-81), who definitively annexed Palestine into the Roman Empire. It has been calculated that in Augustus' time (early 1C AD), including both slaves and freemen, the Jewish inhabitants of Rome numbered between 30,000 and 40,000, in a total population of about one million people.

Until the beginning of the 4C AD, the Jews lived in a climate of tolerance. The earliest destructions of their places of worship date from 388, 395 and 509. Up until the 10C, little is known of the community, excepting the fact that many *scholae* (synagogues) were founded, located above all in the Trastevere district and in the current Jewish quarter.

From the Middle Ages to the mid 1800s, the affairs of the Jewish community in Rome were strongly conditioned by the policies of the reigning pope, with alternating periods of great restriction, such as under Pope Innocent III (1198-1216) who forced Jews to wear a distinguishing sign (a yellow O for men, and a veil

with two blue stripes for women), and of considerable freedom,
as happened during the reign of Pope Martin V (Oddone Colonna
1417-1431), of Pope Alexander VI (Roderigo Borgia 1492-1503)
who welcomed Jewish refugees driven out of Spain, and of Pope
Leo X (Giovanni de' Medici 1513-1521).
However, in 1555 Pope Paul IV (Giovanni Pietro Carafa)
signed a Bull creating a special walled neighbourhood,
with three gates closed at sunset and reopened at dawn,
where Jews were ordered to go and live and where,
for the most part, they practised humble trades. Their
situation became particularly difficult during the
Counterreformation, at the end of the 1500s and
throughout the 1600s. Only in 1848, under
Pope Pius IX (Giovanni Maria Mastai Ferretti),
were the gates finally knocked down.

The Ghetto was largely restructured in 1888, gaining from the point of view of public health, but losing something of the ancient atmosphere that had been produced by the network of narrow winding streets.

Terrible events took place in the Ghetto during the Second World War. On 16 October 1943 more than 2000 people were deported to the Auschwitz death camp, only 16 of them came back. Later, on 23 March 1944, as revenge for a partisan attack in via Rasella in which 32 German soldiers died, 75 Jews were taken from their homes and, along with 260 others, political prisoners and ordinary citizens snatched from the streets, taken along the via Ardeatina to the Fosse Ardeatine, and there barbarously killed. A monument to their memory has been raised on the site.

PORTICO D'OTTAVIA The remains of the so-called Portico d'Ottavia are truly striking. It was the entrance to a square of ancient Rome, first built at the end of the 1C BC by Augustus who dedicated it to his sister Octavia, and later restructured by Septimius Severus (193-211). In the Middle Ages, it became the site of a fish market, as recalled in the name of the adjoining church, Sant'Angelo in Pescheria, dating from the 8C but restructured in the 1400s.

Over the door of the little 18C church of San Gregorio della Divina Pietà is a bilingual inscription in Hebrew and Latin taken from the Book of Isaiah (Is 65:2-3, "I have always been ready to welcome my people, who stubbornly do what is wrong and go their own way. They shamelessly keep on making me angry"). A church already existed

View of the Ghetto
and the Synagogue

on this site in the Middle Ages marking the spot where according to tradition Gregory the Great was born, pope from 590 to 604.

It was here, in the 1600s and 1700s, that the Jewish population was forced to come and listen to sermons in an effort to convert them to Christianity.

SYNAGOGUE Inaugurated in 1904, it is a centrally planned structure covered by a great dome, the interior of which is decorated with frescoes depicting, at the bottom, four palms and two cedars of Lebanon as mentioned in the Sacred Scriptures, and at the top a geometrical design with the colours of the rainbow to recall the return to normality after the Great Flood. Women sit in the four galleries specially reserved for them. The *aron* (the cabinet in which the sacred rolls are kept) faces towards the city of Jerusalem.

Synagogue

In the adjoining museum are the parchment rolls containing the *Torah* (the Law), objects associated with religious celebrations and documents recording the history of the community.

One of the places in the Jewish quarter to have remained virtually intact is the tiny piazza Mattei, at the centre of which is the famous Fontana delle Tartarughe, designed by Giacomo Della Porta in 1581. It has four bronze statues of youths, the work of Taddeo Landini, each pushing a tortoise over the border of the basin above. The tortoises, perhaps by Gian Lorenzo Bernini, were added in 1658, those on the fountain are copies, the originals being in the Capitoline Museums.

JEWISH MUSEUM Located underneath the Synagogue, the entrance being in via Catalana, the new Jewish Museum was inaugurated on 23 November 2005. It contains a collection of inscriptions, plaster casts, furnishings, sacred hangings, silverware and manuscripts, all bearing witness to the life of a small but active and variegated community, present in Rome ever since the Classical age. The final room of the museum is dedicated to the *Shoah*, with documents concerning the tragic deportations of 1943 and the subsequent revival of the Roman community.

Piazza Mattei,
fontana delle Tartarughe

itinerary

PIAZZA DI SPAGNA

PIAZZA DI SPAGNA

The square is one of the results of a very fruitful twenty-year period in the history of the urban development of Rome, during which Popes Innocent XIII (Michelangelo Conti 1721-1724), Benedict XIII (Pierfrancesco Orsini 1724-1730) and Clement XII (Lorenzo Corsini 1730-1740) promoted and completed extraordinary and picturesque architectural works destined to leave their mark on the city: the port of Ripetta (1703-1705) which no longer exists, the Spanish Steps (1723-1726), piazza di Sant'Ignazio (1727-1728) and Fontana di Trevi (1732-1762). In the case of the piazza, the 18C modification masterfully contrived to use to best advantage a space that had remained on the margins of the city following Roman times, but that had begun to be revaluated in the early decades of the 1500s with the construction, by the French community, of the church of Trinità dei Monti (almost complete by 1519; the cloister and convent are from the middle of the century, the façade, despite its inscription, from the end). The first section of what is now via Sistina was

opened in 1567. This road, ordered by Pope Sixtus V (1585-1590) from whom it takes its name, was intended to connect piazza del Popolo with St. Mary Major; two obelisks were to have been positioned at either end to act as a visible link between the two extremities. In practice this axis never achieved the desired result, and only in first years of the 1800s was via Sistina finally linked, by a series of ramps, to piazza del Popolo.

During the course of the 17C, numerous modifications were made to piazza di Spagna: the creation of the Fontana della Barcaccia (1626-1629), attributed to Pietro Bernini, father of the more famous Gian Lorenzo; the extension of Palazzo Monaldeschi, which later became the Spanish embassy (1647); and the building of the Palazzo di Propaganda Fide, of which the façade over the piazza (1644) is the work of Gian Lorenzo Bernini, while the side façade (completed in 1665) is by Francesco Borromini.

Fontana della Barcaccia
with Trinità dei Monti in the
background

Great public feasts used to be held on this site, often organised by
the French community for the arrival of guests of honour, during which
food and wine would be distributed to the crowds. It was also used
for the recreation of battles, which would be staged using magnificent
scenery, some idea of which may be gained from prints of the time.
A question that still had to be addressed was the steep slope between
the piazza and Trinità dei Monti, and in 1723 it was decided to build
the current stairway, the design of which is by Francesco De Sanctis.
At the end of the century, the panorama was enhanced with the
addition of the Sallustian obelisk.
From the mid 18C until our own time, the Spanish Steps have never
ceased to exercise their fascination on Italian and foreign artists, who
consider this square as a studio in every sense of the word, a place
that, without having seen, one cannot claim to know Rome. Travellers
doing the *Grand Tour* would all pass through here, including Corot,
Goethe, Keats (who died in 1821 in the Casina Rossa, the little palazzo
to the right of the Steps that now houses a small but interesting
museum), also Shelley, Mendelssohn, Berlioz, Chateaubriand, de
Lamartine and Gogol.
The last monumental building project to take place in this area was in
1857 when the *Column of the Immaculate Conception* was erected
in the adjacent piazza. The column, almost 12 metres high, is Roman
and comes from Campo Marzio where it was found in 1778. the
statue of the *Virgin Mary* is a 19C work by Giuseppe Obici. Every year
on 8 December, the Feast of the Immaculate Conception, the Pope
comes to pay homage to the statue.

Column of the Immaculate
Conception

FONTANA DELLA BARCACCIA
Ordered by Pope Urban
VIII (Maffeo Barberini 1623-1644), whose coat of arms with the three
bees appears on the side, the fountain was intend to adorn the long
narrow square then called *Trinitas*. It is not clear who designed it,
but it is certain that Pietro Bernini supervised the work, which was
completed in 1629.

SPANISH STEPS
The *Scalinata di Trinità dei Monti*, as it is known
in Italian, was inaugurated by Pope Benedict XIII in 1726. It is made
entirely of travertine and is not in line with either the church or its façade.
The ramps open in "fans", and are designed in such a way that all the
steps, be they concave or convex, are visible from the bottom; the result is open, dynamic, without hidden corners. The extraordinary urban environment thus created, is ideal for moments of leisure and as a
meeting place. In early spring, the steps are adorned with pink azaleas,
which to the eyes of Romans and tourists alike symbolise the end of the
rigours of winter and the return of a new and milder season.

SALLUSTIAN OBELISK
Found in the nearby *Horti Sallustiani*,
this Egyptian obelisk, like the one on the Quirinal Hill, was erected in
1789 during the reign of Pope Pius VI by the architect Giovanni Antinori
and placed in front of the church. It is 13,91 metres high without the
base, of red granite and its engravings date from the Roman age.

TRINITÀ DEI MONTI Work began in 1495, funded by the king of France Charles VIII who had bought the land and donated it to the Order of Minim Fathers. The building of the church and convent dragged on until 1585, the year in which the church was consecrated.

The façade is by Carlo Maderno, and despite the fact that the inscription bears the date of 1570, it was probably completed ten years later. The campaniles are from 1584, built to a design by Giacomo Della Porta. The double ramp in front of the entrance is the work of Domenico Fontana in 1587.

The interior, in the Gothic style, was restructured in the second half of the 18C, and again in 1816 after French troops had used it as a barracks for eight years, almost destroying the building. The side chapels contain interesting frescoes from the 16C and 17C. In 1828, the church passed to the Order of Sisters of the Sacred Heart.

On via Gregoriana, which takes its name from Pope Gregory XIII (Ugo Boncompagni 1572-1585), at number 30, is the German *Bibliotheca Hertziana*, specialised in the history of art. Its façade in the form of a monstrous head, dates from the late 1500s.

Trinità dei Monti

VILLA MEDICI In the first half of the 16C the building belonged the Roman family of the Crescenzi. In 1564 it was sold to the Ricci family who, over what had been a modest construction, erected a great palace designed by the architect Nanni di Baccio Bigio. They also created via di San Sebastianello as a link to piazza di Spagna below. In 1576 the villa was bought by Ferdinando de' Medici, the future grand duke of Tuscany, who had it rebuilt by the Florentine Bartolomeo Ammannati when the building took on its current outline, although the project originally envisaged by the Medici was never realised. The façade overlooking the gardens is decorated with reliefs, statues and paintings, while the interior contains frescos by Sebastiano del Piombo and by the Zuccari brothers. The oblique wall facing towards piazza di Spagna was raised in 1626 to consolidate the stability of the building.

On Ferdinando's death, the villa remained the property of the Medici grand dukes of Tuscany, later succeeded by the house of Habsburg-Lorraine. In 1804 the French army of occupation took possession of the palazzo, which became the seat of the French Academy, a function it still has today.

Villa Medici

VIA DEI CONDOTTI The name derives from the underground water conduits built at the end of the 1500s by Pope Gregory XIII to carry the Acqua Virgo from the Pincio to Fontana di Trevi and Campo Marzio. The "parlour of Rome", in the past it was a meeting place for travellers, artists, writers and men of culture, now it is better known for the presence of boutiques selling some of the most famous brands in Italy and Europe. The heart of the street remains the famous Caffè Greco, so-called from the nationality of the man who founded it in 1760.

Caffè Greco

PIAZZA DEL POPOLO

Few traces from Roman times remain on the piazza, with the exception of the great gate in the Aurelian walls (275 BC) which used to constitute the northern entrance to the city. It opens onto the via Flaminia which was built by the censor Caius Flaminius in 220 BC to connect Rome to Rimini and the Adriatic Sea. During the Middle Ages, this zone was not part of the inhabited area of the city and was scattered with fields and fruit and vegetable gardens. The first important construction dates only from the late 15C when the church of Santa Maria del Popolo was restructured (1480). In the time of Pope Leo X (1513-1521) the so-called "Trident" was created, perhaps with the help of Raphael, when three existing thoroughfares, all of which start from the piazza, were modified and given a decorous urban setting: via di Ripetta, via del Corso (slightly wider now than it was then) and via del Babuino. The project was completed by Pope Sixtus V who also ordered the erection of the obelisk in the centre of the square. Dating from the time of Ramses II (around 1200 BC), it has ever since been known as the *Obelisco Flaminio*, and serves to close the perspective along the various radial routes leading into the

piazza. It is twenty-four metres high and was originally on the *spina* of the Circus Maximus, where it had been placed by Augustus in 10 BC. The peculiarity of this obelisk is that it still has its original base with, on the side facing via del Corso, a dedicatory inscription to the Sun from the pharaoh. The fountains were added by Giuseppe Valadier in 1823.

Sixtus V also planned to connect the piazza, still then only half-built, with St. Peter's Basilica (with the obelisk in St. Peter's Square creating a visual link with the one in piazza del Popolo) and with St. Mary Major along the via Felice (of which only one part was constructed, modern-day via Sistina).

Great changes took place during the Baroque. In 1655, under Pope Alexander VII (Fabio Chigi 1655-1667), the Porta del Popolo was restructured by Bernini for the occasion of the arrival of Queen Christina of Sweden, who had abandoned her throne and come to spend the rest of her days in Rome (the inscription FELICI FAVSTOQVE INGRESSVI wishes her a happy and prosperous arrival). Later, between 1662 and 1681, the twin churches of Santa Maria in Montesanto (left) and Santa Maria dei Miracoli (right), were built by Carlo Rainaldi, also with contributions from Bernini. Until the 1800s, the two churches were considered the true "gates" of the city. In order to conceal the fact that the plots on which they are built are of different sizes, and to create an illusion of symmetricalness, the two churches have different forms; the former being oval, the latter circular.

Twin churches of Santa Maria in Montesanto and Santa Maria dei Miracoli

Piazza del Popolo,
Obelisco Flaminio

The final large-scale modifications to the square were made by Giuseppe Valadier. His original plan, dating from 1793-1794 but never implemented, envisaged the creation of two porticoed wings which would have given the piazza an elongated trapezoidal form, the larger end towards the twin churches, the smaller towards the Porta del Popolo. The second plan, presented by the same architect during the period of French rule (1809-1814) and put into effect between 1816 and 1824, is the one that gave the piazza its current shape, with its two half circles and the ramps leading up to the terrace of the Pincio which gives a magnificent view over the entire city.

SANTA MARIA DEL POPOLO The foundations date from the time of Pope Sixtus IV (Francesco della Rovere 1471-1484) but a church had already been built on this site near the northern entrance to the city by Pope Paschal II (1099-1118). That 12C edifice had been erected to celebrate the liberation of the Holy Sepulchre of Jerusalem (1099), and the site was chosen in order to banish the ghost of the emperor Nero (54-68) who according to popular belief haunted the area, traditionally held to be that in which he was buried.

Over time, the 15C church has undergone numerous modifications, and interventions by many important artists have rendered it a true "container" of valuable works of art, representing many styles from the 16C to Neo-Classicism.

The façade is made entirely of travertine and was, according to some scholars, designed by the architect Baccio Pontelli, according to others by the less-famous Meo del Caprino. It has rather flat mouldings and an elegant portal with a late 15C *Madonna and Child* inside the tympanum. The six mounts are part of the crest of the Chigi family of Pope Alexander VII (1655-1667). He it was who, in 1655, ordered Bernini to add the curved elements and the leaves, in order to connect the lower part of the façade with the top.

The late 15C bell tower, which has its original conical form covered in "scales" and with little spires at the corners, is the only one of its kind in Rome. It is a typical example of Lombard architecture of the same period.

The interior, entirely in travertine with stucco decorations, has a nave and two aisles, transept, apse and four chapels to either side. The elegant rounded arches are interspersed with pilasters and semi-columns, larger in the central nave, smaller in the side aisles.

The apse is by Bramante, perhaps his first work in Rome after arriving from Milan, built between 1500 and 1503. Its shell-like form is particularly noteworthy, as is the arch with its classical-style coffers. The frescoes are by Pinturicchio.

The protruding serrated cornice, the stucco saints over the arches and the allegorical figures bearing a great coat-of-arms were all added by Bernini (1655-1661).

Among the other important works in the church are, in the right aisle:

- The chapel of the della Rovere family (to which Sixtus IV and Julius II belonged) with frescoes by Pinturicchio (1454-1513).
- The chapel of the Cybo family by Carlo Fontana, adorned with marble of various kinds, dating from 1687.
- The third and fourth chapels both with works from the late 1400s, frescoes by the school of Pinturicchio and sculptures by the school of Andrea Bregno.

Santa Maria del Popolo, interior

The transept has an altar from 1657-1659, a work of Bernini's, with two splendid *angels* and a *cantoria*, also by Bernini.

The side corridor contains more late 15C works and the sacristy has another beautiful altar, this time by Andrea Bregno, a Lombard artist whom some think may be the architect of the church itself. The altar was removed from its original location in the apse in 1627.

The Cerasi Chapel, in the left-hand arm of the transept, houses the *Assumption of the Virgin* by Annibale Carracci (1601) and two important works by Caravaggio (1600-1601): the *Crucifixion of St. Peter*, striking for the intense realism of the figures and the use of light which illuminates only the essential parts of the scene, and the *Conversion of St. Paul*, in which the almost the entire canvas is occupied by the horse and the groom, depicted from a unusual angle, while Paul himself is shown lying on the ground.

In the left-hand aisle is the Chigi Chapel, built to a design by Raphael and containing frescoes by his school and by Sebastiano del Piombo.

With the modification of the piazza between 1818 and 1821, Giuseppe Valadier removed two cloisters from the adjoining convent, rebuilding one in the neo-classical style.

Caravaggio,
Crucifixion of St. Peter

ARA PACIS

The *Ara Pacis Augustae* is a celebratory monument ordered by the emperor Augustus (27 BC - 14 AD) on his return from victorious military campaigns in Spain and Gaul. The exact date the Roman Senate voted in favour of the building is known: 4 July 13 BC, as is that of its inauguration: 30 January 9 BC. Originally, it was located in an area under modern-day Palazzo Fiano, between via del Corso and via in Lucina. Excavations undertaken here long ago in 1568 brought to light nine blocks carved with reliefs. Three centuries later, in 1859, further finds were made, but only in 1879 was the monument identified as the Augustan altar of peace (Ara Pacis). Systematic excavation work continued in the first years of the 20C and, finally, in September 1938, under the government of Mussolini, the altar was reassembled and a site chosen for it between the Tiber and Augustus' own mausoleum. Once in situ, the Ara Pacis was protected under a cement and glass shell, of which the glass part was enlarged in the 1960s to make the reliefs visible from the outside, even during closing hours.

A new protective shell made of glass, steel and travertine, including an auditorium and various exhibition halls, has recently been inaugurated, the work of the American architect Richard Meier.

The monument is made up of a perimeter wall, 11.65 metres by 10.62 metres, with two openings. It encloses a raised altar surrounded by steps.

On the inside of the perimeter wall, at the bottom, the decoration is probably meant to represent a palisade. Above is a fine geometric design with garlands of flowers and fruits between *bucrania* (skulls of oxen, with sacrificial significance) and *paterae*

(bowls with handles used during sacred rites).

At the corners are broken pilaster strips with Corinthian capitals. On the outside of the enclosure, in the lower portion, are splendid reliefs with volutes of acanthus leaves which, all emanating from the same trunk, cover the entire surface and are further adorned with rosettes, animals, flowers, etc. This motif was much used in the Middle Ages to symbolise the beauty of the Creation (see the 12C apsidal mosaic of San Clemente).

Also on the exterior wall, but at the top, the reliefs depict episodes associated, on the long sides, with the origins of the city of Rome and, on the short sides, with the inauguration of the altar.

Details:

- Side A. To the left, a much-deteriorated relief shows the cave on the slopes of the Palatine Hill near the Tiber in which, according to legend, Romulus and Remus were born. To the right is the *Sacrifice of Aeneas to the Penates* (Roman divinities that protected home and State).

- Side B. Shows the imperial court. The heads were restored at the end of the 1500s.

- Side C. The depiction to the right is, perhaps, of the *goddess Rome*, to the left is *Peace* with the allegorical figures of *Water* (a marine monster) and *Air* (a swan).

- Side D. Shows the *Cortège of the emperor Augustus and his entourage*. Augustus himself is recognizable at the join between the third and fourth block, only his face and half his robe are visible; *Agrippa*, married to Augustus' daughter Giulia, is wearing a toga and holding a candle. Also present are *Caius Caesar*, Augustus' grandson, *Giulia*, his daughter, and *Tiberius*, the future emperor.

Ara Pacis, details

Protective shell over the Ara Pacis by Richard Meier

The bas-reliefs on the monument are some of the most beautiful of the early Imperial age. Great technical ability combines with a taste for decoration and elegance of form in order to convey, in the most effective possible manner, the typically Roman concern for the composure and dignity of each individual figure, Various artistic techniques can be identified, successfully brought together in a combination typical of this period: Hellenistic tradition, in the decorative motif of the frieze with its swirling acanthus leaves; classical Greek tradition, in the portrayal of the imperial cortège, which echoes the frieze of the procession on the Parthenon in Athens; and Etruscan tradition, in the realistic portraits of the various protagonists.

Not all the reliefs have the same artistic merit, a definite sign that various sculptors worked on the project, some of whom certainly came from Greece. Nonetheless, the whole shows that by the late 1C BC Rome had managed to break the cultural isolation in which it had remained for nearly seven centuries.

In the adjoining square, the layout of which dates back to 1940, are the two churches of:

- San Girolamo degli Schiavoni (to the right, near the road junction), built at the time of Pope Sixtus V (Felice Peretti 1585-1590) by the Lombard architect Martino Longhi the Elder (who also built the campanile on the Campidoglio). It is also called San Girolamo degli Illirici because, in 1387 following the victory of the Turks in Kosovo, a

San Rocco

region to the east of modern-day Albania, Albanians and Dalmatians found refuge in the surrounding neighbourhood. Even, today, their community still meets here.
- San Rocco, which has a 17C interior and a façade dating from 1834 built by the architect Giuseppe Valadier in typical neo-classical style.

MAUSOLEUM OF AUGUSTUS The emperor ordered this mausoleum be built, for himself and his descendants, on his return from Egypt where he had visited the tomb of Alexander the Great. Alexander's tomb has since been lost and his exact burial place remains unknown.

This distinctive circular construction, perhaps an imitation of Hellenistic models, began to be built in 29 BC. Originally, it had a diameter of 87 metres, and the interior was divided by a series of concentric walls linked by radial partitions.

Piazza Augusto Imperatore, fountain

At the centre was a column - which, according so some scholars, emerged from the conical tumulus of earth atop the monument - bearing a statue of the emperor. At the base of the column was a small cavity containing the ashes of Augustus and his wife Livia. Remains of the emperor's descendants have also been identified, down to Nerva (96-98) and to the wife of Septimius Severus (193-211).

In the 12C, the Colonna family converted the mausoleum into a fortress, and it was destroyed and rebuilt on a number of occasions. In 1600, the pile of earth over the monument was used to turn it into a hanging garden; in 1810 it became a site for circuses and in 1907 an auditorium.

Between 1934 and 1938, large-scale renovations freed the mausoleum from the buildings that, over time, had come to surround it. Currently it is a very poor state of repair, but it is soon due to be restored and transformed into a museum.

Mausoleum of Augustus, entrance

Aerial view of Mausoleum of Augustus

QUIRINAL HILL

FONTANA DI TREVI

Built in the first half of the 1700s, this is one of the most important late-Baroque works in Rome.

A fountain already exited on this site in the Middle Ages, but during the course of the 15C such famous architects as Leon Battista Alberti and Bernardo Rossellino laid plans a great monumental fountain. In 1630, Gian Lorenzo Bernini even began work on the foundations of a new structure, following a plan that was later abandoned.

Finally, Pope Clement XII (1730-1740) ordered the realisation of a design by the architect Nicola Salvi, who had won a specially created competition. The fountain was first inaugurated in 1744 under Pope Benedict XIV, and again for a second time in 1762 with the definitive completion of the work under Pope Clement XIII (1758-1769).

The water is brought to the city centre by the aqueduct of the Aqua Virgo, which originates near Salone south-east of Rome (according to an ancient legend, the spring became known when a Roman girl pointed it out to a group of thirsty soldiers).

The fountain, which stands against the back of Palazzo Poli, faces south and so is illuminated by sunlight from dawn to dusk. It appears to visitors "unexpectedly" as they emerge from the narrow surrounding streets, a much sought-after effect in the Baroque.

The Classical-style façade (1729) has a giant order standing on a base. The large central

niche contains a figure of *Neptune* in a chariot shaped like a shell drawn by two *winged horses*, one "wild" and one "tame". Nearby are the *Tritons*, mythological figures, half man and half fish. To the sides, in niches flanked by pilaster strips are two female figures symbolising *Abundance* and *Health*. In the frames above them are, to the left, *Agrippa* giving orders for the building of the aqueduct and, to the right, the *Virgin* showing the soldiers the water source. At the top, over the dedicatory inscription, allegorical figures exalt the beneficial effects of water: abundant harvests and beautiful scenery.

The rocks, as well as the vegetation which appears almost to be moved by the wind, fuse with the architectural elements to create a single harmonious whole.

Being made almost entirely of travertine, which is extremely porous, the fountain creates considerable maintenance problems. It has recently been cleaned and fitted with a water-filtering device in order to avoid the creation of calcium deposits and mould. The coins, which tradition holds must be thrown into the fountain over the shoulder (although in reality this is to avoid the monument being damaged), are said to ensure a return to Rome. The money is collected by the local authorities and donated to charitable causes.

QUIRINAL HILL

One of the seven hills of Rome, the Quirinal was already inhabited at the time the city was formed (7C BC) and owes its name to an archaic temple dedicated to Quirinus, god of agriculture and peace. In the 3C AD another temple, this time to the Egyptian divinity

Serapis, was built and, shortly before the mid 4C, the baths of
Constantine. During the course of the 1400s, important villas were
built here, later restructured in various ways and at various times
towards the end of the 1500s.

Palazzo
del Quirinale

Fontana di Monte Cavallo,
detail of the *Dioscuri*

QUIRINAL PALACE
Conceived by Pope Gregory XIII (Ugo Boncompagni 1572-1585) as an extension to the villa of Ippolito d'Este, the Quirinal Palace, or Palazzo del Quirinale, was begun in 1573 to a design by the architect Martino Longhi the Elder. Work subsequently continued under the direction of Ottavio Mascherino.

Under Pope Clement VIII (Ippolito Aldobrandini 1592-1605) it became a papal residence, a function it maintained with one or two brief interruptions until 1870. During that time, a number of extensions and refurbishments affected both the building itself (with interventions by Domenico Fontana, Carlo Maderno, Gian Lorenzo Bernini and Ferdinando Fuga) and the decoration and paintings. It was badly damaged during Napoleonic times and during the brief French occupation of Rome (1809-1814).

After Unification it became the palace of the kings of Italy and, with the proclamation of the Republic, the official residence of the head of State.

FONTANA DI MONTE CAVALLO
The two statues of the *Dioscuri* were already in the piazza by 1589, placed there by order of Pope Sixtus V. Heroes of Greek mythology but also much venerated in Rome, they had been found in the nearby baths of Constantine.

In 1783, Pope Pius VI commissioned the architect Giovanni Antinori to raise an obelisk in the square. It is 14.63 metres high, without inscriptions (therefore hard to ascribe an origin and date) and in Roman times had, like the obelisk of the Esquiline, been positioned on Augustus' mausoleum. The undertaking failed, and the *Pasquino* "talking" statue near piazza Navona immediately appeared decked with a notice bearing an anagram of the name Antinori, *non tirai* ("I did not pull"), an ironic allusion to the architect's failure to complete the enterprise. A second attempt was made three years later, this time successfully, and the monument was inaugurated in 1786. The addition of the granite basin, originally in the Roman Forum, was an idea of the architect Giacomo Della Porta, put into effect in 1818 by Raffaele Stern.

Also on the same square are: the 18C Palazzo della Consulta by the architect Ferdinando Fuga, today the seat of Italy's Constitutional Court; and the 17C Palazzo Pallavicini Rospigliosi (hidden behind a high wall), which houses the Galleria Pallavicini. Next to that is the Casino Pallavicini, also known as *dell'Aurora* from the subject of a fresco by Guido Reni.

SANT'ANDREA AL QUIRINALE Commissioned from Bernini by Camillo Pamphilj, nephew of Pope Innocent X (1644-1655), the church of Sant'Andrea al Quirinale was begun in 1658 and completed in 1671. It epitomises a Baroque move away from the central planning typical of religious architecture in the Renaissance. In front of the church is a slightly concave area opening onto the street, almost an invitation to enter, over which is a convex porch framed within sober pillars of the Corinthian Order. The interior is oval with the entrance on the short axis, and the space thus appears more extensive and dynamic. This effect is further accentuated by the side chapels which bring the whole structure together in a harmonious play of curves. The walls have a giant order that stretches up to the ribs of the dome, scarcely interrupted by the entablature which, from above, duplicates the oval floor plan below.

Sant'Andrea al Quirinale, detail of the façade

In the first chapel on the right is a particularly noteworthy altar piece from 1707 by the Genovese painter Giovanni Battista Gaulli, known as Baciccia, depicting the *Death of St. Francis Xavier*, a Spanish Jesuit missionary of the 16C. In the main chapel is the *Martyrdom of St. Andrew* by the French painter, Jacques Courtois, known as Borgognone.

San Carlo alle Quattro Fontane

SAN CARLO ALLE QUATTRO FONTANE Commissioned by the Trinitarians, a Spanish Order founded in 1198 with the aim of freeing Christian prisoners in Muslim hands, San Carlo alle Quattro Fontane was built between 1638 and 1667 by Bernini's great antago-

Largo delle Quattro Fontane

San Carlo alle
Quattro Fontane,
mosaic medallion over the
entrance to the cloister

nist, Francesco Borromini. The small plot of land was used to accommodate a tiny church (which would fit inside one of the piers of St.
Peter's Basilica, hence the diminutive used by Romans, *San Carlino*), a
cloister, and the buildings necessary for the religious community.
Construction began from the interior of the church where the architect
adopted, as Bernini had before him, an oval form; but unlike Bernini he
placed the entrance on the long axis. Four concave curves (the two
side chapels, the apse and the entrance) alternate with the convexity of
the rest of the walls to create an extremely dynamic effect. The points
where the curves join are marked by white columns with composite
capitals in which the volutes curl upwards. The curve of the apse
echoes the classical motif of the coffered ceiling with rosettes
at the centre, while the splendid dome, with its highly
original design, is one of Borromini's masterpieces. The
artist chose marble rather than stucco as the finishing
material because he felt marble could be ennobled
by the work of man.
To the right is the little cloister, which a recent restoration has restored to its original splendour.
Built between 1635 and 1644, it has convex corners so as to "confine" the space. The materials
used are stucco and travertine, which blend in
well with the original terracotta floor and steps
of peperino. The well is especially noteworthy,
as are the octagonal capitals on the upper level
and the balustrade with its alternating mouldings to
better refract the light.
The façade, completed in 1667, is Borromini's last

work. It has two levels positioned one over the other and, again, shows the skilful alternation of concave and convex forms, highlighted by the protruding columns and the recessed niches. In the centre over the door is a statue of *St. Charles Borromeo* at prayer, a work from 1680 by the sculptor Ercole Antonio Raggi. To the sides are *St. John of Matha* and *St. Felix of Valois* by the artist Sillano Sillani (1682). The original motif of the angels' wings that come together to frame the niche occupied by the statue of St. Charles is particularly striking; note also the convex central window and the oval, which originally contained a fresco, under a pediment.

LARGO DELLE QUATTRO FONTANE This *Largo* is the crossroads of via del Quirinale and via delle Quattro Fontane, the latter being a section of a much longer axial street once called *strada Felice* from the Christian name of Pope Sixtus V (1585-1590). It runs from the Pincio to Trinità dei Monti where the Sallustian obelisk stands, to St. Mary Major and the Esquiline obelisk. When, in 1564, Porta Pia was built and, in 1786, the obelisk on the Quirinal was raised, the view from this point opened in four different directions perpendicular to one another. The four fountains, by unknown artists from the late 1500s, represent: the *Tiber*, recognisable by the presence of the she-wolf; the *Nile*, with a crouching lion; *Faithfulness*, accompanied by a dog; and *Fortitude*, portrayed as a well-formed female figure.

VIA NAZIONALE Construction began shortly before 1870 (when the land to either side was still covered in vineyards) along a length of the ancient *Vicus Longus*, which used to link the baths of Diocletian to the area of the Forum. The aim was to connect piazza Esedra (now piazza della Repubblica) directly to piazza Venezia, giving Rome a great arterial road on the model of the Parisian boulevards. Within the space of very few years, elegant apartment blocks and other grand buildings were built along the route: the Anglican church of St. Paul within-the-Walls, in the neo-Gothic Italian style (1880); the Palazzo delle Esposizioni, which was designed by the architect Pio Piacentini and used to house the national gallery of modern art (1882), this was latter transferred to Valle Giulia and the palazzo is now used for temporary exhibitions; the Palazzo della Banca d'Italia by Gaetano Koch (begun in 1887, completed in 1902); and the Teatro Eliseo from 1910 (restored in 1938).

Palazzo delle Esposizioni

PIAZZA DELLA REPUBBLICA

In Roman times, the area today occupied by piazza della
Repubblica was covered by the gardens of the baths of Diocletian.
The site was later modified by Michelangelo and by Vanvitelli.
To the south, the piazza is enclosed by two great
porticoed palazzos built in 1889 by the architect Gaetano
Koch along the line of the exedra of the baths of Diocletian,

whence the square's original name of piazza Esedra.
The basin of the central fountain dates from 1885. It contains four
groups of *Naiads* (divinities of springs and rivers) playing with marine
monsters and, at the centre, *Glaucus*, the god of the sea, playing
with fish and Tritons. The sculptures date from the early 20C and are
by the sculptor Mario Rutelli.

Piazza della Repubblica, aerial view with the church of Santa Maria degli Angeli e dei Martiri and the baths of Diocletian

SANTA MARIA DEGLI ANGELI E DEI MARTIRI

This basilica was created by Michelangelo through a brilliant modification of the ancient baths of Diocletian. Work began in 1562, was interrupted by Micehlangelo's death in 1564, and later continued under the direction of his pupil, Jacopo Del Duca.

Beginning in 1749, great "restorations" were introduced by the architect Luigi Vanvitelli who partly altered the work of his predecessor. In the 1930s an attempt was made to restore the building to Michelangelo's original design.

The entrance, part of the *calidarium* of the original baths, gives access to a circular vestibule, once a passage between two pools, with a 17C roof similar to the dome of the Pantheon. It contains a splendid *angel with holy-water stoup*. The vestibule leads into the transept, created by closing part of the *tepidarium*. The height of the pilasters (28 metres) and the majesty of the vault give some idea of the dimensions of the Roman baths. The very deep apse was created from the ancient *frigidarium*. Among the more important paintings are the *Virgin surrounded by angels*, attributed to Lorenzo Lotto (1543), behind the major altar, and works by Domenichino and Pomarancio. Because of its size and capacity, the church is used for official State ceremonies.

On 27 February 2006 the splendid bronze doors, inspired by the *Annunciation* and the *Resurrection*, were unveiled. They are the work of the great Polish sculptor Igor Mitoraj, who lives and works in Pietrasanta in Versilia, an Italian town famous for its marble and bronze work and which was also once the home of the great Michelangelo Buonarroti.

AULA OTTAGONA OR DELLA MINERVA

Part of the south-western portion of the baths complex, it has a square plan with four semi-circular niches, one at each corner with umbrella-style covers, and an octagonal opening in the centre. The original floor level was some four metres lower than today, and the interior was covered in stuccowork and marble. Transformed into a granary in 1609 by Pope Paul V, in the early 19C it became the headquarters of a charitable association, in 1878 a gymnasium, and in 1928 a planetarium. The modern metallic structure recalls this latter function.

Among the sculptures it contains are the *Hellenistic prince* from ca. 150 BC and the *seated boxer* from 1C BC, both from the baths of Constantine on the Quirinal Hill.

Aula Ottagona or "della Minerva", interior

TERMINI STATION A first restructuring of Termini Station (the name derives from the Latin *thermae* a reference to the baths of Diocletian which in Roman times occupied the entire area) began in 1936 with a view to the Universal Exhibition that was to have been held in Rome in 1942. Two design competitions were held and work began from the innermost area. However in 1942, because of the war, construction was suspended. Work resumed in 1948 following a further design competition which was won by two engineers and four architects (Leo Calini, Massimo Castellazzi, Vasco Fadigati, Eugenio Montuori, Achille Pintonello and Annibale Vitellozzi), and was completed in 1950.

For its originality and elegance, Termini Station remains one of the most architecturally important 1940s constructions in Rome. Particularly outstanding is the great undulating cantilever roof, 53 metres long and with an overhang of 19 metres, supported upon great ribs of reinforced concrete with glass openings that illuminate the ticket hall and atrium.

Outside, on the left as one looks towards the front of the station, are the ruins of a Roman wall in *opus quadratum*. This is what remains of defensive fortifications from the 4C BC, built over an earlier structure dating from the time of Servius Tullius (6C BC).

Next to Palazzo Massimo, hidden among the trees in one of the small gardens facing piazza dei Cinquecento, so-called in memory of the 500 Italians who fell at Dogali in Eritrea in 1887, is a small obelisk placed there to commemorate that military campaign in Africa. It is around six

Termini Station

metres high and was brought to Rome in the Imperial age to decorate the temple of Isis in Campo Marzio.

On the piazza are the entrances to the two principal sites of the Museo Nazionale Romano: the section housed in the baths of Diocletian, and the one in Palazzo Massimo.

MUSEO NAZIONALE ROMANO Founded in 1889, it is divided between five different sites: the baths of Diocletian, Palazzo Massimo, the Aula Ottagona or *della Minerva*, Palazzo Altemps and Crypta Balbi.

It contains a vast collection of sculptures, architectural fragments and epigraphs dating from the 3C BC to the 5C AD.

MUSEUM OF THE TERME DI DIOCLEZIANO The great Museo Nazionale Romano has been located here since 1911, when it was opened by order of Victor Emanuel III, king of Italy, to

celebrate the fiftieth anniversary of Italian Unification. It has recently been restructured. The garden giving over the square in front of Termini Station and the courtyard by Michelangelo hold a vast collection of statues, sarcophagi and inscriptions. Inside is a huge assortment of materials recording the early history of the Latin peoples as well as a noteworthy epigraphical collection.

The museum occupies only a part of the ancient baths of Diocletian where, in 1562, Michelangelo built the basilica of Santa Maria degli Angeli, and its adjacent cloister now used as an exhibition space.

The baths of Diocletian - which have been completely

Museum of the
Terme di Diocleziano,
Mithras killing the bull

Baths of Diocletian

transformed over time and, in fact, no longer really exist as such - began to be built in 298 and were inaugurated between 305 and 306, being the largest bath complex of ancient Rome. It has been calculated that they could accommodate 3000 people. Similar in structure to the baths of Trajan (built in 109) and those of Caracalla (completed in 217), they had three main areas: the *frigidarium* (cold-water pool), *tepidarium* (tepid-water pool) and *calidarium* (hot-water pool), positioned along the

central axis of the building. Around them were gymnasia, *laconicum* (hot rooms for sweating), as well as libraries and meeting places. Beyond the vast garden was the perimeter wall and, on the same axis as the three pools, the semicircular theatre. To get some idea of the dimensions, it is worth visiting the Aula Ottagona or *della Minerva* in via Romita near piazza della Repubblica and comparing that with the blueprints of the entire complex. Only one hall of the ancient structure remains intact, it is on the left of the entrance on the station square, but is open only when used for temporary exhibitions. The baths of Diocletian had a short life because in 537 the troops of Vitiges destroyed the water conduits of the Aqua Marcia. Like all Roman monuments, during the Middle Ages the baths became a quarry for stone and marble. Later they were partly restructured, as described above, with Michelangelo's modifications.

Palazzo Massimo alle Terme

MUSEUM OF PALAZZO MASSIMO ALLE TERME

The ground floor was inaugurated in 1995, and the entire museum was opened in 1998. It is housed in a historic palazzo which, until 1960, was the seat of a private religious school, the prestigious *Istituto Massimiliano Massimo*, run by the Jesuit Fathers. The building itself was ordered by the Jesuits and built between 1883 and 1886 in a late 16C style.

The eight rooms and three galleries on the ground floor contain busts, tombstones and altars dating from the 1C BC to the 2C AD. In the second room are sculptures from the end of the 1C BC, and in the third a collection of coins from the Republican age to the end of the Imperial age.

The fifth room contains a particularly noteworthy series of elegant detached frescoes from the second half of the 1C BC and an altar found in Ostia dating from the time of Trajan (early 2C AD). All these exhibits refer to the story of Aeneas, the mythical Trojan hero, and to Romulus, according to tradition his descendent and the founder of Rome.

Museum of Palazzo Massimo alle Terme, Discobolus

On the first floor are busts and statues of various provenances, displayed in chronological order. Among them is the *Discobolus*, a Roman copy of a Greek original of the 5C BC, discovered in the area of the Esquiline Hill.

The second floor is the most interesting part of the museum. It contains numerous detached frescoes, mosaics and stuccowork, including the famous and splendid paintings of the garden of the House of Livia, wife of Augustus, at Prima Porta, and paintings from the Villa of Nero at Anzio.

Niobe from the Horti Sallustiani

ESQUILINE HILL

ESQUILINE HILL

The Esquiline is one of the seven hills on which the ancient city of Rome rose and developed. Inhabited from the mid 4C BC, it became very densely populated. At the end of the 1C BC, it was urbanised by Maecenas, chief minister to the emperor Augustus, who possessed a magnificent villa here. The great poets Virgil and Horace also lived on the hill in what historical sources describe as extremely luxurious residences.

The name, according to current opinion, derives from *exquilini*, meaning residents living outside the city centre, as opposed to *inquilini*.

The Esquiline Hill had a number of different summits of which the two most important were the *Oppius* or Oppian Hill, just north of the Coliseum and the site of the *Domus Aurea* and the baths of Nero, and the *Cispius*, where the basilica of St. Mary Major now stands.

During the Middle Ages, various civic buildings arose here of which a few towers still remain, much restructured. A number of religious complexes were also built, among them the basilica of San Martino ai Monti.

During the Renaissance, many cardinals had villas on the Esquiline, particularly famous was the residence of cardinal Felice Peretti, who became pope with the name Sixtus V (1585-1590).

However, the great urban expansion of the Esquiline came following the proclamation of Rome as capital of Italy in 1870, when the hill became the site of one of the city's main prosperous neighbourhoods stretching out in a grid around the commercial hub of piazza Vittorio Emanuele II. The public garden in the piazza has recently been renovated and important restructuring work is scheduled to take place in the area in the near future.

St. Mary Major

ST. MARY MAJOR

St. Mary Major, one of the patriarchal basilicas of Rome, is the result of a complex historical stratification. It contains works dating from between the 5C and the 18C, all bearing witness to the fact that for many centuries the church has been a vital centre of the city's religious life.

In the middle of the piazza is a great column of the Corinthian Order, taken from the basilica of Maxentius and raised here in 1614 by order of Pope Paul V (Camillo Borghese 1605-1621), acting almost as a counterpoint to the Egyptian obelisk behind the basilica. That obelisk, 14.75 metres high and found near the mausoleum of Augustus, was erected in 1587 by Pope Sixtus V to mark an axial road, once much more important than it is now, between St. Mary Major and Trinità dei Monti, built by the same pope and called with his Christian name: via Felice.

St. Mary Major stands on the spot where, according to tradition, a miraculous snowfall occurred on the night of 5 August 356, during which the Virgin Mary appeared to Pope Liberius and indicated the site upon which to build the new church. However, no trace has been found of that original building, known as the Liberian Basilica or *Sancta Maria ad Nives*, and the origins of the current basilica date from the first half of the 5C.

The external appearance, as it is today, derives from two distinct phases. The cladding of the apse is in the Classical style and was completed in 1673 by Carlo Rainaldi, whereas the façade, the work of the Florentine architect Ferdinando Fuga between 1743 and 1750, serves to join together two separate buildings: the one on the right was completed in 1605, while that on the left was restructured in 1743 by the same architect. The façade has two levels linked with elegant volutes; at the top in the middle is a pediment. It is designed so as to leave visible,

Column taken from the basilica of Maxentius, surmounted with a statue of the Virgin Mary

St. Mary Major, rear

at the level of the second floor, the late 13C mosaics by the Gothic artist Filippo Rusuti adorning the original frontage of the church. This has created a very remarkable effect, which is enhanced in the evening by the skilful use of lighting.

The campanile is the highest in the city (75 metres) and was built between 1370 and 1378.

The interior dates back to the time of the church's foundation during the pontificate of Pope Sixtus III (432-440), who probably wanted to build a new place of worship following the Council of Ephesus (431) which had reaffirmed the importance of the role of the Virgin Mary. It has a nave and two side aisles but no transept. The apse is in line with the nave. The building was preceded by an atrium, only partly conserved in the 18C modifications, and perhaps, as in many early Christian basilicas, by a quadriporticus which has now been completely lost. The columns, taken from other buildings, have Ionic capitals and support not arches, as was common at the time, but an entablature; evidence that the Classical tradition survived into late antiquity. The band running under the windows is adorned with beautiful mosaics, unfortunately not easily visible due to the reflection of the light. They date from when the church was built and depict scenes from the Old Testament. From the same period are the decorations on the triumphal arch with episodes from the life of Christ. The city of Jerusalem is shown surrounded by gem-encrusted walls, with six lambs at the gates to either side, a symbol of the twelve Apostles.

Central nave

The paved floor with its intricate geometric designs dates from the 12C.

The mosaics in the apse (late 13C) are the masterwork of

St. Mary Major,
Ferdinando Fuga, baldachin
over the main altar

Jacopo Torriti, the greatest mosaicist of his time, and portray the *Virgin Mary* seated on a throne adorned with precious stones. She has the attributes of the queen of heaven, as recalled in the inscription below, and is accompanied by *Christ*. Golden stars stand out against the blue background, further down are the sun and moon. All around are angels and saints, while at the top the decoration continues with swirling acanthus leaves, a Classical motif taken from ancient monuments. Among the foliage are various kinds of birds and animals symbolising the beauty of Creation. Finally, at the bottom, are episodes from the life of the Virgin

The ceiling, designed by the architect Giuliano da Sangallo, dates from the closing years of the 15C. According to tradition, it was made using the first gold brought from America.

Further modifications were made to the basilica in the late 1500s. Under Pope Sixtus V, Domenico Fontana built the chapel of the Most Holy Sacrament in the right-hand aisle, known as the Sistine Chapel from the name of the pope who ordered it. Under the main altar of the chapel is an oratory containing a nativity scene (whence one of the names of the basilica, *Sancta Maria ad Praesepe*). Some of the statues in the scene, which can only be visited during Christmas, are by the greatest of Italian Gothic sculptors, Arnolfo

di Cambio. They are all that remain of a larger work the artist had completed on commission from Pope Honorius IV (Iacopo Savelli 1285-1287).

Pope Paul V also modified the basilica, commissioning a great chapel in the left-hand aisle, symmetrical to the other and called, after him, the Pauline Chapel. Like the Sistine it is covered with a dome. The frescoes in the interior are particularly interesting, the work of the Baroque painter Guido Reni, of Cavalier d'Arpino and of Cigoli.

The *baldachin* over the main altar is an imitation of the one in St. Peter's and is the work of Ferdinando Fuga, who also built the façade. The baptismal font by Luigi Valadier is located in the early 17C baptistery. The painting at the end, depicting the *Nativity*, is by Francesco Mancini. Finally, we must not forget the subterranean *Confessio* in front of the main altar, completed in 1864 with the statue of a kneeling *Pope Pius IX* (Giovanni Maria Mastai Ferretti 1846-1878) facing a silver urn said by tradition to contain the relics of the manger.

St. Mary Major, apse, Jacopo Torriti, Coronation of the Virgin Mary

Pauline Chapel, altar of the Madonna

SAN PIETRO IN VINCOLI Built over Roman remains, the first basilica was consecrated in 439 and later restored on a number of occasions during the Middle Ages and the Renaissance. The entrance portico, dating from the last years of the 15C, has octagonal columns and elegant capitals adorned with the crest of cardinal Giuliano della Rovere, the future Pope Julius II (1503-1513). The façade was added a century later. The interior, with a nave, two side aisles, three apses and Doric-style columns, has a late Baroque feel arising from modifications by Francesco Fontana. In the *Confessio* is a gilt bronze urn containing the *chains* with which, according to tradition, St. Peter was held prisoner in Jerusalem and in Rome. The two sets miraculously united when brought together (hence the name of the church San Pietro in Vincoli, St. Peter in Chains). The church, however, is rightly famous for the presence of one particular masterpiece, Michelangelo's *Moses*. Completed in 1515, the statue was intended as part of a great funerary monument commissioned from the Florentine artist by the recently elected Pope Julius II perhaps intending it for the centre of St. Peter's Basilica. But the changing whims of the pope, the beginning of work on the Sistine Chapel and then the death of Julius himself in 1513 meant that the original project underwent considerable alterations. Other statues were made by Michelangelo about 1530, some of which are now in the Galleria dell'Accademia in Florence and in the Musée du Louvre in Paris. The tomb as it appears today was completed by Michelangelo's pupils.

San Pietro in Vincoli,
Michelangelo, Moses

SANTA PUDENZIANA Dedicated to the sister of St. Praxedes, the church of Santa Pudenzaina, situated in via Urbana, is one of the oldest churches in Rome, dating back to the year 384. Restructured on a number of occasions over the centuries, it is famous for the mosaic in the apse, which has been dated to the late 4C. In the centre is *Christ enthroned* in the act of delivering a blessing. Next to him are two women, perhaps *St. Praxedes* and *St. Pudentiana* crowning *Peter* and *Paul*, surrounded by the other *Apostles*. In the background is the city of Jerusalem, Calvary with a jewelled cross, and the symbols of the four Evangelists: the *angel* (Matthew), the *lion* (Mark), the *bull* (Luke) and the *eagle* (John).

Santa Pudenziana, apse,
Christ enthroned between the
Apostles and Sts. Praxedes
and Pudentiana

SANTA PRASSEDE This basilica contains some of the most interesting examples of early mediaeval art in Rome. In its current form it dates back to the time of Pope Paschal I (817-824) who had it built over a pre-existing Roman structure, dedicating it to Praxedes. She was a 1C saint who, according to tradition, together with her sister Pudentiana devoted herself to burying Christian martyrs. The remains of the two women are in the crypt, in the sarcophagus on the lower right.

The fame of the church is due above all to the splendid mosaics on the arch of the apse, in the apse itself and in the chapel of San Zeno, all of which date from the 9C.

At the centre of the apse mosaic is *Christ* standing upon a trail of clouds with the scroll of the Law in his hand, around his head is a halo and above it a crown supported by the hand of the Father. To the left are *St. Paul*, *St. Praxedes* and *St. Paschal I*. The latter, the pope who ordered the work, has a square halo because when the

mosaic was made he was still alive; he is shown in the act of offering a model of the church. Above Pope Paschal is the *Phoenix*, a symbol of the Resurrection. To the right are *St. Peter*, *St. Pudentiana* and *St. Zeno*. Paschal's monogram appears on the arch over the head of the *Christ*. Along the bottom are the *lambs*, representing the twelve Apostles as they move towards the *Lamb of God*, standing on a small hill from which flow the four rivers of heaven.

Santa Prassede, façade

The ceiling covering the chapel of St. Zeno is outstandingly beautiful. It has the form of a Greek cross, with *Christ* in a medallion at the centre surrounded by four *angels* on the four ribs of the vault. Over the doorway are the *Virgin Mary*, *Praxedes*, *Pudentiana* and *Theodora*, the mother of Paschal I, she too with a square halo because still alive at the time the work was completed.

In the adjoining chapel is a relic of the column of the flagellation, brought from Jerusalem in the year 1223.

Finally, in the chapel of the Crucifix at the end on the right is a splendid sarcophagus by Arnolfo di Cambio (1245-1303).

The church has been much modified over time, particularly in the second half of the 16C when the beautiful main entranceway, the frescoes in the nave, and the two balconies at either side of the triumphal arch were added.

The balconies are used to expose the relics of the sister saints, Praxedes and Pudentiana.

The 18C ceiling was restored in the mid 19C.

The paved floor was completely reconstructed during restoration work in 1918. At the centre of the nave a circle indicates the place where, according to tradition, St. Praxedes collected the blood of martyred Christians.

Central nave

OPPIAN HILL The main access is by the stairway connecting the hill to via Labicana. The Oppian Hill, originally one of the summits of the Esquiline Hill, is currently occupied by a park full of ruins for which it is not always easy to establish an exact date because, already by Roman times, various phases of construction had become stratified, one over the other.

Domus Aurea, bowl with handle in form of snake

DOMUS AUREA The Oppian park, very steep and uneven, contains Roman ruins dating mostly from the mid 1C and the early 2C AD. The mid 1C ruins include the remains, almost entirely buried, of the *Domus Aurea*, the great imperial palace that the emperor Nero (54-68) had built for himself following the fire of 64 AD which destroyed a large part of the city. The Roman historian Suetonius describes the building in these terms: "It was so extensive that it had a triple colonnade a mile long. There was a pond too, like a sea, surrounded with buildings to represent cities, besides tracts of country, varied by tilled fields, vineyards, pastures and woods, with great numbers of wild and domestic animals. In the rest of the house all parts were overlaid with gold and adorned with gems and mother-of-pearl. There were dining-rooms with fretted ceilings of ivory. ... The main banquet hall was circular and constantly revolved day and night". Very little is left today, perhaps because the Roman people's hatred for Nero was such that the emperors who succeeded him (the Flavians, 69-96, and Trajan, 98-117) buried what remained of the palace after a great fire in 104 had almost

Entrance

Domus Aurea, Octagonal Hall

entirely destroyed it. The first excavations of the *Domus Aurea* were undertaken in the early 16C. The archaeologists, lowering themselves in, discovered beautiful designs painted on the walls of what they thought were caves or grottoes, hence the name grotesque used to describe that genre of painting which became so popular during the Renaissance.

BATHS OF TITUS AND OF TRAJAN It is not easy to gain admission to see the very few remains of these two baths. The former were completed in 80 AD, built largely using the walls of the *Domus Aurea*; work on the latter began after the year 104 and was completed in 109 AD under Trajan, to a design of the great architect Apollodorus of Damascus who also built the Forum of Trajan. They are the first examples of the great bathhouses, having a central building and a perimeter wall with an exedra, that later served as a model for the baths of Caracalla and those of Diocletian. The few remains include exedrae of a gymnasium and of a nymphaeum with fountains.

Baths of Trajan

itinerary

LATERAN

ST. JOHN LATERAN The church was founded in 324 by order of Constantine (306-337). According to tradition, the emperor saw the cross appear to him in a dream with the famous inscription *in hoc signo vinces* (in this sign you will triumph) foretelling his victory against Maxentius (306-312) at the battle of the Milvian Bridge. Having beaten his rival, in 313 he granted freedom of worship to Christians and donated the Church certain lands and buildings, among them a palace belonging to the Plautius Lateranus family, relatives of his wife. The original basilica had the typical form of the great places of worship in early Christianity, being composed of a long nave with two aisles to either side, ending in an apse and, adjacent to it, an octagonal baptistery. Next to the basilica rose a palace, the residence of popes until the end of the Avignon schism (1377). This complex of buildings was restructured on a number of

occasions during the Middle Ages, particularly in the 12C and at the beginning of the 13C, when the cloister was built, and then during the 14C when various important frescoes and the baldachin over the altar were added.

During the Renaissance, famous architects and painters also made modifications to the church, but the current appearance of the interior is largely due to Francesco Borromini's Baroque reconstruction, which he completed in time for the Jubilee Year 1650. The exterior, on the other hand, was completed in 1735 by Alessandro Galilei.

The façade, a unique fusion of the architectural styles of Michelangelo (see, for example, the palazzos on the sides of piazza del Campidoglio) and of Andrea Palladio, has a giant order made up of pilaster strips to the sides and of semi-columns towards the middle, all of the Ionic Order and resting on pedestals.

St. John Lateran

Cloister

Apse, Jacopo Torriti, mosaic showing the head of Christ between angels and the bejewelled Cross between saints

Right-hand aisle, Pierre Largos, statue of St. Thomas

Between the pillars are openings on two levels with entablatures at the bottom and arches above. A pediment emphasises the height of the central nave. The first-floor balcony where the pope, who is also bishop of Rome, sometimes appears, has a *serliana* (an opening with an arch in the centre and entablatures to the side, much used in 16C Italy, especially in the region of Venice). At the top of the façade is a balustrade (similar to the one on Michelangelo's design for the Campidoglio), surmounted by statues: at the centre is *Christ* flanked by *St. John the Baptist* and *St. John the Evangelist* as well as *Doctors of the Church*.

The ceiling under the portico was rebuilt in the 1700s and has the crest of Pope Clement XII (Lorenzo Corsini 1730-1740) who had commissioned the façade. The same pope ordered that the great statue of the emperor *Constantine*, discovered in baths on the Quirinal Hill, be placed in the left-hand niche. The central bronze doors, taken from the Curia (the ancient seat of the Roman Senate) in the Roman Forum, were modified in the mid 1600s by Pope Alexander VII (Fabio Chigi 1655-1667) who added the stars, the symbol of his family. The Holy Door, the first door on the right, is opened only during Jubilee Years.

The interior, as explained above, has a decisively Baroque appearance thanks to the modifications of Francesco Borromini. He, like all the artists of his time, had no interest in conserving the vestiges of the early Christian church, being more concerned to "restructure" it in the style of the age. His main contribution was that of uniting, two by two, the columns of the nave thus creating niches in which, in the year 1715, figures of the twelve *Apostles* were placed, each around 4.5 metres high. Giant pilaster strips frame aedicules, niches and windows, between which are scenes from the Old and New Testaments. The pilasters end in eccentric Ionic capitals in which the volutes point upwards, rather than downwards as in the Classical tradition.

The paved floor in the Cosmatesque-style dates from the time of Pope Martin V (Oddone Colonna 1417-1431).

The ceiling, competed in 1567, has the coat-of-arms of Pope Pius VI (Giovanni Angelo Braschi 1775-1799) who had it heavily restored.

Other noteworthy features include, in the right-hand aisles: on the first pillar facing towards the interior, a fragment of a famous late 13C fresco attributed to Giotto, the most important painter of the Middle Ages; the third chapel, by the architect Giacomo Della Porta (second half of the 16C) with a crucifix from the same period.

At the centre of the transept, below floor level, is the 15C *tomb of Pope Martin V*; above the tomb is the papal altar covered by a baldachin dating from the end of the 1300s in the style of Arnolfo di Cambio.

At the top are reliquaries containing relics of the heads of St. Peter and St. Paul.

The transept was restructured at the end of the 1500s, with frescoes by Cavalier d'Arpino and Orazio Gentileschi, while the apse contains a mosaic by Jacopo Torriti (late 1200s), much restored in the 19C.

The Cosmatesque cloister was built in the first half of the 13C by the Vassalletto family. Particularly worthy of attention, in the portico, is a 5C papal cathedra with two small 13C columns to the sides, and the *tomb of cardinal Annibaldi*, a work by Arnolfo di Cambio.

LATERAN BAPTISTERY

The baptistery, like the basilica, dates from the 4C. It has an octagonal form and has been much modified over the centuries, especially during the pontificate of Pope Urban VIII (Maffeo Barberini 1623-1644).The interior has columns on two levels with, over the architrave of the first level, an inscription exalting the virtues of Baptism.

LATERAN APOSTOLIC PALACE

Built on the model of Palazzo Farnese, it was ordered by Pope Sixtus V (Felice Peretti 1585-1590) in 1585, who commissioned the architect Domenico Fontana. The site had been occupied by a great building known as the *Patriarchio*, the residence of popes until the Avignon exile (1309). However, during their absence in Avignon the building was destroyed, and when the pontiffs returned in 1377 they went to live on the Vatican Hill. The great palace, which contains frescoes from the late 16C and early 17C, is the headquarters of the vicariate of the diocese of Rome and, like the basilica, enjoys the status of extraterritoriality. It was here, on 11 February 1929, that the so-called "Lateran Pacts" were signed, regulating relations between the Italian State and Vatican City State.

Lateran Baptistery

Lateran Apostolic Palace

OBELISK

At the centre of the square to the side of the basilica is the Lateran obelisk. Of red granite, 32.18 metres high and covered in hieroglyphics, it dates from the reign of Thutmosis II (1504-1450 BC). Sixtus V ordered it be moved from the Circus Maximus to its current site where it was erected by the architect Domenico Fontana in 1588.

SCALA SANTA

The building of the Scala Santa (or the *Sancta Sanctorum*, holy of holies), was also ordered by Pope Sixtus V from Domenico Fontana. It incorporates the old private chapel of the *Patriarchio*, dating from the 4C but rebuilt in the 1300s when the beautiful paintings were added. The central stairs, moved here from the old palace, are believed by the faithful to have been trodden by Christ as he went up to appear before Pilate; for this reason, they must ascend the 28 wood-covered marble steps on their knees. On the outside, to one side, is the so called *Nicchione* (or great niche), much modified by Ferdinando Fuga in 1743, all that remains of a great dining hall in the old papal palace.

Entrance to the Scala Santa

Santa Croce in Gerusalemme,
façade

Santa Croce in Gerusalemme,
campanile

San Clemente, porch

SANTA CROCE IN GERUSALEMME

SANTA CROCE IN GERUSALEMME According to tradition, the first basilica to be raised here was built by Constantine over an old imperial palace from the beginning of the 3C. The intention was to use it to conserve certain relics of the True Cross brought from Jerusalem by Constantine's mother Helena. Much modified in the 12C, when the fine bell tower was built, the church was completely restructured, beginning in 1740, by the architect Domenico Gregorini in the late-Baroque style, of which the oval atrium and the convex façade are notable examples.

SAN CLEMENTE A few hundred metres from the Coliseum is a fine complex of buildings dedicated to St. Clement (88-97), the fourth pope, who lived in the 1C AD and probably died in the Crimea. It is one of the most interesting monuments in the city, a testament to that extraordinary stratification of buildings that has developed in Rome over more than 2700 years of history.

Here, over ancient Roman structures perhaps destroyed in the great fire of 64 AD, two city blocks were built at the end of the 1C AD. Over one of them, at the end of the 2C, a mithraeum was constructed with adjoining buildings (*schola mitraica*) for the followers of the religion. Later, in the 4-5C when Mithraism was banned by law, the site was occupied by a palaeo-Christian basilica that remained in use until the 11C. In the 12C the old basilica, perhaps because it was unstable, was buried under rocks and earth to the height of the capitals and a new church was built on top, decorated with splendid mosaics in the apse and preceded by a great quadriporticus. This is the so-called upper basilica which, at the beginning of the 1400s, was further decorated with important frescoes. More modifications were made in the 17C, and in the early years of the 18C when the façade overlooking the cloister was added. Excavations to unearth the lower strata began in 1857, became particularly intense in the years 1910-1912, and are still going on today. An external corridor along the right-hand aisle of the 4C basilica is currently being explored. Since 1667 the complex has belonged to the Irish Dominican Fathers.

Upper basilica

This dates from the 12C, and still maintains its original layout, with a nave, two side aisles and an apse at the end.

San Clemente,
central nave

The 18C modifications, done under Pope Clement XI (Giovanni Francesco Albani 1700-1721) and marked with his heraldic crest of three mounts and a star, are the work of the architect Carlo Fontana. These included rebuilding the ceiling and the façade overlooking the quadriporticus, restoring the walls over the arches, and adding the white stucco decorations with pilaster strips (the volutes of the capitals point upwards, a typical late-Baroque trait).

Despite these transformations, some particularly valuable mediaeval parts of the church have survived intact: the *schola cantorum*, in other words the choir enclosure, recomposed in the 12C with marble fragments of the 6C taken from the basilica below; the paschal candlestick and the pulpit, decorated with Cosmatesque mosaics; the ciborium or baldachin over the 18C altar, made using 6C fragments and columns from the 1400s; the tabernacle to the right of the apse by the great Gothic sculptor Arnolfo di Cambio showing *Pope Boniface VIII* (Benedetto Caetani 1294-1303) presenting his nephew to the *Virgin Mary*, the *Child Jesus* and *St. Clement*; and the mosaics in the apse.

These mosaics are the most important and valuable work in the church. Dating from the first half of the 12C, they are dominated by the classical spirals of acanthus leaves that branch out from a single trunk and occupy all the available space, along the lines of Augustus' Ara Pacis (late 1C BC). Here, however, other decorative motifs have been added such as chalices, vases, flowers, birds, and figures of musicians, all symbolising the beauty of Creation. In the centre is *Christ on the Cross*, surrounded by twelve *white doves* representing the Apostles and, to the sides, *Mary* and the disciple *John*. At the top, a hand holds the crown, symbol of victory, and further up, within a circle, is the monogram of Christ (the *Crismon,* obtained by the intersection of the first two letters of the Greek word *Xristós*). Next

Apse,
mosaic from first half
of 12C showing Christ
surrounded by twelve
white doves

to this are the first and last letters of the Greek alphabet to indicate that Christ, as is written in the *Apocalypse*, embraces everything from the beginning to the end.

At the bottom *deer* drink from the four rivers of heaven, recalling the phrase: "As a hart longs for flowing streams, so longs my soul for thee, O God " (Ps 42, 2).

Further details of particular interest are the two splendid *peacocks*, symbol of the resurrection and the immortality of the soul, and the scenes of everyday life signifying that all of reality is pervaded with the presence of God.

Twelve *sheep* around the central lamb of *Christ* complete the apse decoration. They are shown in the act of departing from the gates of Bethlehem and Jerusalem, symbolically represented with jewelled walls and stylised monuments. At the centre of the triumphal arch is *Christ delivering a blessing* next to the symbols of the four Evangelists: the *lion* (St. Mark), the *angel* (St. Matthew), the *eagle* (St. John) and the *ox* (St. Luke). Further down are *Peter* and *Paul*, and the prophets *Isaiah* and *Jeremiah*.

The chapel facing the side entrance contains recently-restored frescoes depicting *stories of St. Catherine*, dating from 1423-1431 and attributed to Masolino da Panicale and Masaccio. The latter is considered as the greatest painter of the early 15C, the initiator of Florentine humanism. The scene of the *Annunciation* with a portico in perspective is especially noteworthy.

Lower basilica

First underground level: the palaeo-Christian basilica

On the first level under the basilica is the church dating from the late 4C - early 5C, which contains the foundation walls of the 12C structure above. This original building was slightly wider, so the right-hand wall of the 12C basilica coincides with the right-hand colonnade of the original church beneath. The wall frescoes, depicting episodes from the *life of St. Clement*, date from the 9C and the 11C, and are some of the oldest in Rome. Those illustrating the *legend of Sisinnius* contain inscriptions that can be considered as some of the oldest examples of Vulgar Italian.

At the end of the nave on the left is the supposed *tomb of St. Cyril*, who invented the ancient Slavic alphabet and, according to tradition, on 30 January 861 discovered the body of St. Clement on a Ukrainian island in the Black Sea.

Second underground level: two Roman buildings and the mithraeum

In the second underground level are two buildings from the 1C AD. They are separated from one another by a narrow corridor scarcely 80 centimetres wide, which in reality was a Roman street. The first of these buildings, the larger of the two, is made of large stone blocks and has an internal courtyard surrounded by small rectangular rooms. In all probability it was a *horreum*, or storehouse, or perhaps, as some archaeologists believe, the mint. The second building, discovered in 1867, was perhaps a Roman house, converted in the 2C into a mithraeum. Long and narrow, it has a low barrel-vaulted ceiling covered in pumice to simulate the cave where the divinity was born, and raised podia to either side where the initiates would lie.

Cappella di Santa Caterina, attributed to Masolino da Panicale and Masaccio, mosaic with stories of St. Catherine

SANTO STEFANO ROTONDO

SANTO STEFANO ROTONDO Slightly off the routes normally followed by organised tour groups, this is in fact one of the most interesting and unique churches of Rome. Constructed over a 1C AD barracks within which a mithraeum was built in the 2-3C, the original structure dates from the time of Pope Simplicius (468-483). The church consisted of a vast rectangular raised courtyard, which has completely disappeared today, and a cylindrical building with two broad annular corridors the diameter of which, including the perimeter walls, was around 66 metres.

The first modifications were made by Pope Hadrian I (772-795). Later Pope Innocent II (Gregorio Papareschi 1130-1143), perhaps in order to shore up the roof which threatened to collapse, added the two pillars at the centre of the church and the external portico which is still in place today.

Further large-scale restorations, giving the church its current appearance, took place under Pope Nicholas V (Tommaso Parentucelli 1447-1455). The dimensions of the building were reduced by building a wall at the level of the first exterior colonnade, the roof was reconstructed and the arched windows were bricked in, making one every three a two-light window. Thus the outer corridor was abandoned and has been almost completely lost. It is not known who made these modifications, whether it was Bernardo Rossellino or Leon Battista Alberti, well-known Renaissance architects. A famous account of the time described the operation: "A ruined building [...] restored by Pope Nicholas, but he ruined it even more". The interior contains beautiful frescoes largely attributed to Niccolò Circignani known as Pomarancio, depicting *Martyrdoms* of Christian saints.

Aerial view of the church of Santo Stefano Rotondo

Interior

Interior circular ambulatory, frescoes depicting martyrdoms of Christian saints, attributed to Pomarancio

CAELIAN HILL One of the seven hills of Rome. Its name derives from that of Caelius Vibenna, an Etruscan soldier who helped Servius Tullius conquer the city and become its sixth king.

In the Imperial age (1C to 3C AD) it was the site of various important residences but became depopulated during the early Middle Ages. Around the 9C, a number of picturesque churches were built there, giving the hill its own special character.

Villa Celimontana, entrance pathway with a view of the villa

VILLA CELIMONTANA The earliest mention of this park dates back to 1553 when a vineyard belonging to one Antonio Paluzzelli was bought by Giacomo di Pietrantonio Mattei. Later Ciriaco Mattei (1545-1614) had the architect Jacopo Del Duca build a small country house there, completed in 1582. In the garden, he ordered the erection of a small obelisk donated to him by the Pontifical Curia. Just 2.68 metres high and dating from the time of Rameses II (1279-1213 a.C.),

the obelisk was brought to Rome in antiquity where it decorated a temple dedicated to Isis on the Capitoline Hill. Later, perhaps during the Middle Ages, it was placed in the square on the Capitoline. Mattei also gathered a remarkable collection of antiquities, which has unfortunately been dispersed.

The history of the villa includes episodes of great hospitality on the part of the proprietor. The house, in fact, stood at about the halfway point on the pilgrimage route instituted by St. Philip Neri in 1552 to visit the seven basilicas of Rome (the entire journey, fully 16 miles long, took two days to complete and began from the Chiesa Nuova in corso Vittorio Emanuele II). The Mattei residence thus became a resting place where pilgrims were welcomed and given refreshment. According to accounts of the time, each of the arrivals was offered a large hunk of bread, wine, an egg, two slices of salami, a small piece of cheese and two apples. This practice remained in use until the end of the 19C.

The villa later underwent various transformations as its ownership moved from hand to hand. At the beginning of the 19C, it was bought by Manuel Godoy, the Spanish king's representative in Rome, who ordered extensive excavation work and had the obelisk, which in the meantime had fallen over, re-erected.

Sometime between 1830 and 1840, the building was ceded to a certain Felice Trocchi as payment of a debt and in the mid century it again changed hands becoming the property of a Prussian family.

Following the First World War, the building was bought by the Italian State and in 1928 was opened to the public. Currently the villa, much restructured with an additional floor and two new avant-corps on the façade, is the headquarters of the Italian Geographical Society, and houses a specialised library containing over 250,000 volumes.

In the summer months, concerts and dance shows are held in an open-air theatre there

SANTA MARIA IN DOMNICA

SANTA MARIA IN DOMNICA Also known as Santa Maria della Navicella, the church dates from the 9C, as does the mosaic in the apse depicting the *Virgin Mary enthroned with the Child Jesus and two ranks of angels*. The kneeling figure is *Pope Paschal I* (817-824), his square halo indicating he was still alive at the time the work was completed.

A restoration was done in 1513, commissioned by cardinal Giovanni de' Medici shortly before he was elected as pope with the name of Leo X. The portico is from 1513-1514, the work of the Tuscan architect Andrea Sansovino. The frieze over the windows is by Perin del Vaga, a pupil of Raphael. The ceiling was ordered in 1566 by cardinal Fernando de' Medici.

NAVICELLA

NAVICELLA The *Navicella* (little boat), perhaps an imitation of a Roman boat that it seems occupied this spot in the Middle Ages and the Renaissance, was designed by Andrea Sansovino in 1518-1519 on commission from Pope Leo X (Giovanni de' Medici 1513-1521), whose crest appears a number of times on the base. It was transformed into a fountain in 1931.

Santi Giovanni e Paolo

SANTI GIOVANNI E PAOLO

SANTI GIOVANNI E PAOLO According to tradition, this church was built over the dwelling of two dignitaries of Constantine's court, put to death in 361 by order of Julian the Apostate. The basilica was first restored in the 5C and again in the 12C when the bell tower was built.

Completely restructured in the 1700s, the

original mediaeval plan including the 12C portico were nonetheless maintained. The dome, on the other hand, dates from the 19C.

Noteworthy features in the interior include the apse frescoes by Pomarancio (1588) and, to the left of the altar, a small room with frescoes from the 11C and 12C.

Another fascinating aspect is the crypt where it is possible to see remains of a three-storey Roman building with fragments of frescoes and evident traces of the continuity of religious worship on this site.

Santi Giovanni e Paolo, apse, Pomarancio, Christ in glory

THREE CHAPELS ON THE CAELIAN HILL These three
17C chapels, containing important frescoes, were built over pre-existing structures. They are subject to the Chapter of St. Mary Major. Ordered by cardinal Cesare Baronio (died 1602), the three were constructed at almost the same time: In the centre, Sant'Andrea, from 1607, was built over 4C remains to a design by Flaminio Ponzio, it contains frescoes by Guido Reni, Domenichino and Pomarancio. Santa Silvia, from 1608, has an apse fresco by Guido Reni. Santa Barbara was decorated in 1602 with paintings by Antonio Viviani, it is also known as the chapel of the *Triclinium* for the stone table it contains, upon which, according to tradition, St. Gregory served a meal to twelve paupers.

SAN GREGORIO MAGNO It is said that this majestic church
was founded in the 6C by Pope Gregory I the Great (590-604), and rebuilt by Gregory II (715-731, famous for having received Sutri from Liutprand in 728, the first nucleus of the temporal power of the Church) who dedicated it to his predecessor.

Rebuilt on a number of occasions, the façade was designed by Giovanni Battista Soria (1633), who also drew up the plans for the portico, completed in 1642.

The interior, spacious and sombre like the exterior, has a nave and two aisles divided by columns and pilasters. It was refurbished in the mid 18C; the restoration of the 11-12C Cosmatesque floor dates from the same period. The most interesting part of the building is the dome, completed in the early 1600s by Carlo Maderno and frescoed immediately afterwards by Giovanni Battista Ricci.

Since 1573 the church has been run by Camaldolese monks.

San Gregorio Magno

itinerary

CARACALLA

PASSEGGIATA ARCHEOLOGICA
SANTI NEREO E ACHILLEO
BATHS OF CARACALLA

PASSEGGIATA ARCHEOLOGICA

The so-called *Passeggiata Archeologica* is a kind of "green path" made up of the succession of roads from via di San Gregorio, to via delle Terme di Caracalla and on to Porta San Sebastiano, all flanked by important monuments dating from different times. Already during the brief period that Rome was under the French-Napoleonic administration (1809-1814), led by the French prefect Camillo de Tournon, there was talk of creating a *Jardin du Capitole* to protect the historical-monumental area of Rome.

The idea of protecting this archaeological area of the ancient city was taken up again in 1870, after Rome had been proclaimed the capital of Italy, by a commission charged with drawing up new urban plans to create "public gardens" stretching from the Palatine Hill to Porta San Sebastiano. It was not until the end of 1880 that the general concept was translated into an initial project; this was

put into effect in 1907 and concluded 1914, under the guidance of a commission which included the famous archaeologists Giacomo Boni and Rodolfo Lanciani. Entire city blocks were razed to the ground to liberate monuments such as the baths of Caracalla and the three chapels on the Caelian Hill. Moreover, existing streets were widened and new ones created and planted with large trees. Some archaeologists criticised the project, among them Giuseppe Lugli who described the *Passeggiata Archeologica* as "pretty, but not very archaeological".

Other modifications were made over two different phases: one around the year 1930 the other in 1938, under the government of Mussolini, with monumental and propagandistic aims quite foreign to the original project.

SANTI NEREO E ACHILLEO This church is dedicated to two saints, Nereo and Achilleo, who suffered martyrdom at the end of the 3C and, like many Roman churches, shows evidence of the numerous modifications it has undergone over the centuries.

Built over a pre-existing Roman structure, in its current form of nave, two aisles and an apse the church dates from the time of Pope Leo III (795-816). It was restructured in the late 15C under Sixtus IV (1471-1484) when the nave was rebuilt and octagonal brick columns were added. In 1596 it was taken over by cardinal Cesare Baronio (an enthusiastic follower of Philip Neri, who founded the Congregation of the Oratory and preached a return to a more spiritual and humble form of religiosity in the wake of the Council of Trent, which ended in 1563). His modifications concentrated on consolidating the dilapidated 9C structure and repairing the presbytery. The cardinal also dedicated himself to an interesting restoration project of sacred objects from the old church, "reassembling" with taste and refinement pieces from Roman times and from the Middle Ages. In this way the ciborium (the canopy over the altar in mediaeval churches), the episcopal chair, the throne in the apse, the ambo and even a paschal candlestick were all refurbished.

Santi Nereo e Achilleo, view of the presbytery with the 16C ciborium, and the apse with its 9C frescoes

The apse itself contains a beautiful mosaic from the late 8C - early 9C, and the walls are decorated with frescoes traditionally attributed to Niccolò Circignani, known as Pomarancio. The façade, marked

with traces of late 16C graffiti, has a *protiro* (an element used in mediaeval architecture to emphasise the entrance to a church), which here has a Classical form. The column in front of the church had a capital with a lion's head which, according to tradition, came from Solomon's Temple in Jerusalem. It was, however, stolen in 1985.

BATHS OF CARACALLA This great bath complex was built by the emperor Caracalla between 212 and 217. Construction work was later completed by Heliogabalus (218-222) and Alexander Severus (222-235).

The baths were fed by a branch of the aqueduct of the Aqua Marcia and could accommodate 1600 bathers. Entrance was free of charge. A great multitude of slaves was employed to ensure that everything was kept in perfect working order.

The majestic ruins still give an idea of how the baths must have looked, with great halls once covered with domes or cross vaults, exedrae, niches and arches. Here Roman structural prowess reached its highest point with the skilful use of wall-building techniques and, in particular, of concrete.

Baths of Caracalla

As in almost all bathhouses, here too the principal areas were at the centre of the complex and positioned along a perpendicular axis: the *frigidarium* (cold-water pool), *tepidarium* (tepid-water pool) and *calidarium* (hot-water pool), the latter was circular and had a diameter of 35 metres.

In the same building, at the sides, were vestibules, gymnasia, saunas and nymphaeums.

The floors were covered in mosaics and the walls in marble, while the niches contained statues. The *Farnese Bull*, now in the National Archaeological Museum in Naples, and the *Belvedere Torso*, today in the Vatican Museums, both came from the baths of Caracalla.

Beyond the garden, in the outer perimeter, were more gymnasia as well as libraries, a stadium and the structures associated with the aqueduct that supplied the huge complex with water. On the north-east side, in subterranean vaults accessible only from the outside, is a mithraeum dating from the 3C AD.

Having been sacked by the Visigoths in 410, the baths of Caracalla were finally abandoned in 537 when the Ostrogoths led by Vitiges cut the aqueduct supplying them. In the Middle Ages and during the Renaissance they were used as a stone quarry. Archaeological excavations, which began in the 16C, intensified at the beginning of last century.

Baths of Caracalla

itinerary

AVENTINE HILL

AVENTINE HILL

Over its long urban history, the Aventine Hill (47 metres above sea level) has gone through various phases. It was already part of the city in the 6C BC, enclosed within the walls built at that time (Servian walls). In the mid 5C, being near the river port, it became the residence of the Roman plebeians who, according to tradition, withdrew to the hill in protest in 490 BC. It is said that the consul Menenius Agrippa managed to persuade them to return to work with his famous speech on the need for all the parts of a body to co-operate in order for the organism as a whole to function.

In the Imperial age (1-2C) the hill became one of the most important aristocratic neighbourhoods of the city and great temples were constructed such as those of Diana and Minerva, as well as the baths of Decius, built by that emperor in 242. During the Middle Ages, as the number of wealthy mansions increased, important monastic communities also took up residence on the hill.

Its function as a religious centre has persisted with few changes, through the Renaissance and the Baroque, down to our own day. In the late 18C, the architect Giovanni Battista Piranesi designed the piazza dei Cavalieri di Malta and the church of Santa Maria del Priorato.

A plan is currently being examined for the renovation of Roman and mediaeval remains, the creation of an open-air theatre near the municipal rose garden and a new network of pedestrian pathways to connect the hill to adjoining areas.

Aerial view of
the basilica of
Santa Sabina

SANTA SABINA Built over a pre-existing Roman *domus*, the basilica dates from the 5C and is one of the oldest in Rome. It is dedicated to Sabina, perhaps the owner of the *domus* underneath or, more likely, a martyr who died in Umbria in the year 119. It was completed under Pope Celestine I (422-432) who appears in the mosaic on the counter façade along with two female figures representing the origins of the Christian faith: the figure on the right (with the inscription *ex circumcisione*) symbolises the *Church of the Jews*, the one on the left (*ex gentibus*) the *Community of the Gentiles*. Also from the 5C is the splendid entrance door, carved in cedar wood with scenes from the Old and New Testament, and the decoration over the arches in the interior, with marble inlay in *opus sectile*.

Renovated in the early years of the 9C, the church was completed with the addition of the *schola cantorum* under Pope Eugenius II (824-827). In 1222 it passed into the hands of the Dominican Order who had it extended with an elegant cloister. During the 13C, St. Thomas Aquinas lived here. In the courtyard next to the atrium is an orange tree which, according to tradition, was brought from Spain and planted by St. Dominic himself.

In the mid 1400s the side entrance was opened, preceded by a small portico. Later, in 1560, the apse mosaic was replaced with a fresco by Taddeo Zuccari and, in 1586 during the papacy of Sixtus V, the architect Domenico Fontana made further important "restorations", walling in the windows, removing the porphyry covering of the apse, renewing the paved floor and exposing the beams of the ceiling.

In 1600, the chapel of St. Hyacinth was built, with frescoes by Federico Zuccari, and in 1671 the chapel of St. Catherine. Further modifications, made during the course of the 1700s and 1800s, were largely removed by the architect Antonio Muñoz during restoration work in 1914-1919 and 1936-1939. He sought to return the church to its presumed mediaeval state, while at the same time highlighting certain Roman relics such as the granite column with Corinthian capital (on the side wall to the right) to show how the original palaeo-Christian edifice had been built over an earlier structure. Muñoz also reopened the walled-up windows and decorated them with cement lattices, reconstructed the *schola cantorum* and the episcopal cathedra, and again exposed the 12C floor, replacing the parts that were missing. He also covered the ceiling beams with coffering and repainted the apse decorations.

Sant'Alessio, façade

Piazza dei Cavalieri di Malta

PIAZZA DEI CAVALIERI DI MALTA AND SANTA MARIA DEL PRIORATO
This extraordinary tiny piazza, together with the church of Santa Maria del Priorato, was designed by one of the most renowned neo-classical artists, Giovan Battista Piranesi, chiefly famous for his beautiful engravings depicting the Rome of his day.

The piazza, completed in 1765, is enclosed by a perimeter wall decorated with ancient symbols taken from Etruscan, Roman and Renaissance art, all imaginatively brought together. The small obelisks, the steles and the friezes blend in perfectly with the cypress trees and other vegetation to create a timeless effect (despite the constant presence of parked cars).

Within a very well-kept but closed garden - part of which can be seen by looking through the keyhole in the door (which also affords the famous view of the dome of St. Peter's) - is the church of Santa Maria del Priorato built between 1764 and 1768. Rarely open to the public, its façade, also visible from the lungotevere below, has refined and complex architectural details rich in allegorical symbolism. It belongs to the Sovereign Military Hospitaller Order of the Knights of Malta, the origins of which stretch back to the 11C. Today they dedicate themselves above all to offering healthcare assistance to the poor.

On the same square is the church of Sant'Alessio, of ancient origin but much restructured in 1750, and the convent of Sant'Anselmo in neo-Romanseque style (1900).

Other famous sites on the Aventine Hill include the romantic Parco Savello, also known as the *Giardino degli Aranci* (Orange Garden) which offers

Via di Santa Sabina

a magnificent view over the city, the municipal rose garden, and the church of Santa Prisca which dates from the 5C but was restructured in the 17C and under which is a mithraeum dating from 95 AD.

TESTACCIO NEIGHBOURHOOD

Bounded, and in a certain sense isolated, by via Marmorata, the Tiber and the Aurelian walls, ever since Roman times Testaccio has had a commercial and industrial function associated with the nearby fluvial port, which used to be located on the riverbank next to the neighbourhood. Here in the 1C BC was an *emporium*, or market, the *Porticus Aemilia,* and large *horrea*, or storehouses, which became more extensive as the population of Rome grew larger. The goods arriving from the maritime cities of Ostia and Porto would be brought to Rome on barges pulled by oxen. Such commodities as oil and wine were closed in earthenware amphorae which, once the contents had been transferred, were broken and the pieces tidily disposed of in a dumping site just behind the storehouses. In this manner Monte Testaccio, also known as Monte dei Cocci (from the Latin *textae*, meaning pottery fragments), came into being, an artificial hill of potsherds some 30 metres high and with a diameter of nearly one kilometre. Used until perhaps the 5C, the site still remains partly unexplored. Over time craftsmen's workshops and shops sprang up around it, known by the popular name of *grotte*. They are now used as nightclubs and small restaurants, while the top of the hill is a public park.

Its principal function having passed, the regeneration of the neighbourhood began relatively recently. Around the year 1890, the municipal slaughterhouse or *Mattatoio* was located here, not far from the banks of the Tiber, and between the end of the 1800s and the beginning of the 1900s a lively working-class area came into being. These modifications were all contained in the *Piano Regolatore* of 1873, the first urban town plan following the Unification of Italy and the transfer of the capital to Rome.

On via Marmorata, at the edge of the Parco della Resistenza dell'8 settembre and more or less opposite Porta San Paolo, is the post office designed at the beginning of the 1930s by the architects Adalberto Libera and Mario De Renzi, leading exponents of Italian Rationalism.

The *Mattatoio* ceased to function in 1975 (a new slaughterhouse has been built in the south-east of the city) and the entire district is due to be renovated in such a way as to highlight some of its special characteristics such as its connection with the Tiber and with Monte Testaccio, and its Roman remains in general. A lively debate has taken place between

Keyhole in the door to the headquarters of the Knights of Malta, with the famous view of St. Peter's Basilica those in favour of conserving the *Mattatoio*, as a valuable example of industrial architecture, and supporters of a complete renewal of the area. Of these two schools of thought, the former has prevailed and the old meat market currently houses one of the two sites of the Museo d'Arte Contemporanea di Roma (MACRO). The principal site is in via Reggio Emilia in the industrial complex of the old Peroni beer factory.

Non-Catholic cemetery, exterior view of the perimeter walls

PYRAMID The pyramid is the tomb of the tribune Caius Cestius who died in the year 12 BC. Built by his heirs in little less than a year, it has a travertine base 29.5 metres wide and is 36.4 metres high. The interior, to which it is not easy for the public to gain admission, contains a burial chamber decorated with paintings of scant value. In the Middle Ages, the pyramid was believed to be the tomb or Romulus.

Next to the pyramid is the non-Catholic cemetery containing the remains of, among others, the English poets Percy Bysshe Shelley and John Keats, and of Antonio Gramsci, founder of the Italian Communist Party (1921).

Pyramid and Porta San Paolo

Porta San Paolo, detail

PORTA SAN PAOLO On the west side of the Aurelian walls, near the tomb of Caius Cestius, is the ancient city gate of Porta San Paolo. Some scholars believe that there were originally two gates not far apart, separated only by the pyramid. This would seem a reasonable hypothesis given the intense amount of traffic between the city and the port of Ostia, and was further corroborated in 1888 when a length of the walls was destroyed and certain brick stamps from the 4C were discovered relating to the closure of an opening in the walls.

The current gate was restructured by the emperor Honorius in 403, who raised the height of the towers and the walls. It was modified again in the following century while the city was under siege by the Goths, and further changes were made in the Renaissance and at the end of the 1700s. Currently, it houses the Museo della via Ostiense with interesting models of the archaeological sites of Ostia and Porto, intended by their makers to be seen by visitors before taking the train at the nearby station to visit the sites themselves.

FORMER POWER STATION OF GIOVANNI MONTE-
MARTINI In the autumn of 1997 a new exhibition space was opened in the oldest public power station in Rome, located on the via Ostiense facing the Mercati Generali.

It was provisionally intended to house works from the Capitoline Museums.

Former power station of Giovanni Montemartini, head of Augustus

The power station was built in 1912 and modernised in 1933, but in the 1950s it sank into crisis and went out of service in 1963. Now, with financial help from Rome's municipal energy and water company ACEA, it has been magnificently refurbished and adapted to its new function, representing an interesting example of the "new usage" of an industrial building.

The exhibits, displayed following new "topographical" criteria, include famous and less-famous works from the often hurried excavations of the late 1800s and early 1900s, and have been placed here as they await a definitive home in the extension to the Capitoline Museums.

Column Room. This area, which once held the machines that gathered the residue from coal burning, contains finds from the earliest period of Roman history. The most important exhibits come from the *area sacra di Sant'Omobono* at the foot of the Campidoglio, and from a necropolis on the Esquiline Hill near the basilica of St. Mary Major.

Items of interest include funerary beds, some splendid fragments of mosaics with fish and other animals from a house near via Panisperna, and the so-called *Togato Barberini* of the 1C BC.

Machine Room. This, the main hall of the power station, contains Roman copies as well as original Greek statues brought to Rome as spoils of war in the 1C BC. There is a particularly beautiful statue of Athena, another of Agrippina Minor in basanite (a hard stone from the Egyptian desert), and the sculputures that once decorated the front of the temple of Apollo Sosiano near the theatre of Marcellus.

Boiler Room. The most important exhibit is the large mosaic with hunting scenes (9 x 15 metres), taken from the *Horti Liciniani*. Around it a portico has been built to recreate the atmosphere of the great Roman villas, and this also acts a backdrop for elegant statues of outstanding beauty.

Boiler Room

itinerary

12

TRASTEVERE

TRASTEVERE

Until recently, this was the neighbourhood inhabited by Romans "from Rome", those whose origins in the capital stretched back several generations. Today however its old social and urban character survives only in part. Some evidence of the typically Roman make-up of the neighbourhood survives in the traditional *Festa de' Noantri* (Roman dialect for *Our Feast*) which is celebrated every year in the month of July.

The area has been settled since Roman times (the name derives from *Trans Tiberim*, beyond the Tiber) and in antiquity was chiefly associated with the commercial activities of the river port. These mostly involved Oriental peoples, hence the large number of non-pagan places of worship belonging to Syrians, Greeks and Jews. A number of bridges connected Trastevere to the left bank of the Tiber: Ponte Probo and Ponte Sublicio (both just south of modern-day Ponte Palatino), Ponte Emilio (the *Ponte Rotto* which carried the first stage of the via Aurelia), as well as Ponte Cestio and Ponte Fabricio on the Isola Tiberina. The Aurelian walls (270-275) separated the area from the Roman campagna. The via Portuense passed though the

walls at the old gate of Porta Portese, which was demolished in 1643.
In the early years of Christianity (4-5C) and during the Middle Ages,
many religious communities moved to Trastevere, their main centres
being Santa Maria in Trastevere, San Cosimato and Santa Cecilia.
During the Renaissance the hospitals of San Giovanni Battista
dei Genovesi (1481) and of Madonna dell'Orto (1489) were built,
and via della Lungaretta - the continuation of via della Lungara
- became increasingly important as the main axis leading towards
the area of the Vatican.
Under Pope Paul V (Camillo Borghese 1605-1621), via di San
Francesco a Ripa was laid down and soon became lined with
terraced houses. Pope Urban VIII (Maffeo Barberini 1623-1644) had
the city walls strengthened and a new gate opened, called, like the old
one, Porta Portese; it was completed by Pope Innocent X (Giovanni
Battista Pamphilj 1644-1655) and still exists today. The beginning
of the 1700s saw the completion of two more great buildings: the
Ospizio di San Michele, now seat of the Ministero dei Beni Culturali,
and the hospital of San Gallicano, which still functions today.

This compact city quarter underwent considerable changes with the new city plans developed after the Unification of Italy. In 1886 viale Trastevere (initially called *del Re* then *del Lavoro*) split the area into two. The creation (1876-1926) of the *muraglioni* (the embankments along the river) and of the lungotevere, with the consequent destruction of the fluvial port of Ripa Grande and of many activities such as that of milling, raised a barrier between the neighbourhood and the Tiber. However, the opening of viale Trastevere did provide an ideal axis along which to construct various important buildings such as the Ministero della Pubblica Istruzione and the Palazzo degli Esami.

Today, the neighbourhood still partly retains its characteristic lively atmosphere, typically Roman yet also cosmopolitan, with many restaurants and bars that make it one of the busiest areas of the city, especially at night.

On the western edge of Trastevere, every Sunday morning, the famous market of Porta Portese is held, occupying an entire portion of the via Portuense and surrounding streets on the right bank of the river: a vast flea market in which it is possible to find all kinds of merchandise, modern and antique, new and second-hand.

Santa Cecilia,
central nave

SANTA CECILIA Dating from the time of Paschal I (817-824), the basilica was built on the site where tradition has it that St. Cecilia, her future husband and his brother all suffered martyrdom. Having died after three days of agony, the saint was buried in the catacombs of San Callisto. The church became very important during the Middle Ages, and the portico and campanile were built in the 11C. Later, in 1293, the greatest Roman Gothic painter Pietro Cavallini, frescoed the choir of the convent with the *Last Judgement*, in which the angels have characteristic colourful wings. Dating from the same period is the elegant ciborium by Arnolfo di Cambio, similar to the one the same artist made for the altar of the basilica of St. Paul's.

SAN FRANCESCO A RIPA In piazza di San Francesco d'Assisi, between the years 1682 and 1689, the architect Mattia De Rossi built the church of San Francesco a Ripa, famous for its splendid statue of the *Ecstasy of Blessed Ludovica Albertoni*, one of the last works by Gian Lorenzo Bernini (1674).

SAN CRISOGONO Located in piazza Sonnino, this church was built in the 4-5C over a pre-existing Roman structure. Like many Roman churches, it was renovated in the 8C then rebuilt in the 12C when the Cosmatesque floor and the campanile were added. In 1626, by order of cardinal Scipione Borghese, the building was completely reconstructed by Giovanni Battista Soria, to whom is due the façade decorated with the cardinal's coat-of-arms. The crypt contains remains of the original church and traces of paintings from the 8C and 10C. Also on piazza Sonnino is the 13C Torre degli Anguillara, next to which is a small mediaeval-type house rebuilt using ancient materials and enclosing the so-called *Casa di Dante*.

Former monastery
of San Cosimato,
14C cloister

PIAZZA DI SAN COSIMATO In this square is the entrance to the former monastery of San Cosimato (today a hospital, the Nuovo Regina Margherita) where two cloisters may still be seen: one Romanesque from the 11C-12C, the other from the 1400s with octagonal pillars. The church dates from the time of Pope Sixtus IV (Francesco della Rovere 1471-1484), and is thought to be the work of the Florentine architect Baccio Pontelli.

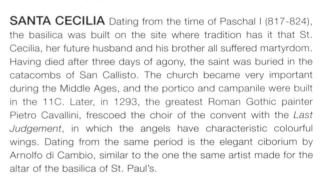

SANTA MARIA IN TRASTEVERE The church stands in the square of the same name which, before viale Trastevere was opened, was the real heart of the district.

Next to the church is the fine 17C Palazzo di San Callisto, which belongs to the Vatican. It was built to the model of Palazzo Farnese, and is the most important of the elegant buildings overlooking the piazza.

The fountain in the middle dates from the 1400s. It was restored by Bramante in 1472, and again in 1658 by Bernini who moved it from its original position next to the wall opposite the church and added the shells. Another restoration by Carlo Fontana in 1694 removed the shells and replaced them with double shells decorated with stone tablets bearing the crest of the local authorities of Rome.

The church, which may date back as far as the 4C, underwent modifications in the 9C and was completely reconstructed by Pope Innocent II (Gregorio Papareschi 1130-1143).

Piazza di Santa Maria in Trastevere

It is preceded by an 18C portico the walls of which are inlaid with Roman and mediaeval fragments. The top of the façade is decorated with late 13C mosaics, the work of Pietro Cavallini. The bell tower is from the 12C.

The interior has a nave, two side aisles and a raised apse. The columns, capitals and entablature were reconstructed at the beginning of the 12C with material taken from the baths of Caracalla. The apse mosaics date from the same period, depicting the *Virgin Mary and Christ enthroned*. To their left are Sts. *Calixtus and Lawrence, and Pope Innocent II* who ordered the work and holds a model of the church in his hand. To the right are Sts. *Peter, Cornelius, Julius and Calepodius*. At the bottom, twelve *sheep* converge upon the *Lamb of God*. At the top of the arch, and dating from the same period, are the four *Evangelists*, and at the bottom splendid framed scenes of the *life of Mary* attributed to Pietro Cavallini (late 13C). The paschal candlesticks and the floor, both restored, are the work of the Cosmati (a 13C Roman family of mosaicists), while the ciborium over the altar is a 19C reconstruction using ancient materials.

Further additions were made at the end of the 1500s - the Altemps chapel to the left of the altar - and in 1680, when the Avila chapel was created in the left-hand aisle by the decorator Antonio Gherardi. The wooden coffered ceiling was designed in 1617 by the painter Domenichino.

Santa Maria in Trastevere, apse, mosaic of Virgin Mary and Christ enthroned, detail

Piazza Trilussa, Lorenzo Ferri, monument to Carlo Alberto Salustri known as Trilussa

PIAZZA TRILUSSA This square is named after an important Roman dialect poet, who lived between 1871 and 1950. The fountain dates from 1613 and was built by order of Pope Paul V. It originally rested against the Ospizio dei Mendicanti in via Giulia, but following the floods of 1870 it was dismantled and rebuilt here on a raised base with a stairway.

PIAZZA DI SANT'EGIDIO The square contains the Museo di Roma in Trastevere, and the late 16C church of Santa Maria della Scala. In Rome it is also well-known for housing the headquarters of a community dedicated to caring for people in need.

SANTA MARIA DEI SETTE DOLORI The church is part of a complex of buildings that make up the convent of an order of cloistered nuns, the Augustinian Oblate Sisters, and for this reason visiting hours are restricted. The building was designed by Francesco Borromini, who began work in 1643. The interior, beyond the square pronaos with its concave and convex walls, is a single rectangular space containing columns with composite capitals, and with two chapels to the sides. Outside, the unfinished parts, where the brick surface is still visible, are divided into concave and straight sections, with openings typical of Borromini.

Santa Maria dei Sette Dolori

PORTA SETTIMIANA An example of the architectural stratification of monuments: it was built by Septimius Severus in the 3C AD, restructured by Pope Alexander VI at the end of the 15C, and modified into its current form by Pope Pius VI in the 18C.

BOTANICAL GARDENS The gardens belong to the Department of Plant Biology of Rome's *La Sapienza* University. It is a twelve-hectare park with 2000 square metres of greenhouses, and is more than a century old having occupied its current site since 1883. An avenue lined with palm trees leads to the Fontana dei Tritoni, built in 1750 to a design by Ferdinando Fuga and once part of the gardens of Palazzo Corsini. Particularly worthy of note are the rose garden, the collection of bamboo, the rockery, the Japanese garden, the Roman woodland and the tropical greenhouse.

Botanical Gardens,
Fontana dei Tritoni

VILLA FARNESINA This most elegant of 16C residences is currently the official headquarters of the *Accademia Nazionale dei Lincei*, the oldest academy in Europe dedicated to the study of physics and mathematics. Its name derives from its symbol of the lynx, an animal famous for its acute eyesight, an indispensable asset for scientific research. The main seat of the *Accademia* is in the nearby Palazzo Corsini.

The palazzo, the gardens of which once extended down to the Tiber, was ordered by the aesthete Agostino Chigi, banker to the papal Cuira and businessman, whose activities extended as far as London and Cairo. He

Villa Farnesina, Raphael,
Triumph of Galatea

chose to entrust the commission to the Sienese architect Baldassarre Peruzzi, who worked here from 1508 to 1511. Later, great painters also became involved in the project including Raphael, Giovanni da Udine, Sebastiano del Piombo, Sodoma, and Peruzzi himself.

Particularly splendid are the Gallery, the Loggia with the fresco of *Galatea* and the *Constellations* on the ceiling, and the famous Hall of Perspectives.

The banquets held here must have been very majestic. It is recounted that Agostino Chigi would serve his guests - usually popes and cardinals - on silver plates decorated with his family's coat-of-arms. At the end of the meal, plates and cutlery would all be thrown into the Tiber where, however, they were caught and recovered by means of a hidden net.

Devastated during the Sack of Rome in 1527, in 1580 the villa became the property of the Farnese family, whence the name Farnesina, and in the mid 18C of the Bourbons of Naples. In 1927 it passed to the Italian State.

PALAZZO AND GALLERIA CORSINI The idea of establishing a *quadreria* (a collection of paintings hung on the basis of aesthetic rather than chronological criteria) in a private residence is due to cardinal Neri Maria Corsini, nephew of Pope Clement XII (1730-1740). Between 1736 and 1751 the cardinal had the palazzo, which was built over a 15C structure, completely refurbished entrusting the project to Ferdinando Fuga, a famous architect working in Rome and Naples. The new building thus became home to collections of works from Florence, the hometown of the Corsini family, and to new acquisitions made in Bologna, Venice and Rome. All the works reveal a clear classicist taste, in contrast to the late Baroque tendencies prevalent at the time.

In 1818 another member of the family, Prince Tommaso Corsini, was elected as a senator in Rome, and the palazzo and the gallery underwent a further period of growth. New purchases were made including many Flemish paintings and works from the Neapolitan school of the 17-18C, as well as new paintings of neo-classical tendencies. Again, these works were exhibited following aesthetic rather than chronological criteria.

Ceded by the heirs to the Italian State in 1883, the collection became the central nucleus - subsequently enlarged with donations from other families - of the Galleria Nazionale di Arte Antica, directed by the famous Italian art critic Adolfo Venturi. In the 1950s, some of the works from the 15C and 16C were transferred to Palazzo Barberini.

The originality of this museum lies in the fact that almost all the extremely varied material is still kept in the place chosen by the original collectors, providing a precious record of a past age.

Of particular interest in Room II are a number of works dating from between the 1300s and the 1600s, including artists of the calibre of Fra Angelico, Jacopo Bassano, Cavalier d'Arpino and Pieter Paul Rubens. Room III contains paintings by Caravaggio (*St. John the Baptist*) and by his Italian and foreign followers. Room V, before the Corsini family moved into the palazzo, was the Roman residence of Queen Christina of Sweden, who came to Rome in 1655 to cultivate her literary and artistic interests, and died here in 1689.

Christian Berentz,
Still life with fly

Caravaggio,
St. John the Baptist,

ROMA O MORTE

GIVSEPPE GA

JANICULUM HILL

This hill takes its name from the Roman divinity Janus, who used to be depicted with two faces because he was the custodian of city gates, where people would come in and go out. A temple dedicated to him probably existed on this site, but no trace of it has survived.

The hill was only partly contained within the Aurelian walls of the 3C, but later, at the time of Pope Leo IV (847-855), it was

included within the walls of the Vatican Borgo. In 1642 it was given additional fortifications by Pope Urban VIII (Maffeo Barberini).
On the square of San Pietro in Montorio (from *Mons Aureus*, the ancient name of the hill deriving from its gold coloured earth) is the Spanish academy of history, archaeology and fine arts, next to which are two buildings of particular artistic merit: the church of San Pietro in Montorio and Bramante's famous *Tempietto*.

Porta San Pancrazio

PORTA SAN PANCRAZIO AND WALLS The Aurelian
walls (275 AD) were restructured in the 16C and have been modified
on a number of occasions since then. Porta San Pancrazio was
built in 1643 by Pope Urban VIII then renovated in the mid 19C
following the battles between French troops and the forces of the
Roman Republic. The gate building contains two exhibition areas: the
Museo Garibaldino and the Museo della Divisione Italiana Partigiana
Garibaldi (recalling the valiant partisans who, following the armistice of
8 September 1943, fought for almost two years alongside Yugoslav
forces for the liberation of Montenegro).

Emilio Gallori, monument to
Giuseppe Garibaldi

MONUMENT TO GIUSEPPE GARIBALDI Standing
at the centre of the square of the same name, which offers a
breathtaking view over Rome, the monument was sculpted by the
artist Emilio Gallori in 1895. It is a tribute to Giuseppe
Garibaldi, hero of Italian Unification. Born in Nice in
1807, he was one of the protagonists of the political
reunification of the peninsula which was finally
achieved, after decades of struggle, in 1860. He was
also famous for having fought in Brazil and Uruguay,
earning the nickname of "Hero of the Two Worlds". He
died in 1882 on the island of Caprera in Sardinia.

VILLA LANTE This building, once the luxurious 16C
residence of the Lante family, is now the headquarters of
the Finnish embassy to the Holy See and of the Roman
Finnish Institute.

Mario Rutelli, monument to
Anita Garibaldi

MONUMENT TO ANITA GARIBALDI The
monument stands over the tomb of Garibaldi's famous
companion and lover. It dates from 1932, the work of the
Sicilian sculptor Mario Rutelli.

Janiculum Beacon

Tasso's Oak

BEACON ON THE JANICULUM Built in 1911 with funds from the Italian community in Argentina, it is stylistically similar to the Victor Emanuel Monument in piazza Venezia, which was built at the same time. A room at the bottom of the tower contains an album with the signatures of the donors. It irradiates a beam of light with the three colours of the Italian flag to illuminate the city on gala evenings.

TASSO'S OAK AND AMPHITHEATRE Tasso's Oak is a tree trunk struck by lightening where, according to tradition, the great poet Torquato Tasso (Sorrento 1544 - Rome 1595) came to sit and meditate before his death. The amphitheatre, dedicated to the same poet, is modern. On summer evenings it is used to stage comedies, some in Roman dialect.

SANT'ONOFRIO AL GIANICOLO Begun in the mid 1400s, it was completed in the second half of the 16C by Sixtus V (1585-1590) who also restructured the nearby via di Sant'Onofrio. The interior contains frescoes by Cavalier d'Arpino, the master of Caravaggio. The apse also has noteworthy frescoes, attributed by some scholars to Baldassarre Peruzzi, a sophisticated early 16C architect and painter from Siena.

Fontana
dell'Acqua Paola

FONTANA DELL'ACQUA PAOLA This fountain was commissioned by Pope Paul V (Camillo Borghese 1605-1621) from whom it takes its name. The work of the architects Giovanni Fontana and Flaminio Ponzio, it was constructed between 1608 and 1612 with stone taken from the Forum of Nerva. The red granite Ionic columns come from the old basilica of St. Peter's. Underneath the great papal coat-of-arms with a griffin and eagle, a large inscription recalls that the water comes from the lake of Bracciano. The enormous basin at the bottom dates from 1690, and was ordered by Pope Alexander VIII (Pietro Ottoboni 1689-1691) who was the first to consolidate and restore the fountain.

Janiculum Ossuary

JANICULUM OSSUARY This ossuary contains the remains of a number of young Romans who died in the 1949 rebellion against the Pope and the French. Among the heroes whose remains and memory are preserved here is Goffredo Mameli, who died at the age of 21, the author of a poem which, set to music in Turin by the composer Michele Novaro, became the Italian national anthem.

SAN PIETRO IN MONTORIO This church was built over a preexisting mediaeval structure in 1472, during the papacy of Sixtus IV. The Florentine architect Baccio Pontelli, working on commission from the Spanish kings Ferdinand of Aragon and Isabella of Castile, built the façade which, with its two levels and rose window, still reflects the Gothic style. It is finished at the top with a pediment, while a 17C stairway with two ramps leads up to the entrance. The interior has a single nave, a short transept, a presbytery and side chapels.

In the first chapel on the right is the *Flagellation of Jesus* by the Venetian painter Sebastiano del Piombo (1518), while the fifth on the left contains beautiful stuccoes by Giulio Mazzoni.

San Pietro in Montorio

BRAMANTE'S *TEMPIETTO* In the courtyard next to the church of San Pietro in Montorio is one of the most important Renaissance works in Rome. Perhaps inspired by the ancient temples of Vesta, it was built - probably in 1502-1507 - to mark the spot where it was believed that St. Peter had been crucified. It aroused much admiration at the time and is mentioned in 16C Italian treatises as an example of *bella e buona architettura*.

The round plan building is divided into three levels: an underground crypt with the "hole" that contained the cross, a cella surrounded by a peristyle with 16 Doric Order columns and a frieze with the symbols of the Church, and a drum with alternate semicircular and rectangular niches surmounted by a dome and lantern. An elegant balustrade provides a light finishing touch to the lower portico, acting as a link between the emptiness of the skies and the solidity of the masonry.

In the original plans, this small but graceful building was to have been surrounded by a circular courtyard with an intermediate colonnade. Had this been built, the *Tempietto* would have become the fulcrum of a centripetal space, symbol of divine perfection and the final goal of a journey, at once physical and spiritual.

Bramante's
Tempietto

itinerary

14

VATICAN

CASTEL SANT'ANGELO

This is one of the monuments of ancient Rome to have undergone the greatest number of transformations over time, not only through structural extensions and modifications, but also through functional changes. In fact, it came into being as an imperial mausoleum, in the Middle Ages it became a fortress defending the right bank of the Tiber, in the Renaissance a fortified papal residence and finally, in the 18C, an aristocratic mansion. Until 1901, the interior was used as a prison, the most famous cell being known as *San Marocco* or *Sanmalò*, once

used to hold prisoners of noble rank who would to be left there to die of hunger. Today almost the entire complex is open to the public, and its well-organised and well-labelled museums make for a pleasant and informative visit. There is also an attractive refreshment area and bookshop near the *Passetto* (a raised corridor, built at the end of the 13C and still standing today, that connects the Vatican Palaces to Castel Sant'Angelo and enabled pontiffs to take refuge in the castle at times of conflict).

View of Castel Sant'Angelo
from ponte Sant'Angelo

Ercole Ferrata,
Angel with cross

Castel Sant'Angelo came into being as the mausoleum of Hadrian (117-138), a monumental tomb that the emperor, on his return from long journeys in Greece and Egypt, ordered be built for himself and his dynasty, the Antonines. Work probably began in the year 130 and was finished in 139 shortly after Hadrian's death. The mausoleum had a square base upon which stood a great cylindrical drum some 24 metres high. At the centre of that was a tower (also originally cylindrical). In the depths of the interior was the burial chamber containing the funerary urns of Hadrian and his descendants down to Caracalla, who was murdered in 217. A bronze four-horse chariot with a statue of the emperor Hadrian stood at the top of the monument.

The form of the mausoleum, inspired by Etruscan tumuli or perhaps by the monumental tombs of the East, followed the model of the mausoleum of Augustus, built a century and a half earlier in Campo Marzio.

A bridge connected the mausoleum to the other bank of the Tiber (Ponte Elio, 134 AD, restructured during the Baroque).

In the year 271, having built the corner towers on the base, the structure was used by the emperor Aurelian to defend the right bank of the Tiber. Thus began the transformation of the mausoleum into a fortress, a function it maintained throughout the Middle Ages.

An even more radical transformation turning the building into a real "castle" was brought about by Pope Boniface IX (1389-1404), and further modifications were made over the following two and a half centuries, concluding in 1630 with Urban VIII.

The Renaissance in particular brought great changes to the structure, still easily visible today thanks to plaques on the walls, ancient inscriptions and papal coats-of-arms on architraves and ceilings. The main stages of these transformations are as follows:

- The construction of three bastions and two small towers protecting the bridge, during the pontificate of Nicholas V (1447-1455).

- The renovation of the great perimeter walls and

Castel Sant'Angelo, Courtyard
of Honour or of the Angel

the building of a papal apartment under Pope Alexander VI (1492-1503), as recalled on the walls themselves in the great coat-of-arms of the pope's family flanked by two winged victories.

- The replacement, in the late 1400s, of the chariot with a marble statue of St. Michael the Archangel by Raffaello da Montelupo, whence the name of Castel Sant'Angelo. The 15C statue was replaced in 1752 with the bronze angel by Pieter Anton Verschaffelt, which still stands atop the monument today.

- The building of an apartment, decorated with splendid frescoes by Perin del Vaga and his workshop, by order of Pope Paul III (1534-1549), who became well aware of the strategic importance of Castel Sant'Angelo following the Sack of Rome in 1527.

- The building of the pentagonal bastions at the corners of the outer defences under Pope Pius IV (1559-1565).

- The fortification of the pentagonal bastions during the reign of Pope Urban VIII (1623-1644);

- The decoration of the bridge under Pope Clement IX, with statues designed by Gian Lorenzo Bernini and made by his assistants between 1667 and 1669.

Courtyard of the Well or of
Alexander VI

These statues represent angels with open wings and wind-swept vestments, each bearing a symbol of Christ's Passion.

Other minor alterations were made in the second half of the 18C with the building of a few small houses. It should be noted, finally, that the 19C construction of the embankment walls along the Tiber greatly modified the appearance of the castle, making it much less imposing as the walls and bastions were buried to a height of three metres.

VATICAN CITY

With a surface area of just 44 hectares, Vatican City State is the world's smallest independent nation, in terms both of number of inhabitants and of territory. Its borders are delineated by the Vatican Walls and, on St. Peter's Square, by the strip of travertine connecting the two arms of the colonnade. Apart from the land within the State itself, Vatican jurisdiction also partly extends to certain places within Rome and outside Rome that enjoy the status of extraterritoriality.

Vatican City State came into being with the Lateran Pacts, signed on 11 February 1929 by the Holy See and the Italian State. The agreement established the new State as a sovereign body subject to international law, created in order to ensure the Holy See, in its capacity as the supreme institution of Catholic Church, "absolute and visible independence," and guarantee it "indisputable sovereignty in international matters", as the preamble to the pacts themselves says. The Church carries out her evangelical mission both through the particular (or local) Churches and through the central government, which is made up of the supreme pontiff and the bodies that help him in the exercise of his responsibilities towards the universal Church.

The form of government is an absolute monarchy. The supreme pontiff is Head of State and has full legislative, executive and judicial powers. During the period of *sede vacante*, these powers devolve upon the College of Cardinals. Legislative power, apart

from being in the hands of the pope, is also exercised in his name by a commission with a cardinal president and cardinal members, appointed for a period of five years. Executive power is delegated to the president of this commission, who by virtue of his office takes the name of president of the Governorate, in which role he is assisted by a secretary general and an under-secretary general. Upon him depends the running of the central administration and offices into which the Governorate is divided, in other words the bodies though which executive power is wielded. Judicial power is exercised, in the pope's name, by the courts and tribunals of the State's legal system. Vatican City State has its own flag, divided vertically into two different-coloured sections, one yellow nearest the flagpole, the other white with the pontifical tiara and the crossed keys. It mints its own money (currently the euro) and issues its own stamps. It also has its own daily newspaper, the *Osservatore Romano* founded in 1861, and, since 1931, a radio station, Vatican Radio, which transmits all over the world in various languages. The number of inhabitants currently stands at around 800; of these, about 450 have Vatican citizenship while the others, though living in the State temporarily or permanently, do not. The safety of the pope and of the State is entrusted to the Corps of the Pontifical Swiss Guard, which was founded in 1506 and the members of which still wear a uniform traditionally held to have been designed by Michelangelo, and to the Gendarmes, who oversee all the policing and security needs of the State.

VATICAN CITY DOWN THE CENTURIES In antiquity, the term Vatican was used to designate the marshy area on the right bank of the Tiber, between Ponte Milvio and modern-day Ponte Sisto. During the period of the kings and throughout the Republican age the area was known as *Ager Vaticanus* and stretched north to the mouth of the Cremera stream and south at least as far as the Janiculum. In the Imperial age, beginning in the 2C AD, the use of the name *Vaticanum* is recorded referring to an area that covered more or less that of modern Vatican City State. In Roman times this region, which lay outside the city, was reclaimed and occupied with villas, the gardens of Agrippina - mother of the emperor Caligula (37-41) - and vast necropolises lying along the main roads. In his mother's gardens, Caligula built a small circus for training charioteers (*Gaianum*), later restructured by Nero (54-68) and held by tradition to be the place where Peter suffered martyrdom in the great persecution of Christians ordered by Nero in 64 AD. Along the via Trionfale, which leads north from St. Peter's Square towards Monte Mario, were various groups of tombs, while along the via Cornelia, which leads west, was the necropolis containing the grave of the Apostle. The presence of Peter established a geographical fulcrum in the area which since then for two millennia has been the most important place of Christian pilgrimage. Many faithful who came to visit the tomb, driven by the desire to remain close to St. Peter, sought to be buried nearby. The resulting necropolis was interred during the construction of the basilica dedicated to the Apostle, ordered by the emperor Constantine (306-337). In fact, after having granted freedom of worship to Christianity with the famous Edict of Milan in 313 AD, about the year 324 Constantine ordered work to begin on a great new church, with a nave and four

Model of the
Constantinian basilica

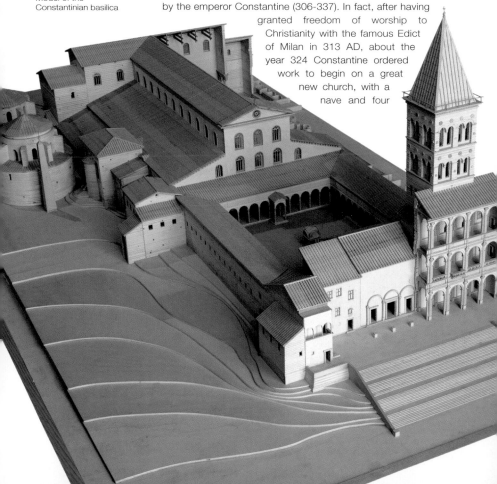

side aisles, a transept and an apse, at the centre of which was Peter's grave. The building also had a great stairway and a quadriporticus (the latter marking the limit of access for the non-baptised). At the same time, Nero's circus gradually fell into ruins, also because much of its stone was used to build the new church which soon became a centre of attraction in the city. Some centuries later Pope Leo IV (847-855) built the first walls of the *Civitas* which from him took the name of *Leonina* and which became the spiritual nucleus of the new mediaeval and Renaissance Rome. Although the popes themselves resided in the Lateran Palace, during the Middle Ages various buildings were constructed in the area around St. Peter's. In particular, during the reign of Eugenius III (1145-1153) and of Innocent III (1198-1216), the Leonine walls were restructured and the first palazzo was built, later extended between the late 1200s and the early 1300s. However in 1309 the seat of the papacy was transferred to Avignon, Rome and St. Peter's Basilica were abandoned for more than a century and even after the popes' return in 1377, it took more than 50 years to restore lustre to the city. In the mid 15C, the question of a possible complete reconstruction of St. Peter's was broached for the first time. Pope Nicholas V (1447-1455) ordered the architect Bernardo Rossellino to draw up plans to extend the basilica with a new apse, larger than the one on the Constantinian edifice. Work began, but a few years later the advance of the Turks and the fall of Constantinople led to its being abandoned. Between 1477 and 1480, Pope Sixtus IV (1471-1484) began work on a great new chapel which from him took the name of "Sistine". Decorated with frescoes by the greatest Italian painters of the time, it was inaugurated on 15 August 1483. Great changes were made by Pope Julius II (1503-1513), who radically transformed the Vatican citadel, beginning the demolition of the Constantinian basilica, making a start on work to build the new St. Peter's, and creating the famous Belvedere Courtyard to connect the Palazzetto del Belvedere of Pope Innocent VIII (1484-1492) to the north with the nucleus of mediaeval buildings to the south. He also called Raphael and Michelangelo to Rome to fresco, respectively, the papal apartments and the Sistine Chapel. Further work was competed over the course of the 16C. Following various vicissitudes the central core of St. Peter's Basilica was planned and begun by Michelangelo in the mid 1500s and subsequently covered with a great "vaulted" dome by Giacomo Della Porta. The nave was added by Carlo Maderno in the early years of the 17C with the extension of the longitudinal arm of the basilica and, in the mid 1600s, Gian Lorenzo Bernini completed the great square, enclosed by two semicircular arms of quadruple columns giving the area its current Baroque appearance and linking this place of prayer to the rest of the city.

Via Cornelia

■ Nero's circus
■ Pagan necropolis
  Constantinian basilica
■ Modern basilica

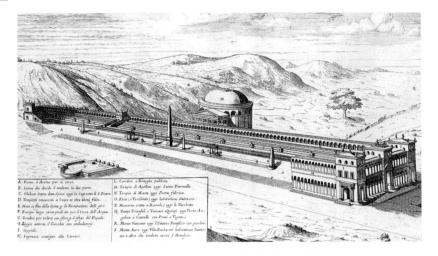

Carlo Fontana, view of the Ager Vaticanus and of Nero's Circus, engraving from *Il Tempio Vaticano e la sua origine*, Roma 1694

HISTORY OF ST. PETER'S BASILICA During the great persecution of Christians, which was unleashed by Nero in the year 64 AD and took place in the Circus of Caligula, St. Peter was among those who suffered martyrdom. He was crucified and later buried, according to the *Liber Pontificalis* (I, 118), *via Aurelia […] iuxta palatium Neronianum, in Vaticanum* (in the Vatican, on the via Aurelia in front of Nero's palace). Among the evidence indicating the place of his martyrdom is a passage from Eusebius of Caesarea (3-4C) quoting a letter written by the presbyter Gaius to Proclus inviting him to come to Rome, "to the Vatican or to the road to Ostia, [where] you will find the trophies of those who founded this Church". Because of the importance of this evidence the 2C aedicule protecting Peter's grave, discovered during excavation work in the Vatican necropolis, was given the name of *Tropaion of Gaius*. Following the emperor Constantine's proclamation of the Edict of Milan (313 AD), Christians were finally free to build their own places of worship, and it was Constantine himself who, in 324, ordered the erection of a basilica incorporating the *Tropaion of Gaius* and having the tomb of Peter as the focal point of the entire structure. Consecrated in 329, the new building had a longitudinal plan with a central nave, four side aisles and a transept. Outside, a stairway led to a quadriporticus directly in front of the basilica, and at the centre of the quadriporticus - also known as the *Paradise* - was a fountain for the ablution of catechumens. That fountain has been identified with the great bronze *pigna* (pinecone) mentioned in Dante's *Divine Comedy* ("la faccia sua mi parea lunga e grossa / come la pina di San Pietro a Roma", *Inf.* XXXI 58-60) and now located in the courtyard of the same name within the Vatican Museums.

It was in this basilica that on Christmas night in the year 800, Charlemagne, king of the Franks, was crowned as emperor of the Holy Roman Empire; and it was to this basilica that, until the early 1300s, masses of pilgrims came on foot from all over Europe to venerate the tomb of the Prince of the Apostles.

When Rome was abandoned for Avignon during the "Babylonian captivity" of the papacy (1309-1377), the basilica, already more than 1000 years old, began to suffer from increasing maintenance and stability problems. Records are scant, but it is certain that in the mid 15C Pope Nicholas V ordered the architect Bernardo Rossellino to draw up plans that included a new choir outside the apse of the Constantinian basilica, the walls of which were partially built to a height of about one and a half metres.

At the beginning of the 1500s, the decision whether to restore or completely rebuild St. Peter's became ever more imperative. In 1505, the new pope (Julius II, elected in October 1503) decided to entrust the commission to one of the greatest architects of the age, Donato Bramante, at that time resident in Rome. Bramante's involvement in this enterprise led to him being given the nickname *maestro ruinante*. Many of his designs are conserved at the Uffizi Gallery in Florence, and all have the shared characteristic of presenting a centrally planned structure in the form of a Greek cross with four protruding apses and a central cube covered with a hemispherical dome. It has been observed (BRUSCHI 1977) that this design reflects a particular form of symbolism "which may be interpreted - following an ancient tradition especially widespread in the Byzantine world - as a cube (the earth) with four arms (the four parts of the world) and surmounted by a dome (the heavens)".

On 18 April 1506 a great ceremony took place to mark the beginning of work on the first pier, and the following year the foundations of the other three piers began to be excavated. However the deaths, first of Julius II (1513) and then of Bramante (1514), brought operations to a halt with only the four piers completed.

Over the next 40 years other projects were drawn up while an impassioned debate continued as to whether the new St. Peter's should have a central plan, dear not only to Bramante but also more generally to all Renaissance architects, or a longitudinal plan in the form of a Latin cross, more in keeping with ecclesiastical tradition and better suited to covering the entire consecrated area of the old Constantinian basilica. With the precondition of maintaining the four piers already built, Raphael (1514) and Antonio da Sangallo the Younger (1538) proposed a longitudinal plan, Baldassarre Peruzzi (1520) a central plan.

Finally, in 1547, Michelangelo was commissioned by Pope Paul III to prepare a new project. He returned to Bramante's central plan, making the piers thicker and the perimeter wall deeper to as to be able to create niches and protuberances. His design, which included a great dome covering the central area in which the papal altar was located, was actually built, though with the exception of the dome itself. Following Michelangelo's death in 1564 it fell to his pupil Giacomo Della Porta to complete the great enterprise, though not without making a few modifications of his own, such as slightly lengthening the curve of the cupola.

The dilemma between a longitudinal or a central plan had still not been definitively resolved. However, when the Council of Trent, which concluded in 1563, recommended the use of longitudinal structures for churches the architect Carlo Maderno was commissioned to lengthen the central body built by Michelangelo. This he did with the addition of three spans that gave St. Peter's the form of a Latin cross. Maderno also built the classical-style façade, completed between 1607 and 1612. This, however, had the defect of obscuring and distancing the view of Michelangelo's dome, and Bernini's square in front of the basilica was later designed with a view to solving the problem of bringing the great structure "closer" to the observer.

Carlo Fontana, view of the interior of the Constantinian basilica, engraving from *Il Tempio Vaticano e la sua origine*, Roma 1694, details

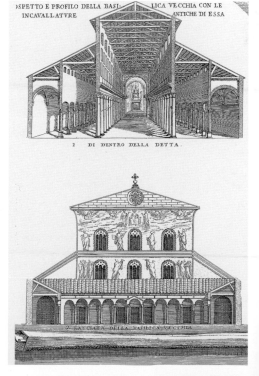

ST. PETER'S BASILICA

The Constantinian basilica disappeared gradually. Slightly more than 150 years passed between the original decision taken by Pope Nicholas V (Tommaso Parentucelli) to restore and enlarge the old basilica, a commission he entrusted to Rossellino in the second half of the 15C, and the completion of the new building with the unveiling of the façade in 1612. A lengthy period in terms of years but entirely understandable if one considers the immensity of the undertaking and the continual changes made to the project as it progressed.

To understand the genesis of St. Peter's Basilica is to comprehend the history of the development of thought and art over those various historical periods.

In the more than 150 years it took to complete the construction of the basilica, the most famous artists of the age

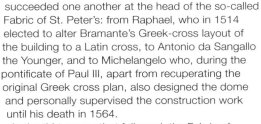

succeeded one another at the head of the so-called Fabric of St. Peter's: from Raphael, who in 1514 elected to alter Bramante's Greek-cross layout of the building to a Latin cross, to Antonio da Sangallo the Younger, and to Michelangelo who, during the pontificate of Paul III, apart from recuperating the original Greek cross plan, also designed the dome and personally supervised the construction work until his death in 1564.

In the thirty years that followed, the Fabric of

St. Peter's was first entrusted to Vignola and subsequently to the architects Giacomo Della Porta and Domenico Fontana, to whom must be awarded the merit of having completed, around the year 1588, Michelangelo's plans for the dome. The current appearance of St. Peter's Basilica is due to modifications made by Carlo Maderno, who gave it the form of a Latin cross and added the spectacular façade.

Work on the basilica finally came to an end with the solemn consecration of the building during the pontificate of Urban VIII in 1626. However it was only between 1656 and 1667, by order of Pope Alexander VII, that Bernini planned and completed the great colonnade of St. Peter's Square with its 1C BC obelisk at the centre. Originally on the *spina* of the Circus of Nero, where St. Peter was martyred, the obelisk was moved to its current position in 1586 by Domenico Fontana on the orders of Pope Sixtus V. St. Peter's Basilica can accommodate up to 20,000 faithful and is about 190 metres long. The width of the nave with the two side aisles is 58 metres and the nave is 45.5 metres high from the floor to the top of the vault. The dome measures 136 metres in height including the cross on top. The interior, with its vast mosaic decorations, contains some of the most famous works of art in the world such as, for example, Bernini's *baldachin* and Michelangelo's *Pietà*.

THE SQUARE Created by Bernini between 1656 and 1667 under Pope Alexander VII (1655-1667), it is divided into two parts: a trapezoidal area enclosed by two straight arms with "closed" faces, converging towards one another on either side of the parvise, and an elliptical area contained between two semicircular quadruple colonnades. As Bernini himself said: "Because the church of St. Peter's is like the womb that generates other churches, she had to have a portico that shows how she maternally opens her arms to Catholics to confirm them in their beliefs, heretics to reunite them with the Church, and infidels to illuminate them in the true faith ".

Bernini's original project included a third section of the portico to close the end of the square, but the death of Alexander VII interrupted the work and that part of the project was never completed. Had the third section been constructed, the intention was for it to have separated the entire complex, closing it off from the surrounding Borgo and creating a surprise effect for pilgrims as they entered the square. This effect was partly restored by the surrounding urban landscape, the so-called *Spina di Borgo* that served to "close" the square. In 1950, the opening of via della Conciliazione and the demolition of the *Spina di Borgo*, widened the access road to the Vatican Basilica and exalted the majestic view of the dome of St. Peter's but at the same time profoundly altered Bernini's original plans. The dimensions of the square are astonishing: it is 320 metres long and has a central diameter of 240 metres. It is enclosed by 284 columns in four rows, and by 88 pilasters. The balustrade over the columns is decorated with 140 statues of saints 3.2 metres high, made by Bernini's pupils around the year 1670. On either side of the obelisk, which was moved to the centre of the square by Domenico Fontana in 1586, are two great fountains: the one on the right is by Carlo Maderno (1614), the one on the left was made by Carlo Fontana under the guidance of Bernini (1675). At the back, at the foot of the stairway, the statues of *St. Peter* and *St. Paul* seem almost to be welcoming the faithful.

One particularly interesting feature is the Scala Regia, which connects St. Peter's Square to the Vatican Palaces. Bernini himself described it as "… the least bad thing he had done ". Completed between 1662 and 1666, it appears quite a lot longer than its 60 metres, thanks to certain perspective illusions such as making it progressively narrower and reducing the distance between the columns towards the end.

St. Peter's Square, right-hand fountain

St. Peter's Square, left-hand fountain

St. Peter's Square seen from the dome

THE DOME This was designed by Michelangelo who, from the year 1547, occupied himself unin-
terruptedly with the basilica. By the end of his long
life (he died at the age of 89 in 1564) work had
been completed on the construction of the drum
with its protruding twined columns alternating with
pedimented windows.

After Michelangelo's death, the project passed to
his pupil Giacomo Della Porta, who raised the
height of the cupola by around seven metres and
completed the construction in just 22 months,
in the year 1590 during the pontificate of Pope
Sixtus V.

The dome has a double shell; it has an internal diameter of 42.56 metres and a height to the cross of
136.57 metres. The lantern is 17 metres high.

The dome has also served as model for later build-

St. Peter's Dome

ings. Among the many, though built using different techniques, are the
dome of St. Paul's Cathedral in London (1675), Les Invalides in Paris
(1680-1691) and the neo-classical cover of the Capitol Building in Wash-
ington D.C. (1794-1817).

THE FAÇADE The work of the architect Carlo Maderno who completed it in 1614.

It is 114.69 metres wide and 48 high, and has a row of columns and
pilaster strips of the Corinthian Order supporting an imposing cornice with
a central pediment. At the top is a balustrade with thirteen statues almost
six metres high, the one in the centre is the *Redeemer delivering a blessing*. An inscription running along the entablature recalls that work was
completed under Pope Paul V (Camillo Borghese 1605-1621).

At the bottom are the five openings that give access to the atrium, over
which are nine windows three of which have a balcony. The central window is the so-called Loggia of the Blessings where the pope appears
to deliver his apostolic blessing *urbi et orbi* (to the city and to the
world) immediately after his election, and at Christmas and Easter
each year.

The restoration of the façade, completed in July 1999, uncovered
some of the colourwashes and shadings put there by Maderno, that
had been hidden under the patina of the years.

Central loggia

Right-hand clock

View of the atrium looking towards the Scala Regia

Vico Consorti,
Holy Door

Gian Lorenzo Bernini,
equestrian statue of
Constantine,
detail

INTERIOR OF THE BASILICA The atrium (which corresponds to the portico of palaeo-Christian basilicas) is considered to be one of the finest works of Carlo Maderno. It was completed between 1608 and 1612.

The central doors, the work of the Florentine sculptor Antonio Averulino known as Filarete, date from 1455 and were reinstalled here from the old Constantinian basilica. Among other things, they show *St. Peter* and *St. Paul* and, at the bottom, their respective martyrdoms.

On the right is and is the Holy Door, cast in bronze by the sculptor Vico Consorti in 1950. It is only opened and closed in the presence of the pope during the Jubilee Years. At the end of the left side of the atrium is an equestrian statue of *Charlemagne* by Agostino Cornacchini (1725), on the right is a statue of the emperor *Constantine*, a work by Bernini from 1670.

The Latin cross form of the interior is due to the modifications made by Carlo Maderno, who completed the basilica in the early 1600s by adding the three spans of the nave and the two side aisles so as to form a unitary whole with Michelangelo's octagonal central nucleus. The resulting space is grandiose and immense, decorated with vast amounts of stuccowork, mosaics and statues in an unequivocally Baroque style that overawes the onlooker.

Visitors will, perhaps, find it necessary to pause for a moment to become accustomed to the dimensions, which may be brought into focus by comparing the height of people with that of the *holy-water stoups* and of the *cherubs* supporting them.

The basilica is 187 long, 58 metres wide across the nave and side aisles, and 140 metres wide across the transept. The vault in the central nave touches a maximum height of 46 metres (that of a 15-storey building!).

To visit the basilica, it is recommended visitors cross the

View of the central nave
from the interior of the dome

central space to the point where the lengths of other great churches
of the world are marked in the floor, then go back to the side aisle
nearest the entrance and continue following the numbers on the attached plan (cf. p. 253).

The central nave is flanked by immense piers decorated with pilaster strips with fluting and cabled fluting (where the lower part is
filled with a solid cylindrical element), and containing niches with 39
figures of *Saints founders of religious Orders and Congregations*.
The ceiling is decorated with gilded stuccowork completed in 1780
under Pope Pius VI.

Michelangelo, Pietà

The right aisle contains many works of great artistic and religious
value. In the first chapel, protected behind an armoured glass
screen, is the *Pietà*, a youthful work by Michelangelo, completed in 1499 when the artist was just 24 years old. The *Virgin
Mary*, a sweet expression on her childlike face, seems almost resigned in the face of her destiny as she
holds the *dead Christ* on her lap, his body
slack and abandoned. The meticulous rendition of the folds of her clothing and veil
exude an extraordinary strength, both
physical and moral, counterpoised by
the delicate lines of the face still redo-
lent of 15C style. This is the only one
of Michelangelo's works to bear his
signature, on the strap across
Mary's breast.

The next chapel along is that of
the Blessed Sacrament, over the
altar of which is a ciborium inspired
by Bramante's *Tempietto* at San
Pietro in Montorio on the Janiculum Hill, a gilded bronze
sculpture by Bernini dat-
ing from 1674. It was
later completed with

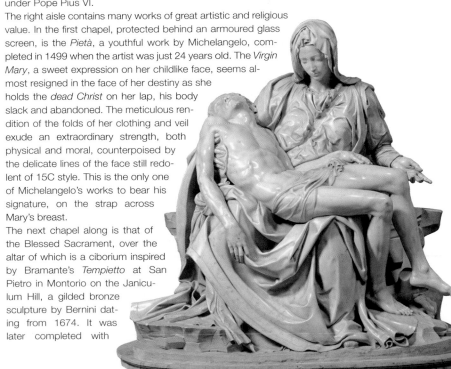

Arnolfo di Cambio (attr.),
bronze statue of St. Peter

Gian Lorenzo Bernini,
monument of the Cathedra
of St. Peter

Gian Lorenzo Bernini,
bronze baldachin

the addition of two kneeling *angels*. Another interesting feature at the end on the right aisle is the *monument to Gregory XIII* (1572-1585), a work by the sculptor Camillo Rusconi from 1723, with allegorical figures representing *Religion* and *Fortitude*, and a *dragon*, the heraldic symbol of the family, under the sarcophagus.

Turning back towards the central nave, visitors come across the famous statue of *St. Peter*, a bronze work which critics almost unanimously attribute to the 13C sculptor Arnolfo di Cambio, although some scholars believe it dates from the 5C. Note how the foot of the statue has been worn away by the kisses of the faithful expressing their veneration for the saint.

At the intersection of the nave and the transept are four massive square piers. On the inner surface of each pier is a niche containing a colossal statue personifying a crucial moment of Christ's Passion: *St. Longinus*, the solider who pierced Christ's side with his lance and who later converted to Christianity, a work by Bernini from 1638; *St. Helena*, mother of the emperor Constantine, who brought the cross and nails of Christ to Rome; *St. Veronica*, who wiped Christ's face with a cloth on his climb up to Calvary, and finally *St. Andrew*, brother of St. Peter, who was crucified in Greece. These latter three statues are by Bernini's workshop.

The papal altar stands at the centre of the church under the famous bronze *baldachin*, a youthful work by Bernini completed between 1624 and 1632. It is 29 metres high and was commissioned from the artist by Pope Urban VIII (Maffeo Barberini 1623-1644) to fill the "empty space" under the cupola and create a strong ascensional dynamic. It was made by taking the bronze decorations from the ceiling of the pronaos of the Pantheon and melting them down, whence the famous phrase *quod non fecerunt barbari fecerunt Barberini* (what the barbarians didn't do, the Barberini did). The *baldachin* has four massive corkscrew columns with composite capitals, decorated with spiral fluting and olive and laurel branches. The canopy is adorned with volutes and four extraordinarily elegant statues, one at each corner, and has a gilded bronze sphere at the top. Note the fringe decorated with bees (the heraldic symbol of the Barberini family, a reference to their industriousness) which seems almost to be moved by a breeze fluttering around the *baldachin*. Inside is a gilded dove, symbol of the Holy Spirit.

Below the altar is the tomb of St. Peter, traditionally held to be the burial place of the Apostle after his martyrdom. The presence of the tomb made this one of the sites most venerated by Christians and led to its being chosen to build the biggest place of worship in the Christian world. Recent archaeological research would seem to confirm the truth of the tradition.

Over the *baldachin* rises the majestic dome, the inside of which was decorated to drawings by Giuseppe Cesari, known as Cavalier d'Arpino, between 1603 and 1613. The Latin inscription running around the bottom of the dome reads: "You are Peter, and on this rock

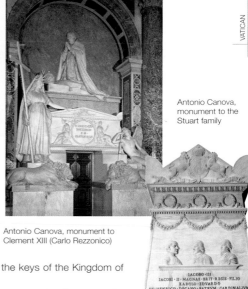

Antonio Canova, monument to the Stuart family

Gian Lorenzo Bernini, monument to Alexander VII (Fabio Chigi)

Antonio Canova, monument to Clement XIII (Carlo Rezzonico)

I will build my Church and I will give you the keys of the Kingdom of Heaven".

In the passage between the right transept and the Chapel of St. Michael the Archangel and Petronilla is the *monument to Clement XIII* (Carlo Rezzonico 1758-1769), the work of the greatest Italian neo-classical sculptor, Antonio Canova. It was commissioned in 1784 and made to the model of funerary monuments by Bernini, with the statue of the pope over the sarcophagus flanked by two allegorical figures: *Religion bearing a cross* and a *funerary spirit snuffing out the flame of life*. Two lions watch over the grave.

The *monument of the Cathedra of St. Peter* is a masterwork of sculpture by Bernini. At its centre is the great oval window covered with a sheet of alabaster and divided into twelve sectors to symbolise the twelve Apostles. In the middle of the window is the dove symbolising the Holy Spirit and all around an extraordinary agglomeration of angels and cherubs, under which is the bronze *Cathedra* of Peter enclosing a wooden seat which, according to tradition, was the cathedra of the first Apostle; in reality it is a throne given to the pope by Charles the Bald in the year 875. Flanking the throne are two Fathers of the Latin Church, *St. Ambrose* and *St. Augustine*, and two of the Greek Church, *St. Athanasius* and *St. John Chrysostom*. The work was completed in 1666 during the reign of Pope Alexander VII.

To the sides are the *monument to Paul III* (Alessandro Farnese) by Guglielmo Della Porta (left), and that to *Urban VIII* (Maffeo Barberini) by Gian Lorenzo Bernini (right).

The monument dedicated to Pope Alexander VII (Fabio Chigi), another artistically important sculpture, is to be found in the left transept. It is Bernini's last work, commissioned by the pontiff himself when the artist was 80 years old. The skeleton emerging from under the red cloth and the hourglass are meant to signify to passage of time and the ineluctability of death.

In the left nave is the *monument to the last of the Stuarts* (1819) by Antonio Canova, dedicated to the last descendants of the Catholic line of the British royal family, who appear in profile on the front.

The *monument to John XXIII* (Angelo Roncalli 1958-1963) is by the sculptor Emilio Greco (1964-1967).

Francesco Mochi, statue of St. Veronica

Historical Artistic Museum
- Treasury of St. Peter's,
Antonio Pollaiolo, monument
to Sixtus IV (Francesco della
Rovere)

Crux Vaticana, donated
by the emperor Justin II

Sarcophagus of Junius Bassus

HISTORICAL ARTISTIC MUSEUM – TREASURY
OF ST. PETER'S Beyond the entrance to the sacristy - known as the *Sagrestia comune*, a late 18C hall with a central plan and columns from Hadrian's Villa in Tivoli - is the Treasury of St. Peter's, containing sacred vessels, statues, papal tiaras and objects of various provenance, many being gifts from kings and princes. One noteworthy work is the *monument to Sixtus IV (*Francesco della Rovere 1471-1484) by Antonio Pollaiolo, a 15C Florentine artist. The sarcophagus, in which the *Virtues* and the *Liberal Arts* are depicted round the figure of the pope, was made in 1493 to a commission by cardinal Giuliano della Rovere, the future Pope Julius II.

VATICAN GROTTOES Below the floor level of the modern basilica but raised with respect to the level of the Constantinian basilica, the grottoes contain chapels dedicated to various saints, as well as the tombs of kings, queens and popes from the 10C on.

The most sacred spot is the tomb of St. Peter, located under the aedicule built in the 4C by the emperor Constantine over the presumed site of the Apostle of Christ's grave. One of the chapels around the apse contains a fresco by the 14C Roman painter Pietro Cavallini, the *Madonna della Bocciata*, so-called for her swollen face which, according to an ancient legend, began to bleed when a drunken solider having lost a game of bowls (*bocce* in Italian) threw one against the sacred image. Also in this area are the tombs of Pope Paul VI (1978) and of Pope John Paul II (2005).

Vatican Grottoes, tomb of John Paul II (Karol Wojtyla)

View of the New Grottoes

PRE-CONSTANTINIAN NECROPOLIS Excavations undertaken around the year 1940 brought to light various 1C BC burial sites that had been located around the north side of the Circus of Nero. There are pagan tombs, richly decorated and frescoed, later flanked by Christian burial sites, sometimes extremely poor. At the end of the necropolis, an aedicule marks the point which both tradition and comprehensive modern research consider to be the site of Peter's grave.

THE VATICAN PALACES

By the mid 9C, the area around the old basilica of St. Peter's had already become a citadel, fortified by the walls built by Leo IV (847-855), the so-called *Città Leonina*.

Between the end of the 1200s and the early decades of the 1300s, buildings began to appear around the square courtyard known as the Cortile del Pappagallo. This was the first nucleus of the Vatican Palaces.

Although the Avignon exile (1309-1377) ended in the late 14C, it was not until the late 15C that new buildings began to be constructed by such popes as Sixtus IV (1471-1484), including the Sistine Chapel which takes its name from him, and Innocent VIII

(1484-1492), whose Palazzetto del Belvedere is 300 metres north of the Vatican Basilica.

It is to Pope Julius II (1503-1513) - and to his architect Donato Bramante - that we owe the idea of linking these two groups of buildings with two elongated sections that enclose a grandiose courtyard divided over three levels. Throughout the 1500s and 1600s, popes continued to extend the Vatican Palaces, in particular Sixtus V (1585-1590) to whom is due the palazzo in which the pope still resides today, and where at midday every Sunday he appears at the window (second from the right on the top floor) to bless the crowds gathered in the great square below.

In the background, the new entrance to the Vatican Museums; on the right the old entrance, now used as the exit

Bookshop at the new entrance to the Vatican Museums

VATICAN MUSEUMS Despite many losses due to war, destruction and theft, the Vatican Museums have progressively developed and expanded with works of art collected by popes from the Renaissance onwards. Today, they are still one of the biggest museum collections in the world. The text below concentrates on the Pinacoteca Vaticana, the Pio-Clementino Museum, the Rooms of Raphael and the Sistine Chapel.

PINACOTECA VATICANA The building housing the Pinacoteca, completed in 1931, was constructed by order of Pope Pius XI (1922-1939) in order to reorganise a collection of paintings that had been created by various pontiffs, beginning with Pope Pius VI (1775-1799). Many of the works on display were taken to Paris by Napoleon in 1797, but later returned following the Congress of Vienna (1815), thanks also to the efforts of the sculptor Antonio Canova. The paintings, which date from the Middle Ages to the 1800s, are displayed in chronological order in 18 rooms.

- Room I contains works by painters of the 12C, 13C and 14C, known as the "primitives" because they predate Giotto. The paintings, on wooden panels, are generally characterised by a gold background, sharply outlined figures, uniform colours and a lack of perspective in the architectural details. Often the main figure appears in the middle while the stories from his or her life are depicted around the sides.

Pinacoteca Vaticana, Giotto, Stefaneschi triptych, *verso*

- Room II is dedicated to Sienese painters of the 14C and to Giotto, the greatest Italian artist of the Middle Ages. Noteworthy works include *Jesus before Pilate* by Pietro Lorenzetti in which the extreme refinement and elegance, a characteristic of Sienese artists, is evident in the graceful forms and the warm colours; and the *Redeemer delivering a blessing* by Simone Martini. At the centre of the room is Giotto's famous *Stefaneschi Triptych*, so called for the name of the cardinal who commissioned it. Painted on both sides, the central panel shows *St. Peter enthroned among angels and offerers* on the front, and *Christ enthroned among angels and an offerer (cardinal Stefaneschi himself)* on the back. Note the refined mosaic decorations on the throne.

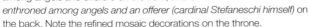

Pinacoteca Vaticana,
Lippo d'Andrea,
Christ's nativity

- Room III has works by artists from the early 15C, a period that marked, in the city of Florence, the passage to a new style of painting. Gold backgrounds tend to disappear, figures become more solid, and the central perspective has a single vanishing point towards which all the lines converge, giving depth to the painting.

One particularly beautiful work is the small tempera on wood, *Madonna and Child with Sts. Dominic and Catherine* by the Dominican friar Fra Angelico, where the new artistic theories blend perfectly with the typically mediaeval taste for miniatures.

- Room IV contains works by Melozzo da Forlì (1438-1494), a painter from the Emilia region of Italy. His *angel musicians* are fragments of a vast fresco that once covered the apse of the basilica dei Santi Apostoli near piazza Venezia and showed *Christ in glory among angels and apostles*. The boldly foreshortened figures with serene expressions and windswept hair are often reproduced in books on the history of music.

Another detached fresco by Melozzo is *Sisto IV and Platina* (1477) depicting the appointment of Platina as prefect of the Apostolic Library. Giuliano della Rovere, the future Pope Julius II, is shown standing in his cardinal's habit. The architectural elements surrounding the figures demonstrate a rigorous use of perspective and contain the classical motifs of coffered ceilings adorned with rosettes, gilt edging and oak garlands (oak in Italian is *rovere*, and Sixtus IV was a member of the della Rovere family).

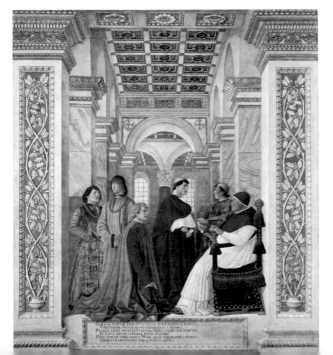

Melozzo da Forlì,
Sixtus IV and Platina

Pinacoteca Vaticana,
Raphael, Transfiguration

Pinacoteca Vaticana,
Leonardo da Vinci,
St. Jerome

- Room V is also dedicated to works from the 1400s. In the painting *Miracles of St. Vincent Ferrer* by Ercole de' Roberti we find a theme typical of Italian art in this century: a taste for ancient ruins and buildings of the past.

- Room VI is dedicated to polyptychs of the 15C, many of them still reflecting 14C tastes, note the gold backgrounds and other details.

- Room VII houses works of the Umbrian school, including the *Madonna and Child with four saints*, a painting from 1495 by Perugino, in which the artist shows his subjects in calm and poised postures surrounded by architectural elements which, in their turn, are part of a pleasant and serene landscape. The artist had earlier painted the *Delivery of the keys* in the Sistine chapel (1461). Note also the *St. Jerome enthroned* by Giovanni Santi, father of the great Raphael.

- Room VIII contains a tapestry of the *Last Supper* taken from Leonardo da Vinci's work of that name, and Flemish tapestries of the 16C made to drawings by Raphael and originally hung along the bottom of the walls in the Sistine Chapel.

Three works by Raphael are on display in the centre of the room. On the right is the *Crowning of the Virgin* dating from 1502-1503, the artist's early period; on the left the *Madonna of Foligno* (1511-1512), painted during the time in which he was also working on the apartments of Julius II, now known as the Rooms of Raphael. At the centre is his masterpiece, the *Transfiguration* (1518-1520), a work in oil on wood in which the influence of Michelangelo is clear in the dramatic posture of the figures (Raphael and Michelangelo were both working in Rome between 1508 and 1512, called by Julius II to work, respectively, on the *Stanze* and the Sistine Chapel. Raphael died suddenly in April 1520).

- Room IX contains an unfinished work by Leonardo da Vinci: his famous *St. Jerome* from 1482. Note, at the top on the left, the landscape of glaciers and distant mountains typical of da Vinci's works, and the emaciated figure of the saint who, having abandoned all his worldly possessions, has embraced the ascetic life. The room also contains the *Lament over the dead Christ* by the Venetian painter Giovanni Bellini.

- Room X houses works by some of the greatest Venetian painters of the 1500s. These include Titian's *Madonna with Child and saints*, known as the *Madonna dei Frari*, with the beautiful veiled woman on the left, and a painting by Paolo Caliari (Veronese) portraying *St. Helena* from a low angle, represented in a way typical of the artist as a rich woman wearing an ample dress of shiny brocade.

- Room XI has works by painters from the second half of the 1500s, among them the *Stoning of St. Stephen* by Giorgio Vasari, the *Sacrifice of Isaac* by Ludovico Carracci, the *Annunciation* by Cavalier d'Arpino, dated 1606, and the *Rest during the flight into Egypt* by Barocci.

- Room XII is dedicated to painters from the early 17C who inherited from Caravaggio a taste for realism and the bold use of foreshortening. Of particular interest are: the *Communion of St. Jerome*, painted by Domenichino in 1616, the *Crucifixion of St. Peter* and *St. Matthew and the angel* by Guido Reni, *St. Peter denying Christ* by Caravaggio's school, the *Deposition from the Cross* by Caravaggio himself in 1604, and the *Martyrdom of St. Erasmus* by the French painter Nicolas Poussin.

- Rooms XIII, XIV and XV. The first of these rooms contains works by the Flemish painter Anton Van Dyck, the Italian Pietro da Cortona and the French Nicolas Poussin. Rooms XIV and XV house "genre" paintings from the 1600s and 1700s.

- Room XVI has paintings by the Bohemian artist Wenzel Peter (1745-1829) who was born near Prague. Particular mention must be made of his magnificent *Adam and Eve in the Garden of Eden* with its exceptional variety of flowers and animals. The two small adjoining rooms contain clay models for statues by Gian Lorenzo Bernini, the finished works being in St. Peter's Basilica (Room XVII), and Greek icons dating from between the 15C and the 19C (Room XVIII).

Pinacoteca Vaticana,
Caravaggio,
Deposition from the Cross

Wenzel Peter, Adam and Eve
in the Garden of Eden

Aerial view of the
Cortile della Pigna

VATICAN COURTYARDS Leaving the so-called Atrium *delle Corazze* on the left, and having crossed the Atrium of the Four Gates, visitors find themselves in the courtyard known as the Cortile della Pigna, which covers part of the area occupied in the 16C by the Cortile del Belvedere. The Belvedere was designed in 1506 by the architect Donato Bramante, commissioned by Julius II to connect the Palazzetto of Innocent VIII (1484-1492) with the Sistine Chapel built by Sixtus IV (1471-1484). At that time, the courtyard was divided into three zones at different levels, linked to one another by elegant ramps and enclosed on either side by two elongated structures with pilaster strips supporting wide arches. The paving and the side arms converged slightly towards the Sistine Chapel so as to make the courtyard appear, to someone looking from the pontifical apartments, even larger than it really was. At the north end of the courtyard, the design included an immense niche to close the prospect. This was built - and is still to be seen today in the Cortile della Pigna - in 1565 by the architect Pirro Ligorio who took the dome of the Pantheon as his model. Engravings from the first half of the 16C still give us some idea of the parties and festivities that were held here. At the end of the 1500s, the Cortile del Belvedere was divided in two with the construction of a transverse section of the Apostolic Library of Pope Sixtus V (1585-1590). Much later, in 1822, another transverse arm was added, known as the "Braccio Nuovo" and built to house a collection of statues. Today then, what was one courtyard has become three: the Cortile della Pigna, the Cortile della Biblioteca and the Cortile del Belvedere.

The Cortile della Pigna is so called for its immense *bronze pinecone* (*pigna*) nearly four metres high. In the classical age it was located near the Pantheon, hence the name of that area *quartiere della Pigna*, and in the Middle Ages it was probably placed in the atrium of the old basilica of St. Peter's. It was moved here in the year 1608. At the sides are two bronze *peacocks*, copies of the 2C AD originals held in the Braccio Nuovo.

At the centre of the vast open area is a bonze sculpture *Sphere within sphere*, a work by the artist Arnaldo Pomodoro (1990).

Arnaldo Pomodoro,
Sphere within sphere,
with the Niche of the
Pigna in the background

EGYPTIAN MUSEUM Up one flight of the Simonetti Staircase (so called from the name of the architect who planned and built it between 1771 and 1784) is the entrance to the Egyptian Museum. Founded in 1839 by Pope Gregory XVI, it contains Egyptian artefacts acquired by the popes at the end of the 1700s and statues brought to Rome in imperial times. Apart from magnificent sarcophagi dating from the third and second millennia BC, particularly worthy of mention are, in Room III, the imitation-Egyptian black basalt statues that once decorated the villa of the emperor Hadrian (117-138).

Egyptian Museum,
Hall of the Mummies

Egyptian Museum, Room of Federico Zeri

CHIARAMONTI MUSEUM Founded by Pope Pius VII (Gregorio Chiaramonti 1800-1823) to house Roman statues and busts, it was laid out by the neo-classical sculptor Antonio Canova in 1807. It contains around 1000 statues, including busts of emperors, representations of divinities and numerous fragments of friezes and reliefs taken from sarcophagi. Note particularly the funerary monument of a miller, a 1C AD work from Ostia.

Braccio Nuovo,
Augustus of Prima Porta

BRACCIO NUOVO This is the name given to the building ordered by Pope Pius VII, inaugurated in 1822. It contains Roman statues as well as copies of Greek originals from the Roman age. The floor is decorated with mosaics.

Important works include the statue of *Augustus* discovered at Prima Porta (an area north of Rome); a Roman copy of the *Doryphorus* from an original by the Greek sculptor Polycleitos (440 BC); two magnificent gilded bronze *peacocks* perhaps from Hadrian's mausoleum, copies of which are to be seen in the Cortile della Pigna; and the statue of the *Nile*, a 1C AD Roman copy of a Hellenistic sculpture from the temple dedicated to the Egyptian divinity Isis located near the Pantheon. It depicts the great river and its tributaries.

PIO-CLEMENTINO MUSEUM It was founded by Pope Clement XIV (1769-1774) and Pope Pius VI (1775-1799) to house the most important Greek and Roman works held by the Vatican. Passing the Square Vestibule and a room containing a magnificent marble bowl, visitors come to the *Gabinetto of Apoxyomenos* which takes its name from a Roman copy of an original Greek bronze by Lysippos (ca. 320 BC) depicting an athlete after his exertions cleaning the sweat from his body with a strigil (a kind of body scraper used in antiquity), his gaze distant, his body relaxed after his victory. The next room affords a view of Bramante's Staircase, ordered by Pope Julius II in 1512 as a means of connecting the Palazzetto of Innocent VIII (1484-1492) to the city. The spiral ramp, built inside a square tower, could also be climbed on horseback.

Pio-Clementino Museum,
Octagonal Courtyard

Laocoon

Pio-Clementino Museum, Gabinetto of Apoxyomenos with the statue of that name seen from the back

Moving into the Octagonal Courtyard, which used to be square and was given its current shape by Clement XIV in 1772, among the most famous statues on view are the *Apollo Belvedere*, a 2C AD Roman copy of an original Greek bronze, perhaps by Leochares (330-320 BC), located in the agora of Athens. The statue of the god of beauty, who perhaps had a bow in his outstretched hand and an arrow in the other, was considered during the neo-classical period as an example of formal and technical perfection. It was brought to the Vatican by Pope Julius II. The famous *group of Laocoon*, a 1C AD Roman copy of an original Greek bronze of the 2C BC by Hagesandros, Athanodoros and Polydoros, was found on the Esquiline Hill in Rome in 1506. Much admired by Michelangelo, it was acquired by Julius II who had it brought to the Vatican. The sculpture depicts the Trojan priest Laocoon who, for having warned his fellow citizens against the Greeks' gift of the wooden horse, was condemned by an enraged Athena to die with his two sons in the toils of sea serpents. The *Perseus with the head of Medusa* and the two *boxers* are by Antonio Canova (1800-1801).

Belvedere Torso

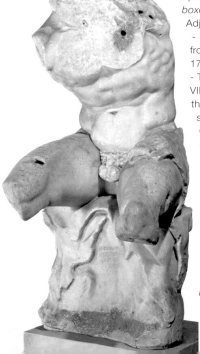

Adjoining the courtyard are:
- The Animal Room, which contains statues of animals from Roman times, much restored at the end of the 1700s.
- The Gallery of Statues, once an open loggia in Innocent VIII's Palazzetto, transformed into a sculpture gallery in the second half of the 18C. It contains valuable Roman statues some of which are copies of works from the Greek classical age (5-4C BC), these include the *Apollo Sauroktonos*, "lizard-killer", from an original by Praxiteles (ca. 350 BC), and the famous *Ariadne sleeping*, a 2C AD Roman copy of a 2C BC original by the school of Pergamon.
- The Gallery of Busts, containing works mostly depicting Roman emperors.
- The Mask Room, which houses the Venus of Knidos, a Roman copy of a Greek original from the shrine of Knidos. The original, much admired in antiquity (mid 4C BC) was by Praxiteles.
- The Hall of the Muses, home to statues of *muses* and *poets*, all Roman copies of Greek originals. At the centre of the room is the famous *Belvedere Torso*, an original

work from the 1C BC bearing the signature of the Athenian sculptor Apollonius. Much admired during the Renaissance and the neo-classical period, the statue's vigorous and powerful musculature corresponded perfectly to the ideals espoused by Michelangelo. The sculpture has recently been identified with the Greek hero Ajax, as he contemplates suicide.

Pio-Clementino Museum, Gallery of Statues

- The Sala Rotonda was built by Michelangelo Simonetti at the end of the 1700s and perfectly reflects the neo-classical tastes of the time; indeed the dome, 21.6 metres in diameter, is a reproduction of that of the Pantheon. At the centre is an enormous monolithic porphyry basin, nearly five metres wide, found in the *Domus Aurea* and placed here at the end of the 18C. Other works worthy of attention are the gilded bronze *Hercules* from the end of the 2C AD, discovered near the Theatre of Pompey, and the 3C mosaic from the baths of Otricoli (a town in Umbria).

- The Hall of the Greek Cross is particularly outstanding for its central mosaic, a 3C AD work from Tusculum, and for two colossal red porphyry sarcophagi. The one on the left belongs to *St. Helena* (4C), mother of the emperor Constantine (306-337), and comes from her mausoleum on the via Casilina; the one on the right is of Constantine's daughter *Constantia*, brought here from the mausoleum of St. Constantia on the via Nomentana.

Apollo Sauroktonos

Returning to the Simonetti Staircase, visitors can chose to visit other rooms of the Palazzetto of Innocent VIII, where the Etruscan Museum is housed, or continue on towards the Rooms of Raphael and the Sistine Chapel.

Mask Room

Etruscan Museum, Room IV

Etruscan Museum,
gold fibula from the Regolini-
Galassi Tomb

ETRUSCAN MUSEUM Founded in 1837 by Pope Gregory XVI, it contains vases, bronzes and other finds from southern Etruria, as well as a vast collection of vases from *Magna Graecia* (the area of Greek colonisation in southern Italy) and antiquities from Roman times (*Antiquarium Romanum*). Note particularly Room II with the finds from the Regolini-Galassi Tomb, and Rooms IV-VIII, known as the *Preziosi*, containing gold jewellery made by Etruscan craftsmen over the course of the 1000-year history of their civilisation.

CHARIOT ROOM Amid the late 18C surroundings is a large marble group from Roman times made up of a *chariot*, drawn by two *horses*. It dates from the 1C AD but underwent extensive restoration in 1788. Another famous work kept here is the *Discobolus*, from an original Greek bronze by Myron (ca. 460 BC), found near Hadrian's Villa at Tivoli.

Chariot Room,
marble group of
chariot and two horses

GALLERY OF THE CANDELABRA Built in 1761, the gallery was originally an open loggia and was closed at the end of the 18C. The paintings on the ceiling are from 1883-1887. It contains Roman statues, copies of Greek originals from the Hellenistic period (3-1C BC) and, in spaces alongside the arches, great 2C AD candelabra from Otricoli.

GALLERY OF TAPESTRIES Hanging on the walls are Flemish tapestries woven in Brussels by the workshop of Pieter van Aelst during the reign of Pope Clement VII (1523-1534) to cartoons by pupils of Raphael. They were first hung in the Sistine Chapel in 1531, and were adjusted to be exhibited in this gallery in 1838.

GALLERY OF MAPS The area takes its name from the 40 maps frescoed on the walls. They represent the regions of Italy and the possessions of the Church at the time of Pope Gregory XIII (1572-1585) and were painted between 1580 and 1585 to drawings by Ignazio Danti, a famous geographer of the time.

The maps are arranged along the gallery as along the north-south divide of the Apennines: on one wall are the regions washed by the Ligurian and Tyrrhenian Seas, on the other those facing the Adriatic. Each regional map has a plan showing the layout of its principal city.

APARTMENT OF PIUS V This includes a gallery, two small rooms and a chapel. It was ordered by Pope Pius V (1566-1572) and frescoed by Giorgio Vasari and Federico Zuccari. Flemish tapestries from the 15C and 16C are on display here. The two small rooms adjoining the gallery contain: in the first, an extensive collection of mediaeval and Renaissance ceramics from the Vatican Palaces and some of the extraterritorial buildings in Rome; in the second, an interesting collection of miniature mosaics produced in Rome between the end of the 18C and the first half of the 19C.

Gallery of Maps

SOBIESKI ROOM AND SALA DELL'IMMACOLATA

The Sobieski Room takes its name from the huge canvas by the Polish painter Jan Matejko (1838-1893) showing the victory of the Polish King John III Sobieski over the Turks at Vienna in 1683. The other paintings in the room date from the 1800s, as do those in the *Sala dell'Immacolata* (Room of Mary Immaculate) which also contains a glass case, a gift from the French firm Christofle, used to keep the gifts given by kings, bishops, cities and dioceses to Pius IX (1846-1878) to mark the institution of the dogma of the Immaculate Conception.

ROOMS OF RAPHAEL These Rooms or *Stanze* were, in fact, the apartments of Pope Julius II (1503-1513). Unwilling to inhabit the quarters previously occupied by his predecessor Alexander VI, which had been frescoed by Pinturicchio, he moved to an upper floor, to a wing built by Pope Nicholas V in the mid 1400s.

The area chosen by the pope had already been decorated by artists more renowned than Raphael then was, including his teacher Perugino; but Raphael, given a free hand by Pope Julius to fresco as he wished, erased all the existing work and began anew.

The Rooms were painted in the following chronological order: the Room of the Segnatura 1508-1511, the Room of Heliodorus 1511-1514, the Room of the Fire in the Borgo 1514-1517, and the Room of Constantine 1517-1524.

The Rooms are described below in the order of the itinerary that visitors are obliged to follow.

The Room of Constantine was largely the work of the pupils of Raphael following their master's sudden death on 6 April 1520. Among the more important painters involved were Giulio Romano and Giovanni Francesco Penni. The episodes depicted are, on the right of the current entrance, the *Baptism of Constantine* in the basilica of St. John Lateran; on the facing wall, *Constantine's Vision of the Cross*; on the wall facing the windows, the *Battle of Ponte Milvio*, during which tradition holds that Constantine saw the Cross appear before him pre-announcing his victory over the pagan Maxentius; finally, on the wall of the windows, the *Donation of Constantine*. The latter scene is set inside St. Peter's Basilica and depicts the act that allegedly gave origin to the States of the Church (in truth, these came into being in 756 with the famous donation of the lands of central Italy by Pepin, king of the Franks, to the Holy See).

The ceiling, decorated by the painter Tommaso Laureti in 1585, shows

Room of Heliodorus, Raphael, Expulsion of Heliodorus from the Temple

the *Triumph of Christianity* over paganism, which is symbolised by the statue lying broken on the ground.

From this room visitors pass to the oldest part of the Pontifical Palace, dating from the 1200s: the Room of the Chiaroscuri, frescoed to designs by Raphael in the second decade of the 1500s, and the Chapel of Nicholas V, used by that pope as a place for private prayer and decorated between 1447 and 1451 by Fra Angelico, a Dominican friar and expert in the art of miniatures who here depicted the *Stories of St. Stephen* and *of St. Lawrence*.

Chapel of Nicholas V, Fra Angelico, St Sixtus granting diaconate to St Lawrence

The itinerary now leads back to Raphael's *Stanze*, to the Room of Heliodorus, the second to be completed, between 1511 and 1514. The theme here is the exaltation of the spiritual and temporal power of the Church and divine interventions in favour of mankind. The *Mass at Bolsena* illustrates a miraculous incident traditionally said to have occurred in 1263 when drops of blood flowing from a consecrated host convinced a Bohemian priest of the truth of the doctrine of transubstantiation (the real transformation of bread and wine into Christ's body and blood), which he had previously doubted. Note the presence of the pope who ordered the work, Julius II, attending the Mass. The *Expulsion of Heliodorus* from the Temple of Jerusalem alludes to the inviolability of the Church estates. Heliodorus, having robbed the treasure of the Jewish Temple in Jerusalem is banished by divine messengers while a group of people, Julius II among them, look on. With respect to the *School of Athens*, which we will see below, the centre of this scene is empty, its dark colours clearly influenced by Venetian painting of that period. The same shadowy tones also appear in the *Deliverance of St. Peter*; one of the first night scenes in the history of Italian art. The fresco is divided into three episodes: the angel appearing to St. Peter and inviting him to follow (centre), the flight of St. Peter and the angel (right), the reawakening of the guards with a magnificent moonlit night in the background (left).

Room of the Segnatura, Raphael, School of Athens

Room of the Segnatura,
Raphael, Disputation on
the Blessed Sacrament

Room of the Fire in the Borgo,
Raphael and assistants,
Battle of Ostia

The next *Stanza* is the Room of the Segnatura, the first to be painted by Raphael.
Its name derives from the fact that, as the
pope's library, the room was used to sign
official documents. The frescoes depict
the three Neo-Platonic categories of *truth*,
goodness and *beauty*. Supernatural truth
is represented in the *Disputation on the
Blessed Sacrament*, rational truth in the
School of Athens, goodness appears in
the depiction of the *Virtues* and the *Law*,
and beauty in the *Parnassus*.

At the bottom of the *Disputation on the
Blessed Sacrament*, on either side of
an altar with a monstrance, two lines of
ecclesiastical figures animatedly "discuss"
the "truths" of heaven. Over them, sitting
in a semicircle on a line of clouds, *saints*
and *prophets* converse calmly because they have seen in heaven
what was promised on earth. At the top is *Christ* flanked by the
*Virgin Ma*ry and *St. John*, above them is *God the Father* and below
the *dove*, symbol of the Holy Spirit. The perspective of the floor
has its vanishing point in the monstrance, the focus of the entire
composition.

The *School of Athens* is one of Raphael's most famous paintings. In
the centre - against a background of classical architecture, probably
a symbolic reference to Bramante's plans for the new St. Peter's - is
Plato in the likeness of Leonardo da Vinci pointing his finger to the
sky in an allusion to the world of ideas, and next to him *Aristotle*
turning his palm to earth to indicate the rationalist principles of his
philosophy. The two are surrounded by a multitude of philosophers
in the likeness of men of Raphael's day including, in the foreground,
Heraclitus (Michelangelo), *Euclid* (Bramante) drawing a geometric
figure on a slate, *Diogenes* lying across the steps, *Ptolomey* and
Zoroaster respectively holding the heavenly and the earthly spheres.
The second figure from the right, wearing a green beret, is a self-
portrait of Raphael himself.

The *Parnassus* shows *Apollo* surrounded by the *muses* and famous
poets and *men of letters*. The figures include, on the left, *Homer* with
his face turned up towards the sky, and *Dante*, shown in profile.

The final *Stanza*, the Room of the Fire in the Borgo, was commissioned
by Pope Leo X (Giovanni de' Medici 1513-1521) and takes its name
from the main fresco it contains. All the works portray historical
events from the reigns of popes named Leo. The *Fire in the Borgo*
depicts the miraculous intervention of Pope Leo IV who, in the year

847, appearing at the window of the Loggia of Blessings and making the sign of the cross, extinguished a great fire that had broken out in the area around the Vatican Basilica. The other frescoes are the *Oath of Leo III*, the *Coronation of Charlemagne* by the same pope in the year 800, and the *Battle of Ostia* a victory won by Pope Leo IV against the Saracens on the coast near Rome in 849. All the frescoes are by Raphael's assistants.

Collection of Modern Religious Art, Georges Rouault, Automne ou Nazareth

LOGGIAS OF RAPHAEL

LOGGIAS OF RAPHAEL The construction of these "Loggias" was begun in 1508 by the architect Donato Bramante. When he died in 1514, work continued under the direction of Raphael, who also painted the frescoes on the second floor.

These frescoes, which he completed with the help of his pupils, represent Rapahel's pictorial response to his arch rival Michelangelo, and indeed he largely repeated the same themes from *Genesis* that appear in the Sistine Chapel.

The frescoes on the first and third floors are by the 16C painters Giovanni da Udine, Giulio Romano and Perin del Vaga.

Note particularly the "grotesque" decorations where vegetal motifs intertwine with bizarre human and animal figures, inspired by the paintings of the *Domus Aurea*, the residence of the emperor Nero which had then just been rediscovered.

Collection of Modern Religious Art, Fernando Botero, Journey towards the Ecumenical Council

BORGIA APARTMENT

BORGIA APARTMENT These were the private chambers of Pope Alexander VI (Rodrigo Borgia 1492-1503) decorated by Bernardino di Betto, known as Pinturicchio, and his assistants. When the pope died, the apartments were abandoned. They were opened to the public only at the end of the 19C. Currently a large part of the space is given over to the Collection of Modern Religious Art, inaugurated by Pope Paul VI in 1973. The collection is made up of around 600 works of painting, sculpture and drawing, donated by contemporary artists, both Italian and non-Italian. It includes works by Gauguin, Chagall, Klee and Kandinskij.

Hall of the Pontiffs with works from the Collection of Modern Religious Art

SISTINE CHAPEL

The Sistine Chapel takes its name from Pope Sixtus IV (Francesco della Rovere 1471-1484), who ordered a great new building to be raised on a site previously occupied by the *Cappella Magna*, a fortified mediaeval structure used for the gatherings of the papal court. At the time the court numbered around 200 people, including the 20 members of the College of Cardinals, representatives of the religious orders and of the most important families, the singers of the choir, and numerous servants and lay people. The Sistine Chapel was also built bearing in mind the need for defence against two potential threats: the *Signoria* of Florence under the Medici family, with which the papacy was in continual

rivalry, and the Turks of Muhammad II who at the time were threatening the eastern shores of Italy. Construction work began in 1475, a Jubilee Year called by Sixtus IV, and was completed on 15 August 1483 when the chapel, dedicated to the Assumption of the Virgin Mary, was solemnly inaugurated by the pope. The design of the building, by the architect Baccio Pontelli, reused the pre-existing medieval walls up to a third of their height. According to some scholars, the dimensions of the building (40.23 metres long, 13.4 metres wide and 20.7 metres high) reproduce those of the great Temple of Solomon, destroyed by the Romans in the year 70 AD.

The main entrance to the chapel, located on the side opposite the small doorway that is used as the principal access today, is preceded by the grandiose Sala Regia where papal audiences are held. The interior is illuminated by arched windows. The barrel vaulted ceiling, where it joins the walls, has lunettes and triangular webs. The *cantoria* on the right side was once used to accommodate the choir, while the stone bench running around three of the walls, though not along the wall behind the altar, was intended for the papal court. The intricately designed screen surmounted by candlesticks divides the area reserved for religious from that reserved for lay people. It was moved back to its current position in the 1500s in order to increase the space available to the clergy. The splendid mosaic floor, still intact today, dates from the 1400s and was constructed to mediaeval models.

The architectural structure having been completed in 1481, Pope Sixtus IV commissioned famous artists to come and work on the decorations. They included the Florentines Botticelli, Domenico Ghirlandaio, Rosselli and Signorelli, and the Umbrians Perugino and Pinturicchio. These painters decorated the side walls of the chapel, which are divided horizontally into three levels and vertically by elegant pilaster strips. The lowest of the three levels, frescoed with fake damascene curtains bearing the pontifical emblem, used to be covered with hanging tapestries some of which, designed by Raphael and his school in the second decade of the 1500s, are now in the Room dedicated to Raphael in the Pinacoteca Vaticana. The middle level, the most important of the three, is decorated with biblical episodes from the *Life of Moses* and the *Life of Christ*, both presented as liberators of humanity. In the top level, between the windows, Sixtus IV ordered portraits of early pontiffs inside painted monochrome niches, a reference to the historical continuity of his mandate with that of his predecessors.

The ceiling of the chapel, as evinced by a famous 16C picture now held in the Uffizi Gallery, was originally decorated down to the lunettes with golden stars on a blue background, the work of the painter Pier Matteo d'Amelia.

Subsequently it fell to the nephew of Sixtus IV, the enterprising Giuliano della Rovere who became pope with the name of Julius II (1503-1513), to complete the decorations in the interior of the chapel. As part of his grandiose plans for the renewal of the city he called Michelangelo Buonarroti to Rome, and after some initial hesitation the artist, who was already famous in Florence and had previously been entrusted by the pope with other commissions, agreed to fresco the ceiling. The cycle was completed over four

Left wall, Sandro Botticelli and workshop, Events in the life of Moses

Left wall, Pietro Perugino, Journey of Moses in Egypt

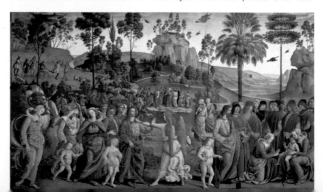

Right wall,
Cosimo Rosselli,
Sermon on the Mount

years of gruelling work (between 1508 and 1512), and has as its theme the history of humanity in the period prior to the coming of Christ.

The painting on the end wall, the *Universal Judgement*, is also by Michelangelo but was done much later, between 1536 and 1541. It was ordered by Pope Paul III (Alessandro Farnese 1534-1549), although he simply confirmed a commission that had already been granted by his predecessor, Pope Clement VII (1523-1534). The theme is that of the inevitable fate awaiting all mankind, of whose destiny God is the absolute arbiter.

Right wall,
Domenico Ghirlandaio,
Calling of the first Apostles

Biblical stories on the side walls

The frescoes on the walls show, on the viewer's left looking towards the *Last Judgement*, the Old Testament scenes of the *Stories of Moses*, saviour of the Jewish people and, on the right, the New Testament scenes of the *Stories of Christ*, Saviour of humanity. The two cycles can, then, be read in parallel. Originally, they also included the *Finding of Moses* and the *Nativity of Christ*, on the wall now occupied by the *Last Judgement*, destroyed by Michelangelo in 1534 to make way for his fresco. The cycle concludes on the wall of the main entrance with the *Disputation over the body of Moses* and the *Resurrection of Christ*, both repainted during the 16C.

The inscriptions at the top, recently restored, are known as *tituli* and refer to the subject matter of the frescoes below.

- Left wall

The first fresco, the *Journey of Moses in Egypt*, attributed to Perugino, depicts the moment in which "Moses took his wife and his sons, put them on a donkey and went back to the land of Egypt; and Moses carried the staff of God in his hand" (Ex 4,20). But during the course of the journey - and here the painting departs from the biblical account - his was stopped by an angel who ordered him to circumcise his second-born (right).

The next panel, *Events in the life of Moses* by Botticelli and his workshop, is one of the most complex for the variety of episodes it brings together. From the right: Moses slays an Egyptian who mistreated a Hebrew; his flight to the land of Midian; he meets the women and waters their flock; the Lord appears in the Burning Bush (left); and in the centre at the top, God tells Moses to remove his shoes in His presence (Ex 2, 11-20 and 3, 1-6). Note the two splendid female figures in the foreground, typical of Botticelli.

The *Crossing of the Red Sea* is attributed to the painter Biagio di Antonio (1446-1516). Moses and his people, fleeing from Egypt with the pharaoh's army in pursuit, manage to cross the Red Sea because God causes the waters to open before them. The waves then close over the Egyptian pursuers who drown together with their horses (Ex 14, 23-30). At the bottom on the left a woman sings a hymn of thanksgiving to the Lord (Ex 15,1-20).

The *Handing over of the Tablets of the Law*, attributed to Cosimo

Rosselli, recounts the biblical narrative of the golden calf. Moses had climbed Mount Sinai to receive the tablets of the Law. When he failed to return, the people gathered around the priest Aaron and melted down rings and other gold objects to make a calf which they placed upon an altar and worshipped.

When Moses finally came down from the mountain, seeing how the people had disobeyed the ban on making sacred images, he broke the tablets of the law in rage (Ex 32, 1-19).

Botticelli's *Punishment of Korah, Dathan and Abiram* refers to the revolt against the Lord by the Jewish people as they lamented the conditions in which Moses forced them to live during their journey towards the Promised Land. But God punished them by causing the ground under their feet to open swallowing them and all their goods (Num 16). Note, in the background of the scene, the Arch of Constantine in Rome.

The *Legacy and Death of Moses* by Signorelli is also made up of a number of separate scenes. On the right Moses gives his blessing to the children of Israel (Deut 33) and, on the left, he hands on the rod of command to Joshua. At the top in the centre, the angel indicates the Promised Land; on the left is the death of Moses.

- Right wall

The *Baptism of Christ*, with episodes taken from the Gospel of St. Matthew, is by Perugino. On the left of the fresco John preaches prior to Christ's Baptism; in the foreground is the episode that gives the work its name and, on the right, Jesus delivers a sermon to his followers. Note

Ceiling, Michelangelo, Creation of Adam, detail

how the Holy Trinity is depicted at the centre, with the dove representing the Holy Spirit over the figure of Christ and, at the top, the Father within a medallion flanked by angels.

The next panel shows the *Temptations of Christ* and the *Healing of the Leper* by Botticelli, also taken from the Gospel of St. Matthew (Mt 4, 1-11). The theme here is the attempt by Satan to get Christ to adore him (his challenge to transform stones into bread, for Christ to throw himself from the highest pinnacle of the temple and be saved by the angels, his offer to Jesus of all the kingdoms of the world shown him from atop a mountain). At the centre is the healing of a leper in accordance with Jewish rites. Note, in the background, the façade of the hospital of the Holy Spirit located between via della Conciliazione and the Tiber, built by Sixtus IV.

The *Calling of the First Apostles* is by Ghirlandaio and follows the biblical text (Mt 4, 18-22) to the letter, showing Jesus summoning the fishermen brothers Peter and Andrew (left) to kneel before him (foreground), and then calling James and John from their boat (right).

The fresco of the *Sermon on the Mount* (Mt 5, 1-12) is attributed to Cosimo Rosselli and shows, on the right, the healing of the leper (Mt 8, 1-4) and, on the left, Christ as he pronounces the famous Beatitudes. It is paired with the fresco on the wall opposite in which Moses receives the tablets of the Law.

The *Consignment of the Keys* of the Church by Jesus to Peter, a fresco by Perugino, is perhaps the most beautiful on the walls of the Sistine Chapel. Against the background of a paved floor shown in perspective is a typically Renaissance octagonal temple with a triumphal arch on either side, similar to the Arch of Constantine in Rome, almost as if to indicate the continuity between past and present.

The *Last Supper* by Cosimo Rosselli and Biagio di Antonio is characterised by the presence of a semi-octagonal table in a room with walls and ceiling of the same shape. Judas appears with his back to the viewer and has a small demon on his shoulder. The Garden of Gethsemane, the arrest of Christ and the Crucifixion are shown in the background.

CEILING With its 800 square metres of painted surface *a buon fresco*, this is Michelangelo's great masterpiece, one of the most important cycles in the world history of painting. Work began in May

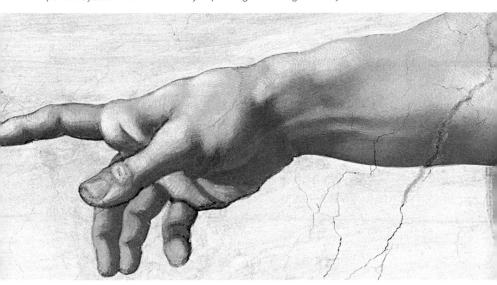

1508, but was interrupted for nearly a year between September 1510 and August 1511. The chapel was solemnly inaugurated by Pope Julius II on 1 November 1512.

The theme of the fresco cycle on the ceiling is linked with the paintings on the side walls, illustrating the Creation of the world, humanity's long wait for the coming of Christ and the prophecies pre-announcing that event. All the figures and scenes are framed within a monumental architectural structure painted over the ceiling.

In order to study the fresco cycle, it may be divided into three sections

First section - In the triangular webs and the lunettes over the windows are the *Forerunners of Christ* as listed in the Gospel of St. Matthew (Mt 1, 1-17). Confined within cramped and shallow spaces,

these men and women represent the succession of the generations as they await, in various poses and attitudes, the great event of the Revelation. They appear tired, overwhelmed, frequently distressed at their inactivity and exasperated by the slow passage of time that separates them from the birth of Christ. Some of these paintings demonstrate the artist's extraordinary technical ability, such as the figure of *Matthan* (on the wall of the old entrance) and that of *Jehoshaphat* (at the centre of the wall with the stories of Christ), executed with rapid brushstrokes and very bright colours.

The four spandrels are decorated with episodes alluding to the salvation of the people of Israel. Beginning with the wall of what used to be the main entrance:

- Right, *Judith and Holofernes*, shows the scene in which the Assyrian general Holofernes, who had been ordered by the Babylonian King Nebuchadnezzar to move against the army of Israel, lies drunk as the young Jewish girl cuts off his head and hands it to her maid (Jdt 13, 8-10).

- Left, the episode of *David and Goliath* during the war between the people of Israel and the Philistines. The young boy David had the courage to face the giant Goliath who had sworn to reduce the Jewish people to slavery if he defeated the Israelite army (1 Sam 17, 41-51).

Over the wall of the *Last Judgement*:

- Right, the *Brazen Serpent*, evokes the biblical episode in which serpents were sent against the Jewish people who, discouraged by their hardships on the march towards the Promised Land, had aroused the Lord's anger and that of Moses (Num 21, 8). Repenting of their behaviour, the people were forgiven and God told Moses to make a bronze serpent and set it on a pole, so whoever was bitten by a real serpent, looking upon the bronze serpent, would live.

- Left, the *Punishment of Haman*, an episode taken from the Book of Esther, depicts the death of the young prince Haman who had promulgated a decree against the Jews according to which whoever failed to bow before the king would be executed. But Esther, the wife of a Persian king, managed to have the decree withdrawn, saving the people of Israel and having Haman put to death.

Above the webs and the spandrels are the famous *ignudi* in symmetrical poses and the *bucrania* (ox skulls), a classical motif that alludes to ritual sacrifices.

Second section - Along the sides, sitting on majestic thrones flanked

242 Ceiling, Michelangelo, Delphic Sibyl

Ceiling, Michelangelo, Libyan Sibyl

Ceiling, Michelangelo, Creation of Celestial Bodies and Plants

by naked monochrome *putti* standing on plinths, are the splendid figures of the seven biblical *Prophets* and the five pagan *Sibyls*. Their common trait is that of having pre-announced the coming of Christ. The figures, accompanied in the background by *angels* or *cherubs* emphasising their function, are depicted in the act of reading a book or unrolling a parchment, and display an extraordinary power that is at once physical and spiritual. Among the most beautiful are the *Delphic Sibyl*, and the Prophets *Ezekiel* and *Jonah*. The latter is shown next to the whale in which he remained for three days, the same period of time Christ spent in the tomb before his Resurrection.

Ceiling, Michelangelo, Prophet Isaiah

Third section - The rectangular panels (four large and five small) running along the centre of the ceiling contain scenes taken from the Book of Genesis. Three of the episodes involve the creation of the world, three the story of Adam and Eve, and three events in the life of Noah. The frescoes of Noah were the first Michelangelo completed when he began to paint the ceiling, perhaps a deliberate choice on his part to leave the scenes in which the Creator appears for later.

The three frescoes of the Creation begin with the scene of the *Separation of Light from Darkness* (Gen 1, 3-4), in which the figure of the Creator, wrapped in pink robes and depicted with a complex use of foreshortening, occupies almost all the space available. Modern studies undertaken after cleaning and restoration have shown that Michelangelo completed this panel in just one day of work.

Ceiling, Michelangelo, Prophet Joel

This panel is followed by the *Creation of Celestial Bodies and Plants*, a scene divided into two unequal parts in both of which appears the figure of the Lord. On the right, God is shown from the front as he makes a magnificently authoritative gesture to create the brilliant yellow sun and the paler moon. On the left, audaciously shown from behind, God is depicted in the act of creating plant life (Gen 1, 12-16).

The third panel of the Creation is the *Separation of Land and Sea* (Gen 1, 7-9), another brilliant achievement for the absolutely innovative use of perspective.

And so we come to the famous *Creation of Adam*. The focal point of the composition, slightly to the left of centre, is made up of the two hands almost touching. Adam's body is magnificently rendered and the figure of God, wrapped in a pink robe, is surrounded by wingless angels with expressions of amazement on their faces. It is interesting to note that the two figures - God the Creator and Adam - were obtained from the same preparatory drawing, almost as if

Ceiling, Michelangelo, Creation of Adam

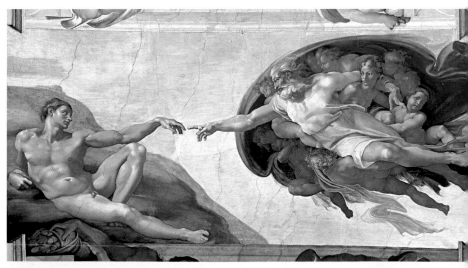

Ceiling, Michelangelo,
Creation of Eve

to confirm the biblical expression: "God created humankind in his image" (Gen 1, 27).

The next panel along is the *Creation of Eve*. Note how in Michelangelo's painting, woman is born from the living rock and not from Adam's side as in the biblical account.

The sixth fresco represents *Original Sin* (on the left) and the *Banishment from the Garden of Eden* (on the right). The two scenes are divided by the tree of good and evil, around the trunk of which is coiled the serpent and from behind which, on high, appears the Archangel Gabriel. The tree, which is slightly to one side of the centre of the composition divides a green and luxuriant environment from an arid desert, reflecting the differing destinies of the human condition. The bodies of our first fathers also appear different after the fall, as if they had aged suddenly, showing how for Michelangelo the physical aspect is also an expression of interior spirituality.

The seventh scene, the *Sacrifice of Noah*, shows the patriarch's thanksgiving to the Lord after the Flood. In the foreground is the offer of the entrails of a ram: "Then Noah built an altar to the Lord, and took of every clean animal and of every clean bird, and offered burnt offerings on the altar" (Gen 8, 20).

The *Flood*, depicted in the eighth panel is a liberal rendition of chapters 7 and 8 of the Book of Genesis. On the right of the scene is a tent offering refuge to a number of terrified individuals shortly to become victims of the deluge. In the centre, the few survivors crowded onto a boat are saved by Noah who directs them towards his Ark, shown as the top of the picture on the left. In the foreground, a diagonally arranged scene represents the salvation: after the flood and the withdrawal of the waters, the survivors reach dry land carrying the few material goods they have managed to save. The entire fresco

Ceiling, Michelangelo,
Original Sin and Expulsion
from Paradise

Ceiling, Michelangelo, the Flood

is populated by at least 60 figures, set against a clear background with a lot of depth. This was probably the first episode Michelangelo painted, from then on he favoured much larger images and more complex compositions with an ever bolder use of foreshortening. In the year 1797, an explosion in the gunpowder magazines of Castel Sant'Angelo unfortunately caused the collapse of part of the sky where, as 16C engravings show, there was a bolt of lightening.

The next scene, the last and the one nearest the original entrance of the chapel, is the *Drunkenness of Noah* and shows the resumption of life and agricultural activity on the earth. "Noah, a man of the soil, was the first to plant a vineyard. He drank some of the wine and became drunk, and he lay uncovered in his tent. And Ham, the father of Canaan, saw the nakedness of his father, and told his two brothers outside. Then Shem and Japheth took a garment, laid it on both their shoulders, and walked backward and covered the nakedness of their father; their faces were turned away, and they did not see their father's nakedness" (Gen 9, 20-23).

Around the nine scenes from the Book of Genesis are the *Ignudi*, extraordinary male figures with naked, powerfully muscled bodies, perhaps an allusion to the beauty of man created in the likeness of God. They are seated in twisted postures upon marble blocks and hold festoons and ribbons tied to bronze-coloured medallions decorated with scenes, also taken from the Old Testament. They have an important role in the overall composition of the ceiling because they break the continuity of the structural frame and link together the different panels of Genesis. It has been observed that "their presence over each of the four projecting elements, serves

Ceiling,
Michelangelo, Ignudo

to frame the minor scenes in an apparently more spontaneous manner and hence has a fundamental role in the alternating rhythm of the nine panels" (PANE 1964). This vital function may be better understood by observing, between the first and second scenes, the arch that lost its decoration with the fall of part of the fresco in 1797.

From a purely artistic point of view, further important details should be noted: the fact that the figures of the *Ignudi* and of the *Creator* get larger towards the altar; the use of colour, which is more densely applied in the stories of Noah, and more lightly and rapidly in the final scenes; and finally, how the foreground images are "in focus" and have sharp well-defined outlines, while the more distant figures in the background are rendered with more fluid brushstrokes and hazy contours, a technique that Michelangelo had probably learned from his contemporary Leonardo da Vinci.

End wall,
Michelangelo, Last
Judgement

End wall,
Michelangelo,
Last Judgement,
detail

LAST JUDGEMENT In the year 1532, twenty years after completing the ceiling of the Sistine Chapel, Michelangelo was commissioned by Pope Clement VII (1523-1534) to paint the wall behind the altar. However, it was only in 1536 under Clement's successor, Pope Paul III (Alessandro Farnese 1534-1549), that the artist began the project, finishing it in 1541. On 13 October that year, during the course of a solemn celebration, the great fresco was unveiled. The painting was intended to symbolised the re-found supremacy of the papacy after the tragic events of 1527 when Rome had been sacked by the mercenary troops known as the Landsknechts, and after the Lutheran crisis had shaken the Church to her foundations.

Michelangelo's first act was to clad the wall to be frescoed with a layer of brick, the surface inclined slightly outwards towards the top (by 26 centimetres) in order to prevent dust settling. Any deformations in perspective could then be corrected visually. This modification caused the loss of a number of 15C frescoes and of the lunettes painted by Michelangelo himself.

Although inspired by bilabial texts, in particular the Apocalypse, and by Dante's *Divine Comedy*, what prevails in this work is the artist's own tragic philosophical view. In the centre is *Christ*, the *Virgin Mary* next to him, who with a simple movement of his arm decides mankind's ineluctable eternal destiny. Some will be saved (the figures on the left floating up towards heaven), the majority will be condemned to damnation (the naked figures on the right falling down into hell).

The figures move as if in a vortex against a sky-blue background devoid of architectural features. The dead, at the bottom on the left, see their skeletons progressively reacquire flesh to the point of complete reincarnation and are awoken from their long sleep by angels sounding trumpets. These angels, none of whom have wings, appear in a group at the centre of the fresco bearing two books: a smaller one (held by the *Archangel Michael*) containing the names of the blessed, and a larger one containing the names of the damned.

To the left of *Christ* are *St. Andrew*, shown from the back carrying his cross, and *St. John the Baptist* (or perhaps *Adam*), with a powerfully muscled body. Below the central figure are *St. Lawrence* bearing a grid to recall his martyrdom of being burned alive over hot coals, and *St. Bartholomew* holding an empty human skin (which according to some scholars contains a portrait of Michelangelo). The figure of *St. Peter* is identifiable on the right, with the features of Pope Paul III who ordered the fresco, as he holds out the keys, one silver and one gold. Under him is *St. Blaise* who displays the metal wool-combs with which he was torn before being killed, and *St. Catherine of Alexandria* bearing half of a toothed wheel alluding to her martyrdom (both these figures, especially the former, underwent considerable modification in 1565 to correct their poses which were considered immodest). Next to them is a kneeling *St. Sebastian* with the arrows in his hand. Slightly further down is the famous figure of one of the damned covering his eye with his hand in terror at the horrific spectacle before him.

End wall,
Michelangelo,
Last Judgement,
details

Another scene worthy of attention is the one featuring *Charon*, the mythical ferryman who appears in Virgil's *Aeneid* and Dante's *Divine Comedy*. He is shown as he drives the sinners out of his boat, pushing them towards hell to abandon them to their terrible fate. At the end of this group, towards the corner of the fresco, is the figure of Biagio da Cesena, the papal master of ceremonies who had judged Michelangelo's work as fit for a washhouse or tavern. By way of revenge, the artist depicted him in the role of *Minos*, one of the judges of the underworld in Greek and Roman mythology who indicates to which circle of hell the damned must be sent by the number of spirals of the snake wrapped around his body. Finally, at the top of the fresco are the symbols of Christ's Passion: the cross, the crown of thorns, the dice with which the guards played, the column of his flagellation and the sponge with which he was given to drink.

Michelangelo's style here is very different from the one he used on the ceiling and expresses his changed attitude to life. God is the severe judge whom no-one can contrast, not the Virgin Mary and certainly not man. For this reason the bodies seem to be weighed down with their suffering, almost as if they still bore traces of their life on earth. The colours stand out against the intense blue that dominates the scene, and range from the reds to - with a few exceptions - brown and green, and on to black, underlining the tragic nature of the events. Only behind the figures of *Christ* and the *Virgin Mary*, who is wearing the heavenly mantle, does the background become an intense yellow in order to highlight the power of that raised arm.

In the wake of decisions taken at the Council of Trent, which came to an end in 1563 with the recommendation that only decorous works that conformed to Holy Scripture be displayed in places of worship, in 1565 the fresco of the Last Judgement was retouched by one of Michelangelo's pupils, Daniele da Volterra. He added veils and loin cloths to cover the nakedness of some of the figures, a job that earned him the nickname of *Braghettone*. Further modifications were made, for the same reason, at the end of the 1500s and over the following two centuries.

When the fresco was restored there was much debate among scholars as to whether or not to remove these additions, which had all been applied when the plaster was dry. Some argued that the work should be returned to its original state as painted by Michelangelo, while others felt that the later additions should be maintained in order to show the changes made over the passage of time. In the end it was decided to leave only the modifications made by Daniele da Volterra, as tangible evidence of a historical period, and to remove all subsequent alterations. As John Paul II said during a Mass held in the chapel on 8 April 1994 to celebrate its reopening after the restorations: "the Sistine Chapel is the shrine of the theology of the human body", and "a testimony to the beauty of mankind created by God as man and woman"; here Christ expresses "the entire mystery of the visibility of the invisible ".

VATICAN APOSTOLIC LIBRARY
The library was founded by Popes Nicholas V (1451) and Sixtus IV (1475), and continuously expanded by their successors. In the year 1589, Pope Sixtus V completed it by dividing the Cortile del Belvedere with the transverse arm where the Sistine Hall is located, the great reading room named after the pope and built by Domenico Fontana. Open to accredited scholars, the library has around 50,000 manuscripts, 7000 incunabula (the name given to any form of printed matter predating 1500), thousands of engravings and about one million printed volumes.

Sistine Hall

PIO-CHRISTIAN MUSEUM This museum contains a collection of Christian antiquities originally on display in the Lateran Palace. Founded by Pope Pius IX in 1854, it includes statues, sarcophagi, inscriptions and various other artefacts from the 6C on. Note particularly the statue of the *Good Shepherd*, which originally adorned the corner of a sarcophagus; it shows a beardless young man in a sleeveless tunic with a sack over his shoulder. It was heavily restored during the 18C.

GREGORIAN PROFANE MUSEUM Established by Pope Gregory XVI (1831-1846) in the Lateran Palace in 1844, it was transferred to the Vatican by order of Pope John XXIII and reopened to the public in 1970.
It contains Greek works, Greek copies from Roman times and Roman sculptures dating from the 1C to the 3C AD. Particularly famous is the sculptural group of *Athena and Marsyas* from a Greek original by Myron (ca. 450 BC).

Gregorian Profane Museum, Athena and Marsyas

ETHNOLOGICAL MISSIONARY MUSEUM Inaugurated by Pope Pius XI in 1926, this museum also used to be located at the Lateran before being moved here. It contains works of art and items of historical record from all parts of the world that have been touched by pontifical missions. Of particular interest are models of holy buildings from various religions such as the Temple of the Sky of Peking which dates from the 15C, though it was rebuilt in the 18C, the altar of Confucius, and the Shintoist temple from the old capital city of Japan, Nara; statues, mostly Buddhist, used as part of religious life in Tibet, Indonesia and India, as well as in the countries of the Far East; exhibits pertaining to Muslim cultures and to Central Africa; objects and works of art from the Americas, in particular Mexico, Guatemala and Nicaragua.

HISTORICAL MUSEUM – CARRIAGE PAVILION Created by Pope Paul VI in 1973 and located in a vast subterranean hall under the *Giardino Quadrato*, the museum contains saddles, carriages, cars and sedan chairs used by various popes.
Among the curiosities the museum contains, apart from the 19C carriages, is the model of the Vatican City's first locomotive (1929). Note particularly the Berlin *di Gran Gala* built for Pope Leo XII and used down to the time of Pope Pius XI.
The Carriage Pavilion is an external section of the Historical Museum, which since 1991 has been located in the papal apartment of the Lateran Apostolic Palace.

Carriage Pavilion,
Berlin "di Gran Gala"

VATICAN GARDENS

A pleasant place to tour on foot or by bus, although only group visits are allowed and permission must be requested in writing from the Gendarmerie of Vatican City State.

In the gardens are the institutions involved in running the small State, including the buildings housing the Governorate, the tribunal, the railway station, the management of Vatican Radio, a small heliport, the headquarters of the Pontifical Academy of the

Sciences and the Sala Nervi or Paul VI Hall used, among other things, for papal audiences. It was built between 1966 and 1971 and can accommodate 6000 people sitting and 4000 standing. Of particular artistic merit is the architectural complex immersed among greenery known as the Casina di Pio IV (1559-1565); built by the architect Pirro Ligorio, it is made up of two buildings joined by an oval courtyard.

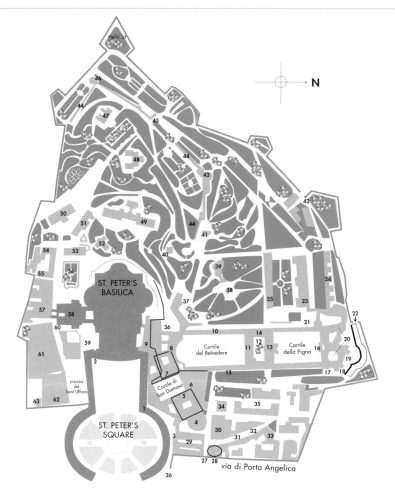

N

ST. PETER'S BASILICA

ST. PETER'S SQUARE

Cortile del Belvedere

Cortile della Pigna

Cortile di San Damaso

piazza del Sant'Uffizio

via di Porta Angelica

1 Bronze Door
2 Arch of the Bells
3 St. Peter's Gate
4 Tower of Nicholas V
5 Palazzo of Sixtus V
6 Palazzo of Gregory XIII
7 Mediaeval palazzo
8 Borgia Tower
9 Sistine Chapel
10 Corridor of Ligorio
11 Vatican Apostolic Library
12 Library Courtyard
13 Braccio Nuovo
14 Torre dei Venti
15 Corridor of Bramante
16 Niche of the *Pigna*
17 Fontana della Galera
18 Bramante's Staircase
19 Palazzetto del Belvedere
20 Museo Pio-Clementino
21 Atrium of the Four Gates
22 Entrance to the Vatican Museums
23 Pinacoteca Vaticana
24 Gregorian Profane, Pio-Christian and Ethnological Missionary Museums

25 Carriage Pavilion
26 Passetto di Borgo
27 Gate of Sant'Anna
28 Church of Sant'Anna dei Palafrenieri
29 Court of the Swiss Guard
30 Vatican Printing Press
31 Tapestry restoration laboratory
32 Church of San Pellegrino
33 *Osservatore Romano*
34 Central Post Office
35 Vatican Pharmacy
36 Piazza del Forno
37 Fontana del Santissimo Sacramento
38 Casina di Pius IV
39 Pontifical Academy of the Sciences
40 Gardeners' headquarters
41 Fontana dell'Aquilone
42 Torre del Gallinaro
43 Management of Vatican Radio
44 Perimeter of the Leonine City
45 Grotto of Lourdes
46 Torre San Giovanni

47 Marconi transmission centre
48 Ethiopian College
49 Palazzo of the Governorate
50 Railway station
51 Mosaic studio
52 Church of Santo Stefano degli Abissini
53 Palazzo del Tribunale
54 Palazzo dell'Arciprete
55 Palazzo San Carlo
56 Piazza Santa Marta
57 *Domus Sanctae Martae*
58 Palazzo della Canonica and Sacristy of St. Peter's
59 Piazza dei Protomartiri Romani
60 Teutonic College
61 Hall for papal audiences
62 Palazzo del Sant'Uffizio
63 Church of San Salvatore in Terrione

ST. PETER'S BASILICA

1 Atrium
2 Door of the Dead, by Manzù
3 Central Door, by Filarete
4 Holy Door
5 Central nave
6 Chapel of the Pietà
7 Monument to Leo XII
8 Monument to Queen Christine of Sweden
9 Monument to Pius XI
10 Chapel of St. Sebastian
11 Monument to Pius XII
12 Monument to Innocent XII
13 Monument to Matilde di Canossa
14 Chapel of the Blessed Sacrament
15 Monument to Gregory XIII
16 Monument to Gregory XIV
17 Monument to Gregory XVI
18 Gregorian Chapel
19 Altar of the Madonna del Soccorso
20 Altar of St. Jerome
21 Altar of St. Basil
22 Monument to Benedict XIV
23 Right transept
24 Altar of St. Wenceslas
25 Altar of Sts. Processus and Martinian
26 Altar of St. Erasmus
27 Altar of the Navicella
28 Monument to Clement XIII
29 Altar of St. Michael the Archangel

30 Altar of St. Petronilla
31 Altar of St. Peter restoring Tabitha to life
32 Monument to Clement X
33 Aisle of the Cathedra
34 Monument to Urban VIII
35 Monument to the Cathedra of St. Peter
36 Monument to Paul III
37 Monument to Alexander VIII
38 Altar of St. Peter healing the lame man
39 Chapel of the Madonna della Colonna
40 Altar of St. Leo the Great
41 Altar of the Madonna della Colonna
42 Monument to Alexander VII
43 Altar of the Sacred Heart
44 Left transept
45 Altar of St. Thomas
46 Altar of St. Joseph
47 Altar of the Crucifixion of St. Peter
48 Statue of St. Veronica
49 Statue of St. Helena
50 Statue of St. Longinus
51 Statue of St. Peter
52 Confession and papal altar
53 Statue of St. Andrew
54 Altar of the Bugia
55 Monument to Pius VIII and entrance to the Sacristy and the Treasury
56 Clementine Chapel

57 Altar of St. Gregory
58 Monument to Pius VII
59 Altar of the Transfiguration
60 Monument to Leo XI
61 Monument to Innocent XI
62 Chapel of the Choir
63 Altar to the Blessed Virgin Immaculate
64 Monument to St. Pius X
65 Monument to Innocent VIII
66 Monument to John XXIII
67 Chapel of the Presentation of the Virgin Mary
68 Monument to Benedict XV
69 Monument to M. Clementina Sobieski
70 Monument to the last Stuarts
71 Baptistery
72 Arch of the Bells
73 Mosaic of the Navicella
74 Equestrian statue of Constantine
75 Equestrian statue of Charlemagne
76 Largo Braschi
77 Sacristy
78 Historical Artistic Museum – Treasury of St. Peter's
79 Chapter
80 Sacristy of the Canons

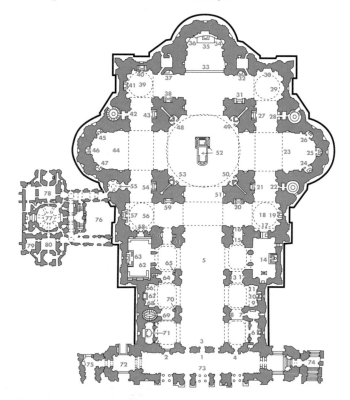

VIA VENETO

VIA VENETO

This street, made famous by Fellini's film *La dolce vita,* came into being at the end of the 19C to connect piazza Barberini with Villa Borghese.

All the surrounding district, called Ludovisi from the name of the prince who was the last proprietor of the area, arose from a great wave of building speculation which in very few years, between 1885 and 1905, destroyed a series of aristocratic villas and large parks. Today via Veneto and its surrounding streets are characterised by the presence of large hotels such as the Eden and the Majestic

(both opened in 1889), the Ambasciatori (1902-1905) and the Excelsior (1906), and by luxurious shops, cafés and restaurants. The large building that houses the American embassy was built in 1890, the work of Gaetano Koch. One curious sight is the church of Santa Maria della Concezione, in the crypt of which are four chapels decorated with the skeletons and bones of 4000 Capuchin friars.
In the nearby via Bissolati, designed in 1933 by Marcello Piacentini, are the offices of many large banks and airlines

Piazza Barberini, with Fontana
del Tritone in the foreground

Fontana del Tritone,
detail

Palazzo Barberini, façade

Galleria Nazionale
d'Arte Antica, Raphael,
La Fornarina

PIAZZA BARBERINI At the junction of via Barberini with the busy via Tritone, both from 1871, is piazza Barberini, inaugurated in the late 1800s on an area that until then had remained outside the city. In the centre is Gian Lorenzo Bernini's Fontana del Tritone (1643) that once marked the entrance to the only large building in the area, Palazzo Barberini, which used to give directly onto the square. The basin has the form of a shell and is held up by four *dolphins*, their jaws open and their tails entwined. At the top is a *Triton* (sea god) blowing into a shell. The *bees* between the tails of the dolphins are the heraldic symbol of the family of Pope Urban VIII (Maffeo Barberini 1623-1644), who ordered the work.

PALAZZO BARBERINI It was designed for Pope Urban VIII by Carlo Maderno in 1625. Following his death, the work was completed in 1633 under the guidance of Francesco Borromini, and of Gian Lorenzo Bernini who built the façade overlooking the courtyard. This has now become the main frontage because following the modifications brought about by the creation of piazza Barberini the entrance was moved to via delle Quattro Fontane. The buiding is a successful fusion of the Renaissance and the Baroque, being divided into three horizontal bands with semi-columns of the Tuscan Order at the level of the portico, Ionic and Corinthian on the upper floors in keeping with Tuscan Renaissance tradition. It is also characterised by a glass gallery on the first floor and by the accentuated splay of the windows on the top floor, giving the illusion of a depth that in reality does not exist, a typical characteristic of the 17C. The interior of the palazzo contains interesting frescoes completed between 1632 and 1639 by Pietro da Cortona, one of the greatest Roman painters of the Baroque.

Acquired by the State in 1949, until December 2006 Palazzo Barberini was partly occupied by the Italian Army Officers' Club. Now almost the entire building is given over to the Galleria Nazionale d'Arte Antica, which contains more than 1500 works from between the 12C and the 18C. Among the more important painters are Raphael (who painted the famous *La Fornarina*), Tintoretto, Andrea del Sarto, Domenico Beccafumi, Caravaggio, Guido Reni, Orazio Gentileschi and Salvator Rosa.

LARGO SANTA SUSANNA – LARGO SAN BERNARDO
This is, in fact, a single piazza, the names of which come from the two churches at either end. Santa Susanna, a 17C reworking of a medieval building, is the American national church in Rome. San Bernardo, rather like the Aula Ottagona, was converted from a hall of the baths of Diocletian.

SANTA MARIA DELLA VITTORIA
The church stands on a site occupied in the Middle Ages by a chapel dedicated to St. Paul. It was built between 1608 and 1620 by order of the Discalced Carmelites, who commissioned the project from Carlo Maderno. The façade, on the other hand, dates from 1626 and is the work of Giovanni Battista Soria who followed the model of the nearby Santa Susanna.

The name of the church recalls a legendary episode from 1620 when, during the Thirty Years War between Catholics and Protestants, a monk called Dominic found an image of the Virgin lying in a rubbish heap near the castle of Pilsen, and with it led the Catholics to victory. Following a fire in 1833, the original image was replaced with a copy.

The interior contains paintings by Domenichino as well as the famous sculpture by Gian Lorenzo Bernini, the *Ecstasy of Santa Theresa*. Completed between 1646 and 1651, it depicts the saint as she receives her mystical vision, accompanied by an angel who watches over her and smiles. The sculpture, interpreted by many of Bernini's contemporaries as showing an all too sensual ecstasy, is the emblem of Baroque art, for the clever use of light reflected off the gilded bronze "rays" and the great realism of the marble figures.

Santa Maria della Vittoria, façade

Gian Lorenzo Bernini, Ecstasy of Santa Theresa

Interior of dome, Giovanni Domenico Cerrini, Assumption of St. Paul

GALLERIA COMUNALE D'ARTE MODERNA E CONTEMPORANEA
Located in the former convent of San Giuseppe in via Francesco Crispi, the gallery holds works of modern and contemporary art acquired by the local authorities of Rome from 1883 onwards, with paintings dating from between the late 19C to around 1950. Among the more famous artists represented are Sartorio, Balla, Morandi, de Chirico, Pirandello, Savinio, Guttuso and Afro. The gallery has also been assigned a pavilion in the old Peroni beer factory in via Reggio Emilia, a space used to house the *Centro Ricerca e Documentazione Arti Visive*. The aim of this research centre is to document exhibitions of modern and contemporary art in public and private areas in Rome, and the work of artists linked to Rome, by collecting and classifying catalogues, monographs, invitations and press communiqués.

BEYOND THE CITY WALLS

Tradition has it that the first walls of Rome dated from the 9-8C BC, at which time the nucleus of the city was still on the Palatine Hill. This was the *Roma quadrata* of which all that remains are some fanciful maps, above all from the 1500s, very few literary sources and absolutely no archaeological traces.

The city was still governed by kings when, under Servius Tullius (578-535 BC), another set of walls was built. These were burnt to the ground by the Gauls in 390 BC, then rebuilt between 372 BC and 352 BC, following exactly the same route as the Servian walls for a total length of seven kilometres. The walls were made of great square blocks of tufa, some fragments of which are still visible on the square in front of Termini Station to the left of the main entrance, at the foot of the Aventine Hill near piazza Albania, and in the few blocks remaining on the roundabout in largo Magnanapoli, facing the markets of Trajan. They retained their function for a long time, until the 2-1C BC. Later, during the late Republican and early Imperial age, Rome no longer needed defensive structures and became a safe and open city.

Only under the emperor Aurelian (270-275 AD) was the need again felt to defend the capital of empire with fortifications, in the face of the ever more threatening advance into northern Italy of the barbarian Alemanni people who had reached as far as Lake Garda. Work on the new walls began in 272 and continued after the emperor's death, finishing in 279. The fortification was 19 kilometres long and six metres high, had a walkway partially covered and protected with battlements, and towers every 100 Roman feet, equivalent to about 30 metres. The gates were 17 in number. Those on main roads had either a single or double arch and were flanked by two semicircular towers, those on less-important roads had a single arch and square towers. In some places there were small openings designed to let pedestrians enter and leave the city.

In 402 the emperor Honorius, dismayed by the advance of the Visigoths led by Alaric, moved the capital from Milan to Ravenna and at the same time reinforced the Aurelian walls in Rome, raising them up to 20 metres in height, closing some of the double gates and adding features useful for military defence. They were also extended to encompass the Janiculum Hill. But the onslaught of the Goths in 410,

Porta
San Sebastiano

and of other barbarian peoples during the course of the 5C, destroyed them in large part.

They were later restored and, during the 6C, destroyed and rebuilt on a number of occasions.

In 847, Pope Leo IV (847-855), immediately after his election to the pontifical throne and following an attempt by the Saracens to invade Rome (846), still defended by its old ramparts, ordered a radical restoration of the Aurelian walls and, at the same time, began building a new series of fortifications surrounding the Constantinian basilica of St. Peter's and the buildings that had arisen around it. The resulting area took from him the name of *Città Leonina* and was the original nucleus of what would later become Vatican City. At the end of the 13C, these walls were linked to Castel Sant'Angelo by the raised corridor known as the *Passetto*, which still exists today.

Following the Sack of Rome in 1527, Pope Paul III (Alessandro Farnese 1534-1549) ordered the architect Antonio da Sangallo the Elder, an expert in military architecture, to restore the 3C walls and adapt them, with oblique ramparts known as "scarps", for defence against the latest development in modern weaponry: firearms. However, because of a lack of funds, only parts of the project were completed, near the modern-day via Cristoforo Colombo and along the perimeter of the Vatican walls, where great bastions are still to be seen. Twenty years later, the fortifications of Castel Sant'Angelo were also adapted. Further modifications were made by Michelangelo in the mid 16C (inner façade of Porta Pia 1561-1564), and by his rival Nanni di Baccio Bigio (external façade of Porta del Popolo, 1562-1565). Finally, in 1642, the walls around the Janiculum were modified and the Porta del Popolo completed with an internal façade by Bernini (1655).

Porta Pia, interior façade

In more modern times, following the Second World War, further work was done on the walls, including the great openings for the passage of the via Cristoforo Colombo, completed in 1951.

The interesting Museum of the Walls is housed in Porta San Sebastiano, which is located at the end of the road of the same name and marks the beginning of the old Appian Way.

Aerial view of Porta Pinciana and the Aurelian walls

The Passetto where it joins the Vatican Palaces

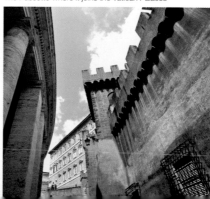

VILLA BORGHESE

With an area of more than 80 hectares, this is the biggest park in Rome. It became the property of the Borghese family in 1580, and was extended and renovated in the early 1600s by cardinal Scipione Borghese, nephew of the future Paul V (1605-1621), who ordered the building of the small palazzo known as the Casino Borghese, which today houses the museum and gallery of the same name. He entrusted the commission to Flaminio Ponzio and, following that architect's death in 1613, to the Flemish Jan Van Santen known as Vasanzio. The gardens, which were divided into three large sectors, were designed by the architect Girolamo Rainaldi who began work in 1621. Rainaldi also built the Aviary and the Palazzina della Meridiana. In 1766, Prince Marcantonio IV Borghese restructured the park, transforming it into an English-style garden and building three small temples in keeping with the neo-classical tastes of the age: to Aesculapius, to Diana and to Antoninus and Faustina. Further modifications were made at the beginning of the 1800s by the architect Luigi Canina, who adorned the park with buildings inspired by ancient Egypt and classical Greece and Rome, such as the propylaea (monumental entrances). One particularly interesting

element is the Fontana del Fiocco, in which naturalistic elements are wonderfully blended with neo-classical architecture. In 1901, the villa passed to the Italian State which, in 1903, ceded it to the local authorities of Rome.

Over the last few years, the local authorities have implemented a programme for the promotion and protection of this park, which has always been very popular with both Romans and visitors alike. Indeed, it is no longer simply a splendid and picturesque place for walks and games but has become a real "Park of Cultures", containing many different artistic and recreational attractions and offering the chance to participate in cultural and leisure activities. The park contains: the Galleria Borghese, the Galleria Nazionale d'Arte Moderna, the Museo Carlo Bilotti located in the Orangery, the Museo Civico di Zoologia, the Museo Etrusco di Villa Giulia, the Museo Pietro Canonica, the Casina di Raffaello (transformed into a children's play area), the Casina delle Rose (now the Casa del Cinema), the Casina Valadier, the Silvano Toti Globe Theatre, the French Academy (Villa Medici), the Cinema dei Piccoli, the Teatro Stabile dei Burattini San Carlino, many foreign academies and cultural institutes, and the zoo.

VILLA BORGHESE

1 Mounted police headquarters, Villa Umberto
2 Fontana di Venere
3 Borghese Museum and Gallery
(Casino Borghese)
4 Aviary
5 Palazzina della Meridiana
6 Fontane Oscure
7 Fontana dei Cavalli Marini
8 Monument to Umberto I
9 Fontana del Sarcofago
10 Propilei delle Aquile
11 Casa del Cinema (Casina delle Rose)
12 Cinema dei Piccoli
13 Temple of Diana
14 Fontana dei Pupazzi
15 Casina di Raffaello – Children's play area
16 Casino dell'Orologio
17 Silvano Toti Globe Theatre
18 Temple of Antoninus and Faustina
19 Museo Pietro Canonica
20 Casino del Graziano
21 Zoo
22 Museo Civico di Zoologia
23 Valle dei Cuccioli
24 Galleria Nazionale d'Arte Moderna
25 British School at Rome
26 Museo Etrusco di Villa Giulia
27 Villa Poniatowski
28 Gardens of Valle Giulia
29 Fontane delle Tartarughe
30 Temple of Aesculapius
31 Arch of Septimius Severus
32 Fonte Gaia
33 Casina del Lago
34 Portico dei Leoni
35 Fontana del Peschiera
36 Museo Carlo Bilotti (Orangery)
37 Egyptian portico
38 Fontana del Fiocco
39 Casino Giustiniani
40 Ninfeo Giustiniani
41 Neo-classical propylaea
42 Fontana del Mosè
43 Teatro Stabile dei Burattini San Carlino
44 Water clock
45 Obelisk of Antinous
46 Rustic Chalet
47 Casina Valadier
48 French Academy (Villa Medici)

Bar/cafè
Bicycle hire
Lavatories
Restaurant
Information
Fountains
Dog-walking area
Wireless internet access
Underground railway station

BIOPARCO

22

25

24
V.le delle Belle Arti

21

23
P.le Cervantes
Largo Picasso

Viale del Giardino Zoologico

20
Wi-Fi zone

Wi-Fi zone

29

28

30

31

Via Madama Letizia

a Esculapio

37

32

Via di Valle Giulia

18

17
Wi-Fi zone

19

Wi-Fi zone

Viale dell'Uccelliera

Wi-Fi zone

5

i

4

3

2

1

Viale dei Daini
Wi-Fi zone

Wi-Fi zone

Wi-Fi zone

Parco dei Daini

P

Piazza di Siena

16

V.le dei Cavalli Marini

7

6

P.le del Museo Borghese

Viale Canonica

33

Via dell'Aranciera

Wi-Fi zone

36

34
Wi-Fi zone

35

V.le Fiorello La Guardia

15

14

Via Casina di Raffaello

Via del Pupazzi

8

6

Viale del Museo Borghese

Via Pinciana

P.le delle Canestre

13

Viale delle Magnolie

9

V.le Goethe

12
Wi-Fi zone

Wi-Fi zone

P

Piazza H. Sienkiewicz

11
Wi-Fi zone

V.le San Paolo del Brasile

Wi-Fi zone

GALOPPATOIO

Viale del Muro Torto

P 10

M P
SPAGNA

P.le San Paolo del Brasile

PORTA PINCIANA

M
SPAGNA

48

ità dei Monti

TRINITÀ DEI MONTI

Casino
Borghese

GALLERIA BORGHESE This museum, housed in the Casino Borghese, is famous all over the world, not only for the beautiful 17C architecture of the building, decorated with stuccoes and frescoes dating from various periods, but also for its fine collection of statues and paintings dating from the Renaissance to the first years of the 1800s. Important restoration work completed in July 1997 returned the museum to its original splendour.

The building of this small two-storey palazzo with two avant-corps to either side and surrounded by a large vineyard near Porta Pinciana, began in 1608 by order of cardinal Scipione Borghese, the favourite nephew of Pope Paul V, son of his sister Ortensia. When elected to the pontifical throne, Pope Paul adopted his nephew, giving him the Borghese surname and granting him a plot of land just outside the city populated, according to the sources, with hares, roe deer and stags.

The architects were Flaminio Ponzio, of Lombard origin and, following his death in 1613, Jan Van Santen, a Durchman who had Italiansed his name to Giovanni Vasanzio. Scipione decorated his new palazzo with paintings by Raphael (the *Deposition*, acquired by what was to all effects a robbery on commission), Titian (*Sacred and profane love*), Lucas Cranach the Elder (*Venus and love, thief of honey*), Caravaggio (*Madonna And Child with St. Ann (dei Palafrenieri), Sick Bacchus*), Domenichino (*Hunt of Diana*) and Guido Reni (*Moses breaking the Tablets of the Law*), and with sculptures by Bernini, including *Pluto and Proserpine*, *David* and *Apollo and Daphne*. This magnificent collection thus came to be added to the other considerable possessions of the family.

The Casino Borghese went through another period of splendour when, in 1770, it was inherited by a descendent of the family, Marcantonio IV Borghese, who kept it until his death in the year 1800. He commissioned the neo-classical architect Antonio Asprucci to modernise the building

Gian Lorenzo Bernini,
Pluto and Proserpine

Hall of Pauline Borghese

Titian,
Sacred and profane love

and, in 1780, had the walls and ceilings decorated by Mariano Rossi with frescoes the subject mater of which was related the works of art on display. This effect has now been lost, with the exception of the room containing *Apollo e Daphne*, where the wall paintings illustrate the story of the nymph. With the Treaty of Tolentino (1798), Marcantonio was forced to surrender a number of masterpieces to France; they were returned, but only in part, a few years later. When the palazzo passed to Marcantonio's son Camillo - who in 1803 married Pauline Bonaparte, sister of Napoleon I - other works of art were transferred to Paris where they are still on display in the Musée du Louvre. In 1827, Camillo bought the *Danae* by Correggio and in 1805-1808 he commissioned the greatest artist of the time, Antonio Canova, to create the famous sculpture of *Pauline Bonaparte as Venus Victrix*. A magnificent renovation has restored the original smoothness of the skin, as well as the wooden support upon which the sculpture rested that enabled it to be rotated. It should be remembered that Canova had covered the body of his Pauline with pink wax to make her appear more lifelike.

Caravaggio,
Sick Bacchus

In 1902 the palazzo became the property of the Italian State and soon after was opened to the public.

Restoration work in the 1980s and 1990s - undertaken with the aim of restoring the 17C aspect of the building - led to the reconstruction of Vasanzio's two-ramp stairway on the basis of ancient documents and of a 1636 view of the palazzo by Johann Wilhelm Baur. During the same period, the basement was renovated and now contains the ticket office and other accessory areas of the museum. Furthermore, the original stuccowork was renewed and the plaster given the colour of fake marble.

On 30 November 2005 the Galleria Borghese stockrooms were opened to the public and can be visited on request, although booking is obligatory. They represent another museum in their own right where visitors can admire some 300 works including paintings, bronzes and small marble statues. Among the works present are: *Venus* by Baldassarre Peruzzi, *Christ carrying the Cross* by Sebastiano del Piombo and *St. Francis* by Annibale Carracci.

GALLERIA NAZIONALE D'ARTE MODERNA (GNAM) This
gallery, founded in 1883, was originally housed on via Nazionale, in the

Palazzo delle Belle Arti,
headquarters of the Galleria
Nazionale d'Arte Moderna

Palazzo delle Esposizioni which is now dedicated to putting on temporary exhibitions. In 1914, it was moved to Valle Giulia, to the Palazzo delle Belle Arti, which was built to a design by Cesare Bazzani for the Universal Exhibition of 1911, and extended in 1934.
Particularly well represented in the gallery are paintings and sculptures of Italian neo-classicism (Appiani, Camuccini and Canova), as well as of the various currents of Romanticism:

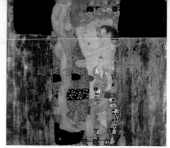

Galleria Nazionale d'Arte
Moderna, Vincent van Gogh,
Portrait of a young peasant;
Gustav Klimt,
The three ages of woman

Galleria Nazionale
d'Arte Moderna,
Antonio Canova, Hercules
and Lichas

purists (Hayez), landscape painters (Gigante), *Macchiaioli* (Fattori, Signorini and others), Divisionists (Segantini, Pellizza da Volpedo). There are very few paintings by Impressionists and post-Impressionists (Monet, Degas, Van Gogh).

As for the avant-garde artistic movements of the 20C, there are a considerable number of Futurist Italian artists (Balla, Boccioni), followers of the metaphysical school (de Chirico, Carrà, Morandi), of the school of Paris (Modigliani), of non-figurative art in general (Burri, Fontana, Capogrossi, Corpora), as well as artists representing the most significant post-war trends. There is also a significant number of works by foreign painters (Rodin, Mondrian, Kandinskij, Klimt, Duchamp, Arp).

MUSEO ETRUSCO DI VILLA GIULIA This is the largest and most important museum in Rome dedicated to the civilisation of the Etruscans.

The collection began to be formed in 1889 and was expanded on a number of occasions, it is housed in Villa Giulia, a splendid suburban Renaissance residence.

The building takes its name from Pope Julius III (Giovanni Maria de' Ciocchi del Monte 1550-1555), who wanted a sumptuous palace for himself at the gates of Rome, surrounded by gardens stretching down to the Tiber. To build it he called in young artists destined for future fame such as Giorgio Vasari (who in his writings claims the work as his own), Bartolomeo Ammannati and Jacopo Barozzi known as Vignola. Michelangelo, who was then 76 years old, was given the task of supervisor.

It is difficult to say where the work of each artist begins and ends, what is certain is that the villa, decorated with statues, frescoes and stuccowork, is truly striking. Of particular interest is the *Nymphaeum*, a monumental fountain adorned with porticoes, statues, niches, mosaics and water spouts, located below the ground level of the villa.

Following the pope's death, the family property was broken up, though the villa remained with the Apostolic Camera. Abandoned during the 17C, in 1774 it was used as a hospital. Only in 1870 did it pass to the State, and in 1888 became a museum. The most recent restorations, returning it to its old appearance, date from the 1990s.

The Etruscan museum is divided by archaeological areas. Room 1 contains a *Centaur* (a mythological figure, half man and half horse) and a *Youth with a marine animal*, from Veio (north of Rome). The statues were probably positioned at the sides of tomb entrances to protect the dead.

Villa Giulia

Room 2 has items from ancient tombs pertaining to Villanovian civilisation (so-called from the town of Villanova near Bologna) which predated Etruscan culture in northern Lazio, and to Sardinian civilisation.

Finds from the area of Vulci occupy rooms 3 and 4, and exhibits from around Lake Bolsena are on display in rooms 5 and 6.

The ancient city of Veio, in-

Museo Etrusco di Villa Giulia, sarcophagus of husband and wife

Museo Etrusco di Villa Giulia, *Cista Ficoroni*

cluding the famous terracotta *Apollo* which shows such evident Ionic Greek influence, is represented in room 7, while items found in the necropolis of Cerveteri are displayed in rooms 8, 9 and 10. These include the *sarcophagus of husband and wife*, a famous terracotta sculpture from the late 6C BC.

On the first floor is an immense collection of bronzes, a *chariot* almost completely intact, and the ceramics that the son of the illustrious Etruscan scholar, Augusto Castellani, donated to the Italian State in 1919. Not to be missed is a small room, opened on request, with a collection of beautifully made gold jewellery.

Finally, room 33, contains gold and jewels from the Barberini and Bernardini collections.

MUSEO NAZIONALE DELLE ARTI DEL XXI SECOLO

(MAXXI) The building was once occupied by a *carabinieri* barracks, subsequently restructured by the Anglo-Iraqi architect Zaha Hadid who won a specially-organised competition in 1998. Here, a new contemporary art exhibition space has gradually been opened to the public. It houses paintings and sculptures by contemporary artists as well as a photographic archive and a section dedicated to conserving documents regarding important Italian architects recently deceased, such as Carlo Scarpa and Aldo Rossi.

AUDITORIUM PARCO DELLA MUSICA
Designed by the architect Renzo Piano, winner of an international competition, Rome's new Auditorium is a city of music in every sense of the term. The semi-circular cavea (amphitheatre) is intended to hold meetings and conferences, pop and classical music concerts, and other performances of various kinds, and has a seating capacity of 3000. Around it are three large halls, immense "crustaceans" designed to have the best possible acoustical properties.

On the left is the largest hall, called the Sala Santa Cecilia (with over 2700 seats) and intended for symphony orchestra concerts and operas; in the centre, the Sala Sinopoli (1200 seats) is for chamber music recitals, but also for conferences; on the right, the Sala Petrassi (700 seats) is designed for operetta, dance, cinema and poetry readings.

The complex also includes shops, exhibition areas, service rooms, a library, a museum of music and a small archaeological area that came to light during building work.

MUSEO D'ARTE CONTEMPORANEA DI ROMA (MACRO)
– VIA REGGIO EMILIA This complex of Art Nouveau buildings was designed by the architect Gustavo Giovannoni between 1909 and 1913 as the refrigerated storehouses of the Peroni beer factory. Recently renovated (2002), it now houses Rome's Museo d'Arte Contemporanea, which contains works by world-famous Italian artists covering the period from the 1960s to the present.

SANT'AGNESE FUORI LE MURA The complex of buildings that make up Sant'Agnese fuori le Mura on the via Nomentana is one of the most interesting places of mediaeval Rome, and includes remains and monuments dating from between the 3C and the 8C AD.

The site includes:

- The ruins of an ancient palaeo-Christian basilica from the 4C dedicated to St. Agnes.
- A beautifully preserved mausoleum, also from the 4C, built to hold the remains of Constantia, daughter of the emperor Constantine. She died in Bithynia in 354, but her body was later brought to Rome.
- A basilica from the 7-8C, also dedicated to St. Agnes.
- A dense network of catacombs on three levels, dating from the late 2C to the 4C.

According to tradition, Agnes, a young Christian girl who lived in the 4C, having refused the advances of a wealthy Roman, was exposed naked in the stadium of Domitian (modern-day piazza Navona), whereupon a sudden and miraculous growth of hair covered her nudity. This, however, did not prevent her being martyred, either at the stake or by beheading.

OLD BASILICA This immense building, ordered by Constantine's daughter Constantia between 337 and 350, was 98.3 metres long, 40.3 metres wide and originally had the form of a Roman circus, with a nave, two side aisles and a single apse. All that remains are the foundations of the outer walls and picturesque ruins at the apse end, this however is enough to make out, against the grass of the field, the unusual "plan" of the church.

MAUSOLEUM OF ST. CONSTANTIA This is the only monument in Rome from the time of Constantine to have survived almost intact, only the external portico and the interior decoration have been lost. Located near the south side of the ancient basilica, it was built as a mausoleum, later transformed into a baptistery and subsequently, in 1254, into a church. A narthex, still easily recognisable today with its two small apses, gave access to the interior. Inside, the area is divided into a circular ambulatory, covered

Mausoleum of St. Constantia

with barrel vaults and hidden in shadow, and a higher central area with a dome, hidden from the outside by a "tiburium" and strongly illuminated by arched windows. The central area and ambulatory are divided from one another by twelve pairs of radially-positioned columns with composite capitals supporting an entablature that accentuates the natural attraction of the spectator's attention towards the centre. The walls of the church have alternating semicircular and rectangular niches, slightly larger at the two main diameters so as to form a cross within the circle.

In the central niche is a copy of the red porphyry sarcophagus containing the remains of St. Constantia. The original was transported to the Vatican in 1791 where it is on display in the Pio-Clementino Museum.

The mosaics in the ambulatory are very fine, some of the oldest to have survived in Rome. Against the white background are geometric designs, and scenes of grape harvesting and vine shoots, an allusion to Christ's words "I am the vine, and you are the branches" (Jn 15: 5). The figures at the centre of the scenes are difficult to interpret.

SANT'AGNESE FUORI LE MURA

This basilica was built in the 7C by Pope Honorius I (625-638) on the site of the tomb of the martyr St. Agnes and over part of an earlier 4C basilica. The building was later restored under Pope Hadrian I (772-795). It has a nave and two side aisles, with a semicircular apse in line with the nave and, exceptionally for an Italian church of longitudinal plan, a *matroneum* - the area in oriental churches traditionally reserved for women.

Sant'Agnese fuori le Mura, façade

Sant'Agnese fuori le Mura, rear, with campanile in the foreground

The apse is decorated with mosaics dating from the time of Pope Honorius and has three figures standing against a gold background: *St. Agnes* is in the centre wearing royal robes over the flames of her martyrdom; on the right is *Pope Symmachus* (498-514) and on the left *Honorius* himself, offering a model of the church to the saint. The image is flat but nonetheless rich and opulent, a typical example of the Byzantine tastes of the time.

This beautiful basilica was restructured at the end of the 16C, and the ciborium and gilded wood ceiling are from the first years of the 1600s.

CATACOMBS OF SANT'AGNESE

Discovered in 1865, they extend over three levels and contain important graffiti and funerary inscriptions.

OLD APPIAN WAY

The Appian Way, the most beautiful of the consular roads (the 1C AD poet Statius called it *regina viarum*), derives its name from that of the censor Appius Claudius, who in 312 BC built the first stage from Porta San Sebastiano to Capua (it was subsequently lengthened, first as far as Benevento then to Taranto and Brindisi, where two cipolin marble columns still indicate where it ends). It had a fundamental role in carrying commercial traffic to and from the East. In Roman times it was lined with buildings, villas, temples, sacred woods, public post stations and, above all, with tombs, often monumental tombs decorated with inscriptions describing the deceased or even inviting passers-by to pause and dedicate a thought to the occupant. Of this wealth of testimony to the Roman world, very little has come down to our own day.

With the fall of the Roman Empire of the West it became impossible to continue maintenance of the road and it fell into abandonment and decay, especially during the Middle Ages. Nonetheless, the part nearest to Rome continued to be used until about 1500, when it was completely abandoned in favour of the via Appia Nuova (the course of which arose more or less spontaneously from everyday usage in the second half of the 16C). Another reason for this change were the tolls levied on

the old road, and the danger of brigands.

From the Renaissance until the 19C, many studies were
undertaken and efforts made to "revive" the Appian Way, in
particular thanks to humanist popes such as Pius II (Enea
Silvio Piccolomini 1458-1464) and scholars like Pirro Ligorio,
Ennio Quirino Visconti and Antonio Nibby, but also with the
encouragement and interest of artists such as Piranesi and
Goethe. In the mid 1800s, the road was finally freed from the
rubble and vegetation covering it, the monuments were restored
and the land occupied with expropriated archaeological remains.
For more than a century, the neighbourhood of the Appian Way
has again become partly inhabited with the construction of large
new villas, high-class but not always, to be truthful, respectful of
the historical surroundings.

Today the most evocative part of the Appian Way is that
stretching from the tomb of Cecilia Metella to the Grande
Raccordo Anulare (GRA, the ring road circling the city of
Rome). Among monumental ruins and natural greenery, the
modern city often at a distance, the atmosphere seems
timeless. In many areas the original basalt slab paving remains,
4.1 metres wide, beside which runs a beaten earth path giving
a total width of 10.2 metres.

Aerial view of the
Appian Way and
the Torre Selce

Arch of Drusus

PORTA SAN SEBASTIANO This is where the Appian Way begins (originally it began further back at Porta Capena in the Republican walls, of which all that remains today are a few ruins on the so-called *Passeggiata Archeologica*). Once called Porta Appia, it is an opening in the Aurelian walls, which are still to be seen stretching way impossingly on either side.

This is the most beautiful and best preserved of the gates to ancient Rome. In its current form, it dates from the 4C AD and represents a formidable highpoint in military defensive techniques. The gate gives access to the covered walkway that runs along the walls as far as via Cristoforo Colombo. Just inside the gate are the noteworthy remains of the Arch of Drusus and just outside, to the left of the square, is a fountain with two funerary busts and an ancient sarcophagus used as a basin. About a hundred metres further down the road, in the wall on the right, is a copy of the first milestone of the Appian Way (the original, in cipolin marble, is to be seen on the balustrade of the Campidoglio, on the side nearest via delle Tre Pile). Having passed the point where the Appian Way passes under a bridge bearing via Cilicia, on the left are the remains of a tall tower tomb. This is believed to be all that remains of the mausoleum of Geta (211-212), the unfortunate emperor, son of Septimius Severus, murdered by his own brother Caracalla.

Domine Quo Vadis?

DOMINE QUO VADIS? This is the name of a small church with a single nave dating, according to some sources, from the 8-9C or, according to others, from the 11C. It stands on the spot where, according to popular tradition, Christ appeared to St. Peter who was leaving Rome after having escaped from the Mamertine Prison. The Apostle asked Jesus *Quo vadis Domine*? (Lord, where are you going?), and Christ replied *Eo Romam iterum crucifigi* (I am going to Rome to be crucified again). St. Peter, understanding the meaning of the Lord's reply, turned back to the city, rejoined the community of the faithful and found martyrdom in the persecution ordered by the emperor Nero.

In the second half of the 1500s the church was in such a poor state of repair that the English cardinal Reginald Pole ordered the construction, a little further along on via della Caffarella, of a small round chapel with a dome to ensure that the memory of Christ's appearance in this place would be perpetuated (1588).

In 1592, the interior of the church of Domine Quo Vadis? began to be restored. In 1637 the façade was also renovated, by order of cardinal Francesco Barberini who had his coat-of-arms with three bees added to the frontage.

Just inside the entrance is a stone copy of a set of footprints which popular belief holds belonged to Jesus (the original is in the basilica of San Sebastiano). Scholars believe it to be an *ex voto* offering for the favourable outcome of a pilgrimage.

Catacombs of Domitilla,
Arcosolium of the Little Apostles

CATACOMBS OF DOMITILLA

The Catacombs of Domitilla are situated on via delle Sette Chiese 282 near the Appian Way. The site seems to have been donated by the Roman matron to whom they are dedicated. Of particular interest are the basilica of Santi Martiri Nereo and Achilleo of the 4th century, the hypogeum of the Flavi and several frescoes with scenes from the New and Old Testament.

Catacombs of Domitilla,
Arcosolium of Veneranda

CATACOMBS OF SAN CALLISTO

This is the biggest burial ground in ancient Rome. Including the cemetery of San Sebastiano, it covers nearly 15 hectares and has a total extent of nearly 20 kilometres; a real underground labyrinth, in places extending over various levels. It contains both pagan and Christian tombs; in fact, from the 1C onwards, in periods when the new religion was not being subjected to persecution, Christians could bury their dead here quite freely. Particularly noteworthy are the graves of early popes: Cornelius, Zephyrinus, Fabian and Melchiades.

The name of the area comes from the deacon Calixtus (who later became pope) to whom Pope Zephyrinus (199-217) had entrusted the administration of the cemetery after having received the area as a gift from Lucina, a Roman noblewoman who had converted to Christianity (hence also the origin of the name "Cemetery of Lucina"). However, the great expansion of the burial ground only came about later, after Christianity had become the religion of State. The complex is divided into various parts, of which the most interesting is that of the *gens Caecilia*.

The history of these catacombs is linked to the memory of tragic persecutions. In the year 258, Pope Sixtus II was killed in his episcopal throne as he preached to the faithful, and with him all those present were also murdered. St. Cecilia, her Christian faith having being discovered, was executed here along with her relatives who were also believers (after having been proclaimed a saint, her relics were taken to Trastevere and placed in the church built over what used to be her house).

Catacombs of San Callisto,
papal crypt

Façade of the basilica of San Sebastiano inside which is the entrance to the catacombs of San Sebastiano

San Sebastiano, interior

Catacombs of
San Sebastiano,
Gian Lorenzo Bernini (attr.),
bust of St. Sebastian

SAN SEBASTIANO Dating from the 4C, the basilica was originally dedicated to Sts. Peter and Paul and, for that reason, called *Basilica Apostolorum* (its dedication was due to the belief at the time that the two saints were buried there). In the 9C it took the name of St. Sebastian, an officer of the Praetorian Guard who converted to Christianity and fell victim to the persecution of Diocletian (284-305). Under the altar is a recumbent statue of *St. Sebastian*, a beautiful work by the sculptor Antonio Giorgetti to a design by Gian Lorenzo Bernini. The church - which became one of the seven basilicas on the pilgrimage route instituted by St. Philip Neri - also contains an arrow which is traditionally believed to have been removed from St. Sebastian's body, and the original marble block with what are believed to be the footprints left by Christ when he appeared to St. Peter (a copy is held in the church of Domine Quo Vadis?).

CATACOMBS OF SAN SEBASTIANO This small necropolis probably dates from the 2C AD. The word catacomb, which comes from the Greek, designated the quarries for the extraction of pozzuolana that existed in the surrounding area; from the 9C onwards, the term came to be used as a generic name for all Christian underground cemeteries. Contrary to widespread belief, they were only burial sites and not places of refuge for followers of the new religion, indeed the accesses to the catacombs were all well known to the Roman authorities. They contain burial vaults decorated with stuccos and wall paintings, giving a good idea of what the mausolea that once lined the Appian Way must have looked like. The notoriety of these particular catacombs is linked above all to the tradition (probably unfounded) that a group of Christians from the East, having stolen the bodies of St. Peter and St. Paul with the intention of taking them to their own country, temporarily buried them here. The plot was discovered by the Roman Christian community, but it was decided nonetheless to leave the relics where they were and build the *Basilica Apostolorum*, which later became the basilica of San Sebastiano.
The site is still partially unexplored, and the oldest part has yet to be excavated. The area that can be visited today dates prevalently from the 4C.

Circus of Maxentius

MAUSOLEUM OF ROMULUS AND CIRCUS OF MAXENTIUS

This is one of the largest monuments on the Appian Way. Romulus, the son of the emperor Maxentius, died prematurely in the year 307 AD and his father had a great building raised in his memory. Round and covered with a dome, it was preceded by a pronaos with six columns, of which all that remains today is the circular base. The outer walls and some of the pilasters of the vast quadriporticus have also survived to our own times.

Next to the tomb of Romulus and lying diagonally with respect to the Appian Way is the Circus of Maxentius, which was designed to stage chariot races. It is well preserved but its rich decoration of sculptures, statues, columns and fountains has been lost. It was built by the emperor in 309 AD. On the central *spina* was an Egyptian obelisk bearing the name of Domitian, which Pope Innocent X had moved to piazza Navona in 1649 where it still stands atop Bernini's fountain of the four rivers. Next to the circus are the imposing remains of an imperial palace, also built by Maxentius.

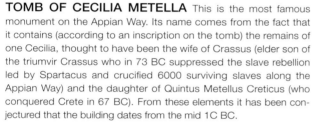

Mausoleum di Romulus

TOMB OF CECILIA METELLA

This is the most famous monument on the Appian Way. Its name comes from the fact that it contains (according to an inscription on the tomb) the remains of one Cecilia, thought to have been the wife of Crassus (elder son of the triumvir Crassus who in 73 BC suppressed the slave rebellion led by Spartacus and crucified 6000 surviving slaves along the Appian Way) and the daughter of Quintus Metellus Creticus (who conquered Crete in 67 BC). From these elements it has been conjectured that the building dates from the mid 1C BC.

The mausoleum consists of a round drum over a square base and is made of travertine. At the top is a frieze with *bucrania* (ox skulls), whence the name of the area: *Capo di Bove*. In the interior it is possible to visit the funerary cell, which is lined with fine brickwork.

Because of its strategic position on one of the main access routes to Rome, the Byzantines transformed it into a fortress. In the 11C, the counts of Tuscolo built a square fort that still exists today and transformed the tomb into a keep defending one of the gates through which the Appian Way passed. In 1299 the Caetani family built a baronial palace against the mausoleum. Later, with the feuds between the aristocratic families of Rome, the building changed hands several times, belonging, among others, to the Savelli, emperor Henry VII, the Colonna and finally the Orsini, who kept it until 1435. The tomb then went through a period of abandonment and was mainly used to house troops heading for Rome. For this reason, in 1589, under Pope Sixtus V, the Roman Senate ordered it be pulled down. However, when demolition work had already begun, a final appeal from the custodian Paolo Lancellotti fortunately caused the order to be reversed.

On the mound near the mausoleum was a small village that already existed in Roman times, it reached its maximum splendour in the mid 2C AD when it became part of a larger estate belonging to Herodes Atticus, who had a villa there.

In the Middle Ages, at the time of the Caetani family, the village had scores of house and a number of churches. The picturesque ruins of one of these churches, a small Gothic edifice dedicated to St. Nicholas of Bari, are still visible in front of the tomb on the other side of the Appian Way.

Tomb of Cecilia Metella

ST. PAUL'S OUTSIDE-THE-WALLS

This is one of the most important basilicas in Rome and, like the churches of St. Peter's, St. Mary Major and St. John Lateran, has the status of extraterritoriality.

In the year 324, just a few years after Christians had been granted freedom of worship, a church was built on this site, over the place where the Apostle Paul was traditionally believed to have been buried after his death in Rome in the year 67 AD. The original building was, however, completely rebuilt at the end of the 4C by the emperors Theodosius and Honorius. A great quadriporticus, which traditionally marked the limit of access to the building for the non-baptised, preceded the interior of the basilica which had a central nave, four aisles, two to either side, a transept and an apse.

Between the 5C and the year 1000 the church was restored on numerous occasions, other modifications were made at the end of the 13C in preparation for the Jubilee Year of 1300, and in the 16C, the 17C and the 18C.

On the night of 5 July 1823, a great fire almost completely destroyed the basilica, only the façade and part of the portico remained untouched. A number of the columns in the two left-hand side aisles and the exterior walls were devastated, as was the triumphal arch, the transept with the works of art it contained, and the 13C cloister. The subsequent reconstruction was slow and accompanied by a lively theoretical debate between those who felt the church should be rebuilt to the ancient model and others who believed it should be replaced with a modern building. Some people, among them the architect Giuseppe Valadier (who had restored the Coliseum and the Arch of Titus), supported the idea of using the surviving parts to create something completely new. The final decision, made by Pope Leo XII, favoured the idea

of rebuilding the old church, but not only did he fail to dispel doubts about creating what was to all effects a fake antique, but also attracted criticism for what, in purely aesthetic terms, was a negative outcome.

The quadriporticus has had a rather troubled history of its own. In the year 1724, having been rebuilt a few years previously by Alessandro Specchi, it collapsed suddenly and was almost entirely destroyed. Pope Benedict XIII had to have it rebuilt in a hurry in order to be ready for the Jubilee Year of 1750. Following the blaze of 1823 it took fully five years to rebuild. Its false classical forms give it a cold and bombastic appearance, a pretentious style that seems to have little connection with that of the ancient basilicas of the 5C. At the centre of the square is a statue of *St. Paul* in the act of unsheathing a long sword, the work of Giuseppe Obici. The mosaic on the façade dates from the second half of the 1800s and is divided as follows: at the top *Christ delivering a blessing between Sts. Peter and Paul*, in the middle the *Lamb of God* and at the bottom four prophets, *Isaiah*, *Jeremiah*, *Ezekiel* and *Daniel*. Under the portico are late 19C statues. The central bronze doors, parts of which are covered in silver, are the work of Antonio Maraini who completed them in 1931. The Holy Door, on the right, dates from the 11C. It was much restored following the fire, and used to be at the main entrance of the basilica.

St. Paul's Outside-the-Walls, façade

Statue of St. Paul

The interior is divided by columns of granite from northern Lombardy with capitals in Carrara marble. The area up to the altar was completely rebuilt between 1831 and 1854. Illumination comes from typically palaeo-Christian windows between which wall paintings depict episodes from the *life of St. Paul*. Under these, in medallions running along a frieze, are portraits of all the popes. The first, portraying *St. Peter*, is in the transept on the right.

The columns of the counter façade were donated in 1840 by the viceroy of Egypt. The statues preceding the triumphal arch are from the late 1800s, and the arch itself is decorated with 5C mosaics.

The tabernacle or ciborium over the altar is the most important work in the church. It was made in 1285 by Arnolfo di Cambio, one of the greatest Italian Gothic sculptors, and shows an elegant fusion of Classical and Gothic elements, proof that the influence of ancient sculpture was also much felt during the Middle Ages.

The Classical tradition may be recognised in the great columns with composite capitals (not originals but faithfully recomposed following the conflagration of 1823), the small columns flanking the arches, the statues with their serene and learned expressions standing in niches at the corners, and the pediments enclosing winged figures bearing perforated medallions; the Gothic elements are the pointed arches, the series of spires and pinnacles soaring upwards to heaven and the detailed mosaic designs that decorate the beautiful monument.

The two ends of the transept have identical twin altars, while against the back wall are four chapels of which the second from the left is

Central nave

particularly noteworthy. This is the chapel of the Blessed Sacrament, an 18C addition that houses a much-venerated *Crucifix* from the 1300s. According to tradition, the head of the crucified Christ moved towards the statue of *St. Bridget* kneeling at his feet. The statue is by Stefano Maderno. A mosaic of the *Madonna and Child* from the 13C also merits attention

In the apse is a mosaic dating from the early 13C. It depicts *Christ enthroned surrounded by*

View of the transept and
the internal façade of the
triumphal arch

saints, among them *St. Paul* and *St. Peter*, and was much restored after the fire.

In the transept on the right is a beautiful paschal candlestick dating from the late 12C. Unusually large, it is decorated with a
Christological cycle, monsters and other decorative motifs,
all mediaeval, and has been attributed to Pietro Vassalletto.
Mention must also be made of the wonderful 13C cloister,
also by the workshop of Vassalletto, a family of Roman artists
who specialised in mosaic decorations and whose work can
also be seen elsewhere, in particular in the cloister of St. John
Lateran. The small well-proportioned arches are supported
upon colonnettes of different forms, while lunettes decorated
with symbolic motifs and an entablature with geometric designs
complete the decoration.

The cloister gives access to the sacristy and to the picture gallery
which contains interesting panels and paintings from the Middle
Ages to the 19C.

On the exterior at the back of the building is the campanile, which
was built in 1860 and is 65 metres high. It was intended to reflect the
Classical style but fails to do so and is of scant architectural value.

Finally, the Gregorian portico, on the exterior of the building on the
north side, is so called because it was built during the reign of Pope
Gregory XVI (Bartolomeo Cappellari 1831-1846). It was conceived
as part of an idea to turn the transept into the central nave, and its
only noteworthy feature is that it uses columns that were salvaged
from the fire.

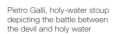

Pietro Galli, holy-water stoup
depicting the battle between
the devil and holy water

Cloister with the paired
colonnettes in
the foreground

EUR

This neighbourhood was built to host the 1942 Universal Exhibition of Rome (Esposizione Universale di Roma, whence the name EUR), which was never held because of the war. As that year also marked the twentieth anniversary of the fascist regime, Mussolini had decided to build a magnificent suburb on the outskirts of the city as a symbol of the new times and of their historical continuity with imperial Rome. The plans were drawn up by the architects Giuseppe Pagano, Marcello Piacentini, Luigi Piccinato, Ettore Rossi and Luigi Vietti, and on 28 April 1937 Mussolini himself began the work by planting the first laurel tree. This was the beginning of an unstoppable growth of the city towards the sea, as foreseen by a rhetorical but prophetic inscription on one of the buildings overlooking what is now piazzale dell'Agricoltura: *La Terza Roma si dilaterà sopra altri colli, lungo le sponde del fiume sacro fino alle coste del Tirreno* (The Third Rome will spread over other hills, along the banks of the sacred river unto the shores of the Tyrrhenian Sea).

Special competitions were soon organised for the construction of the most important buildings: Palazzo dei Congressi, won by Adalberto Libera, one of the greatest architects of the time; Palazzo della Civiltà del Lavoro, referred to jokingly by Romans as the "square Coliseum" or sometimes as the "Gruyere" because the façade includes 216 arched openings; piazza Imperiale, now called piazza Guglielmo Marconi, with a modern 45-metre-high obelisk at the centre dedicated to the inventor of the radio and sculpted with episodes from his life; the headquarters of the Central Archives of State; the church of Santi Pietro e Paolo, and many others. In April 1942, because of the dramatic events of the war, all the work was abandoned and only started again in the early 1950s. The underground railway, which at the time made this one of the most desirable residential areas of Rome, was inaugurated in 1955. Other important additions were made to EUR for the occasion of

Aerial view
of piazzale delle
Nazioni Unite

the 17th Olympic Games, which were held in Rome in the summer of 1960: the Velodromo, a swimming pool (the *Piscina delle Rose*), the playing fields at the Tre Fontane and the Palazzo dello Sport. The latter, designed by the engineer Pier Luigi Nervi in collaboration with the architect Marcello Piacentini, has an extraordinary dome with a diameter of 100 metres, made in prefabricated sections joined together with a layer of concrete. It has space to accommodate 15000 spectators.

In the 1960s, certain government ministries and public institutions were transferred to EUR, and large banks, Italian and foreign companies, and embassies all opened offices here. The area began to be populated with expensive shops (in viale Europa) and exclusive residences, both flats and villas.

There are various museums in EUR:

- The Museo Nazionale Preistorico-Etnografico Luigi Pigorini, which has a number of interesting rooms dedicated to non-European continents, and a fine collection of prehistoric exhibits.
- The Museo Nazionale dell'Alto Medioevo, which mostly contains objects dating from the time of the Lombards (6-7C).
- The Museo Nazionale delle Arti e Tradizioni Popolari, which aims to convey a greater knowledge of the uses and customs of traditional Italian life.
- The Museo della Civiltà Romana, which is located in a "cold" building dating from the earliest period of construction in EUR. It contains plaster casts of sculptures and models of the principal monuments of ancient Rome and could appear to be a huge collection of fakes, were it not that some items alone make a visit worthwhile. Among these is a reproduction of the reliefs on *Trajan's Column*, and an immense model of Rome (on a scale of 1:250), made in 1937 by the architect Italo Gismondi and subsequently updated on the basis of modern excavations and archaeological research.

In October 2004, a monumental sculpture by the artist Arnaldo Pomodoro was placed at the entrance to the neighbourhood for travellers coming from outside Rome. Modelled in bronze and 21 metres high, it represents the *Novecento* (1900s), a century marked by terrible events such as the Second World War but also by the wonderful discoveries of science and technology.

itinerary

17

OUTSIDE ROME

TIVOLI
OSTIA ANTICA
TARQUINIA
CERVETERI

TIVOLI

HADRIAN'S VILLA The emperor Hadrian (117-138), an extraordinarily refined and cultivated man had, according to the ancient sources, deeply assimilated Roman, Greek and Oriental cultures. For almost his entire life, he dedicated himself to building this magnificent complex, which he began the year following his accession and where he sought to recreate the sights he had seen on his long journeys.

The villa, lying on the slopes of the Tiburtini Hills near the Aniene River, ably exploits the water resources to feed the vast ornamental basins in the park. The emperor could have chosen another site for his residence, but probably there were no other such extensive areas available near Rome. To get some idea of the extent of the villa, it should be recalled that the part excavated represents only a fifth of the entire complex.

The splendour of the building was recognised even in antiquity. The 4C historian Aelius Spartianus in his *Life of Hadrian* writes: "His villa at Tivoli was marvellously constructed, and he actually gave to parts of it the names of provinces and places of the greatest renown, calling them, for instance, Lyceum, Academia, Prytaneum, Canopus, Poikile and Tempe. And in order not to omit anything, he even made a Hades".

These categorisations had great influence on scholars in the period the villa was first discovered, during the Renaissance. Indeed even today the various areas of the villa have been given names, often

chosen arbitrarily, that recall the buildings of Classical Greece, of Egypt and of Asia Minor.

This important imperial residence is, then, an agglomeration of different buildings placed to form a continuous whole, but without the predefined planning that was used for Roman cities. The logic followed seems to depend exclusively upon aesthetic considerations, and precisely for this reason creates such a fascinating and evocative effect. The various areas are very different, naturally adapted to the terrain, and would seem to be completely isolated from one another if it were not that they are interconnected by long porticos stretching in various directions. Each area has its own specific plan with straight and curved lines that bring an effect of movement to the whole.

In some cases curved walls give way to a succession of concavities and convexities, covered with domes of the most diverse forms, a feature that has led to talk of a Baroque *ante-litteram*. In any case it represents a prelude to the further development of Roman architecture, made up of complex and dynamic spaces, that was later continued by Byzantine art.

The statues and paintings that adorned the villa, the marbles of various kinds and from distant shores, are now scattered over the main museums of Europe. Many, however, are still to be seen in Rome, in the Capitoline and Vatican Museums.

ESSENTIAL ITINERARY A specially-constructed pavilion near the ticket entrance contains a model of the villa, made in the 1950s by the architect Italo Gismondi.

The first building the visitor comes across is the Poikile, the name being a reference to the oldest portico in Athens - frescoed, according to the sources, by the great painter Polygnotos (5C BC) - where philosophers, and in particular Aristotle, would come to teach. The portico encloses a vast rectangular space at the centre of which is a pool of water 100 metres long and 26 metres wide. A substructure within the area had numerous small chambers distributed over three or four floors, popularly known as the *Cento camerelle*, they were in fact 160 rooms perhaps used as guards' quarters. Only traces remain.

At the end of the complex, moving south beyond the museum, is the Canopus, a vast basin surrounded, now only in part, by a colonnade with arches and entablatures. It is meant to imitate the Egyptian shrine of Canopus on the Nile. At the end is the Serapeum, a temple dedicated to the Egyptian divinity Serapis.

The itinerary now leads back to the Small Baths and the Great Baths, divided into the areas typical of bathhouses: the *frigidarium* (cold-water pool), *tepidarium* (tepid-water pool) and *calidarium* (hot-water pool).

From the *triclinium*, the nymphaeum and the fishpond, the itinerary continues across the Golden Court (so-called for the beautiful marbles that once covered it) in which, at the extremities of a broad open space which was also once porticoed, are two centrally-planned buildings. The larger has concave and convex walls, the smaller four "lobes" and a segmented dome, and they herald the further Baroque-like developments of Roman architecture in late antiquity.

Following the imperial apartments, the visit can concludes in the maritime theatre, a misleading name for the building that represents

Villa Adriana, the great dome of the baths and the "Heliocaminus"

Golden Court

Canopus with statue of a river god in the foreground

the central and perhaps most intimate place in the villa, reserved for the emperor's private use. It is a circular construction with a diameter of 42.56 metres. At the centre is a portico of Ionic columns and, separated by a canal, a small island once covered with architecturally vibrant and dynamic buildings, but of which only a few ruins remain today.

In February 2006 excavations within the so-called *Complesso della Palestra* (gymnasium) brought to light a monumental stairway (or propylaeum), which served as the entrance to the entire complex.

VILLA D'ESTE It was built between 1550 and 1572 by the rich and powerful cardinal Ippolito II d'Este (1509-1572), son of Alfonso I d'Este, duke of Ferrara, and of Lucrezia Borgia whose father had been pope with the name of Alexander VI (1492-1503).

In 1519, just ten years old, Ippolito became archbishop of Milan. At the age of 27 he was sent to France as the court representative of his family, and two years later was appointed a cardinal. A great lover of the arts, he was patron to such poets as Ariosto and Tasso, and to artists and musicians. On various occasions he also tried, unsuccessfully, to be elected as pope. In 1550 Julius III, immediately after his own election to the pontifical throne and in order to thank cardinal d'Este for having helped to elect him, appointed him as governor of Tivoli. His official residence was a Benedictine monastery attached to the Gothic church of Santa Maria Maggiore, but the new proprietor did not delay in adapting it to its new functions.

Having expropriated the terrain on which the gardens of Villa d'Este still stand today, in

Fontana dell'Organo and Fontana del Nettuno seen from the fishponds

1551 the cardinal ordered building work to begin, probably to designs by the architect Pirro Ligorio. However, the activities were soon interrupted as d'Este had to undertake commissions in Siena, and later was sent away to Lombardy by order of Pope Paul IV (Giovanni Pietro Carafa 1555-1559) as punishment for acts of corruption allegedly committed by the cardinal in his attempts to get elected to the pontifical throne. Only with the election of Pope Pius IV (1559-1565) could Ippolito II d'Este return to Tivoli, where he remained until his death.

The restructuring of the palazzo was not completed as originally planned because, in 1568, the cardinal lost the considerable incomes he used to receive from his possessions in France. As a consequence, two side wings of the building were never built and the main frontage

Fontana di Proserpina

remained permanently unfinished. The frescoes in the villa were completed by the pupils of Federico Zuccari and by the painter Livio Agresti between 1565 and 1572. The creation of the garden kept the cardinal occupied until his death.

In order to understand the original layout of the building, it must be borne in mind that the entrance was once on the side opposite from where it is now, at the south end of the enclosure. A large Italian-style garden, with low trees and bushes, preceded the building.

Villa d'Este,
fontana dell'Ovato

Fontana del Bicchierone

The ground floor was occupied by the reception rooms, while the cardinal's apartments were located on the first floor. The visitors' route today goes in the opposite direction, beginning on the first floor at the level of the courtyard and descending towards the garden.

The garden today is very different from how it was originally designed because the low vegetation, readily visible in the above-mentioned frescoes and in Dupérac's engraving, *Vues et Perspectives des Jardins de Tivoli* (1572), has been replaced with tall trees obscuring a panoramic view of the whole.

The visit begins with the diagonal ramps known as the *Passeggiate del Cardinale* because Ippolito II d'Este used to love to walk there, passes

Cento fontane

the Fontana del Bicchierone, completed in 1661 to a design by Gian Lorenzo Bernini, and comes to the Fontana dell'Ovato or "di Tivoli", with its concave and convex lines designed by Pirro Ligorio himself. The statues date from 1567, the work of Giovanni Battista Della Porta.

Villa d'Este, panoramic view from the garden terrace

Hidden among the vegetation above is the Fontana del Pegaso, named after the winged horse which, according to legend, as it sprang into flight created the rivers that flow from the Tiburtini Hills.

Fontana del Nettuno

The visit continues towards the Fontana dell'Organo, work on which began in 1568 but was only completed in the early 1600s. Air, moved by the water, caused the notes of a melodious organ to vibrate. Below is another fountain, the Fontana del Nettuno, built in 1927 to replace Bernini's naturalistic waterfall.

Continuing past the fishponds, which were part of Pirro Ligorio's original plans, the visitor reaches the *Rotonda dei Cipressi*, a ring of cypress trees planted in 1640. At the end is the Fontana della Madre Natura, originally part of the Fontana dell' Organo but moved in 1611.

Fontana della Civetta

To the right is the Fontana della Civetta, once fitted with a device that has now been lost, and two more fountains, the Fontana di Proserpina and the Fontana di Roma, the latter being a symbolic representation of the city visible in the distance.

Finally, the visitor reaches the Cento Fontane, much modified over the years, and the Fontana del Drago, also part of the original plans for the garden which make specific reference to the myth of Hercules. The visit ends with the Grotto of Diana, containing reliefs of Ovid's *Metamorphosis* and elegant floral and naturalistic motifs.

OSTIA ANTICA

Ostia was the port of ancient Rome, the place where goods and wares from other Mediterranean lands arrived to supply the city. The name derives from the Latin *Ostium* (the end point of a watercourse), a reference to its position on the coast by the mouth of the Tiber. Today however, with the build-up of the deposits brought down by the river, the coastline has moved forwards by around three kilometres from where it was in Roman times, leaving the ruins of Ostia Antica land bound.

According to tradition, the city was founded in the 7C BC during the reign of king Ancus Marcius (642-616 BC), although no traces from that period have been found, and some scholars doubt whether in fact the city existed at that time. The oldest finds date from 330-320 BC when the walls of the *castrum* were built, the fortifications that controlled the access to Rome along the Tiber. The *castrum*, like all Roman military camps, had a square plan with two perpendicular roads (the *cardo* running north-south, and the *decumanus* running east-west). According to recent research Ostia, unlike other recently founded cities, did not then have a forum, in other words a central square surrounded by temples and public buildings; this was only built at the beginning of the Imperial age (late 1C BC - early 1C AD). All that remains of the Republican age (up to 27 BC) are a few places of worship (the so-called four little temples) and the walls (80 BC), known as the Sullian walls because built by the head of the *Optimates* (the aristocratic party), Sulla, who had won the civil war against Marius, the leader of the *Populares* (the plebeian party).

Under the first emperor, Augustus (27 BC - 14 AD), Ostia

underwent great development. The *Capitolium* (the great temple dedicated to Mars, Juno and Minerva), the theatre and the piazzale delle Corporazioni were all rebuilt. Soon afterwards, under Tiberius (14-37) the forum was renovated with the building of a temple dedicated to Rome and Augustus. However, the port remained shallow and big ships still had to anchor offshore and transfer their cargo onto barges. Perhaps it was to resolve this problem that the emperor Claudius (41-54) decided to build a new port and to locate it, against the advice of his engineers, three kilometres further north. Around this new harbour another town quickly grew up, that of Porto.

Under Domitian, (81-96) Ostia again thrived; the city was in large part restructured and the level of the streets was raised by about one metre (the difference in height is visible on the *decumanus*, immediately after the Porta Romana and before reaching the forum). The baths of Neptune and the Caserma dei Vigili (firemen's barracks) were built.

The modernisation of the city continued under Trajan (98-117) who also extended the city of Porto where he built a hexagonal harbour, the only one of its kind in the maritime history of the Mediterranean.

Under the emperor Hadrian (117-138) Ostia reached the peak of its prosperity which then lasted, though with alternating phases, for the entire second and third centuries. The neighbourhood north of the forum was built, houses with gardens near Porta Marina, and new *horrea* (stores and warehouses), baths, apartment blocks and nymphaea.

It has been calculated that in the first two centuries of empire, Ostia had a population of some 50,000 inhabitants, as compared with Rome's one million. Being a port, the population was characterised by great ethnic and religious diversity.

In fact, alongside the traditional pagan temples, numerous mithraea came to be built in Ostia during the 1C and 2C AD (the rites of Mithraism, originally from Persia and perhaps brought to Rome by returning soldiers, consisted in the adoration of the god Mithras in a chamber similar to a cave; 18 such sites have been discovered in Ostia whence it may be deduced that Mithraism was probably the second most popular religion practised by the Romans), as well as temples dedicated to other divinities of Oriental origin such as Sabazios and Attis (of particular interest is the triangular *campo della Magna Mater*), Serapis (Egyptian) and Isis (also of North African origin, protectress of sailors).

The city also had a significant Jewish community (estimated to number 2000-3000 people). In the 1C AD they built one of the first synagogues in Europe, located near what was then the beach, somewhat apart from the rest of the city. The synagogue was restructured in the 4C.

Also in the 4C, Christianity established itself in the city, evidence of which is the two-nave basilica standing at the fork in the *decumanus maximus*. Furthermore it was at Ostia, as St. Augustine recounts in his *Confessions*, that St. Monica, the mother of the saint of Hippo, died suddenly and was buried, probably in what is now the Renaissance village, near the church of Santa Aurea. An inscription near the nymphaeum of the theatre recalls the event.

Ostia Antica, the decumanus maximus with the theatre in the background

Necropolis, columbarium

Aerial view of the theatre

ESSENTIAL ITINERARY The entrance leads directly onto the *decumanus maximus*, the east-west axis and the continuation of the via Ostiense that connected the city to Rome. Leaving the necropolis on the left (better left for the end of the visit), visitors come to the Porta Romana (the main gate for people coming from Rome) beyond which is piazzale della Vittoria where carts and carriages would be parked. Continuing down the main street, on the right are the Caserma dei Vigili (firemen's barracks), the baths of Neptune, and the theatre with

the piazzale delle Corporazioni. Returning to the *decumanus*, visitors should go down via dei Molini to visit the bakery and from there along the via della Casa di Diana with its *insulae* (apartment blocks with shops on the ground floor) on each side. In the Forum the two pagan temples, and especially the round temple, are of particular interest. Visitors should now continue along to the fork to see the *tabernae* of the fishmongers, then turn right to visit the Mithraeum of the Baths, the *insula del Serapide* and the *insula degli Aurighi*. The Christian basilica and the *campo della Magna Mater* are also not to be missed. Turning back towards the exit, visitors will be able to see the baths of the Forum, the *Domus della Fortuna Annonaria* and, finally, the necropolis.

Ostia Antica,
theatrical mask

RENAISSANCE VILLAGE
Not far from the entrance to the site of the excavations, is the 15C village of Ostia Antica, once a fortress guarding the mouth of the Tiber.

It is probable that this site contained a palaeo-Christian necropolis, and an early mediaeval village of which only the perimeter walls remain, known as Gregoriopolis from the name of Pope Gregory IV (827-844), who founded it.

The small fortified village must have gone through a period of decline during the Avignon schism (1309-1377) when the papacy was moved to France. At the beginning of the 15C, it was fortified by Pope Martin V (Oddone Colonna 1417-1431) who added a tower-keep, defined by an ancient text as *excelsa et rotunda*.

Further modifications were made between 1461 and 1483, when cardinal Guillaume d'Estouteville was bishop of Ostia. He had the perim-

Church of Santa Aurea

Ostia Antica,
entrance to the village

eter walls restored, where his coat-of-arms is still much in evidence, and three rows of houses built, still in existence today. He also began work on the construction of the church.

At the end of the 1400s, however, the appearance of the village changed completely. Cardinal Giuliano della Rovere, who before becoming Pope with the name of Julius II was bishop of Ostia from 1483 to 1503, ordered more defences for the mouth of the Tiber and commissioned the Florentine architect Baccio Pontelli, an expert in military fortifications, to build a castle incorporating the earlier tower-keep. He also completed the church, dedicated to Santa Aurea.

The triangular castle represents a turning point in military architecture because, while maintaining certain typically mediaeval elements such as embrasures from which to fire arrows and pour boiling oil, it also has structures designed for defence against firearms, introduced into Italy around 1460. These include the pentagonal bastion, the scarp (the sloping wall just over the moat), the casemates (fortified shelters along the perimeter from which to fire), the battlements (unfortunately partly replaced by a mistaken modern restoration), and the ravelin (an additional fortification at the entrance).

The church is also extremely interesting. Dedicated to Santa Aurea, a Roman martyr of noble family who is buried nearby, the exterior is of brick and travertine as was typical in the Renaissance, and cardinal Giuliano della Rovere's heraldic symbols of the tree and the acorn are much in evidence.

Finally, mention must be made of the bishopric, which was frescoed in the first decades of the 1500s by such refined painters as Baldas-

Ostia Antica,
castle of Julius II

sarre Peruzzi, Cesare da Sesto and Domenico Beccafumi with mono-
chromes inspired by *Trajan's Column*.

After 1557 the village fell into decline. That year a sudden flood caused
the Tiber River, which used to run alongside the town, to change course
to its current location further away. The castle thus lost its defensive
functions and was only renovated following the Second World War.

PORTS OF CLAUDIUS AND TRAJAN AND THE FIU-
MICINO MUSEUM OF ROMAN SHIPS It was the emperor
Claudius (41-54) who, between 42 and 46 BC, built a port at the
mouth of the Tiber to supplement that of Ostia Antica. Remains of the
quays and various associated buildings are still just visible within the
area of the Leonardo da Vinci international airport. Soon however, it
began to silt up with the debris brought down by the river and, around
50 years later, the emperor Trajan (98-117) ordered the creation of another harbour. Built to an original hexagonal form, Trajan's dock could
accommodate up to fifty vessels and had a canal, known as the *Fossa
Traianea*, connecting it to the river and the sea. A city soon grew up
around the port, it was independent of Ostia and took the name of
Porto. At the beginning of the 4C, under Constantine, the city was
given walls and remained active until the 6C. Following a period of decline, it revived in the late Renaissance and even had its own bishopric.
Plans are currently afoot to create a large archaeological park around
the remains of the Roman town.

The museum, which is located at the entrance to the international airport, contains the remains of original Roman ships. Twenty-six metres
long, they are nonetheless small with respect to the great vessels of
antiquity which, as far as we know, could reach up to 48 metres in
length. All that remains of these vessels are the keels but this is by no
means strange because, during the winter when the ships did not put
out to sea but remained moored in port, it only needed a heavy swell
to bring down a lantern and burn all the upper works. Other interesting
exhibits include a *cast of the Torlonia relief* which dates from the 3C AD
and depicts an imperial vessel in the port of Claudius, and two large
wall panels: one showing the places where the ships in the museum
were found, the other the trade routes used by the Romans.

TARQUINIA AND CERVETERI

The necropolises of Tarquinia and Cerveteri, situated respectively 90 and 45 kilometres north of Rome, are the most important Etruscan sites in the Lazio region. The ancient civilisation of the Etruscans, located in central Italy, preceded that of the Romans.

Of Indo-European origin, or perhaps from Asia Minor, from the 9-7C BC the Etruscans settled the territory between the Arno and the Tiber. They reached their peak in the 7C and 6C BC when they conquered Rome itself, expanding north to the valley of the Po and south as far as Capua.

Cerveteri, Castello Ruspali, site of the Museo Nazionale Cerite

Later, beginning in the mid 6C, the Etruscans began a slow but inexorable decline as they became involved in unequal struggles with the Greeks and Carthaginians for the control of the Mediterranean, losing various cities including Rome at the end of the 6C, Cumae in Campania in 474 BC and the entire Po Valley in the mid 4C BC.

At the same time, Rome began to extend its supremacy into northern Lazio with the conquest of Veio (396 BC) and of Cerveteri (273 BC). From then on the Etruscan people, repeatedly defeated and subjugated, were gradually absorbed by the Romans.

Though great builders of city walls, bridges and aqueducts, the Etruscans, deeply attached to the idea of the transitory nature of earthly life, left no great temples or basilicas. Those they did construct were made using perishable materials such as wood and clay. They did, however, give great importance to tombs which they would build in stone or dig out of rock, mostly around Tarquinia and Cerveteri in the Lazio region. Many of these tombs contained funerary objects, today conserved in various museums, which testify to their trading activities with other Mediterranean peoples, and especially with Greece.

ESSENTIAL ITINERARY In Tarquinia is the fascinating Museo Nazionale Tarquiniese located in the 15C Palazzo Vitelleschi. It contains, among other things: the famous pair of terracotta *winged*

Tarquinia, necropolis, tomb of the Leopard, supplicant and musicians

horses discovered in 1938 and originally part of a temple known as Ara della Regina, of which only the base remains; a series of sarcophagi made of local limestone or other stone, some with traces of colour; a vast collection of Greek and Etruscan vases testifying to the intense trade between those two peoples until the 5C BC; and finally, wall paintings detached from tombs and a series of fine jewellery in gold and precious stones giving evidence of the great artistic refinement achieved by this civilisation.

Also in Tarquinia are a number of underground tombs dating from between the 7C and 4C BC. Visits are organised in turns; ask at the museum.

At Cerveteri the largest and most important necropolis is the Necropoli della Banditaccia, with its characteristic mound tombs from the 7-6C BC. The burial chambers, enclosed by tufa walls, are only partly below ground level, within circular structures covered with a conical tumulus of earth. It is believed that the shape of these Etruscan tombs was similar to that of their houses of which, however, no trace remains.

Tarquinia, façade of Palazzo Vitelleschi, site of the Museo Nazionale Tarquiniese

Tarquinia, Museo Nazionale Tarquiniese, winged horses

INDEX OF EMPERORS

BIBLIOGRAFY

The bibliography of works concerning Rome is, of course, immense. Given below are the titles of just a few texts that are easily obtainable in bookshops or libraries, and may interest readers seeking greater knowledge on general aspects of the city's history.

Architettura del Settecento a Roma nei disegni della Raccolta Grafica Comunale, exhibition catalogue (Rome, Palazzo Braschi, 24 September - 10 November 1991), Rome 1991.
M. ARMELLINI, *Le Chiese di Roma*, Rome 1887.
M. ARMELLINI – C. CECCHELLI, *Le chiese di Roma dal secolo IV al XIX*, Rome 1942.
A. AUGENTI (ed.), *Roma. Arte e Archeologia*, Florence 2000.
I. BELLI BARSALI, *Le ville della Campagna Romana*, Milan 1975.
I. BELLI BARSALI, *Ville di Roma*, Rome 1983.
A. BRUSCHI, *Bramante*, Rome-Bari 1977.
E. CALVESI, *La Cappella Sistina e la sua decorazione da Perugino a Michelangelo*, Rome 1997.
A. CEDERNA, *Mussolini urbanista. Lo sventramento di Roma negli anni del consenso*, Rome 1979.
A. CEDERNA, *Storia moderna dell'Appia Antica. 1950-1996: dai gangster dell'Appia al parco di carta*, Rome 1997.
B. CESTELLI GUIDI, *Cosa trovare nei Musei di Roma*, Florence-Rome 2005.
F. COARELLI, *Guida archeologica di Roma*, Rome 1997.
S. DANESI SQUARZINA – G. BORGHINI (ed.), *Il Borgo di Ostia Antica da Sisto IV a Giulio II*, exhibition catalogue (Ostia, Castle and Bishopric, 19 June - 30 September 1980), Rome 1981.
I. DELLA PORTELLA, *Roma sotterranea*, Venice 1999.
C. D'ONOFRIO, *Gli Obelischi di Roma*, Rome 1967.
C. D'ONOFRIO, *Acque e Fontane di Roma*, Rome 1986.
M. FAGIOLO, *Ville e Giardini di Roma*, Milan 2001.
M. FAGIOLO – P. PORTOGHESI (ed.), *Roma Barocca. Bernini, Borromini, Pietro da Cortona*, exhibition catalogue (Rome, Castel Sant'Angelo, 15 June - 29 October 2006), Rome 2006.
Fiumicino tra cielo e mare. Una storia da vedere, Rome 2000.
A.P. FRUTAZ (ed.), *Le piante di Roma*, 3 vols., Rome 1962.
R. L. GELLER, *Roma ebraica*, Rome 1984.
V. GOLZIO – G. ZANDER, *Le chiese di Roma dall'XI al XVI secolo*, Bologna 1963.
V. GOLZIO – G. ZANDER, *L'Arte di Roma nel XV secolo*, Bologna 1968.
M. GORI SASSOLI (ed.), *Roma veduta. Disegni e stampe panoramiche della città dal XV al XIX secolo*, exhibition catalogue (Rome, Palazzo Poli, 30 September 2000 - 28 January 2001), Rome 2000.
H. GROSS, *Roma nel Settecento*, Rome-Bari 1990.
I. INSOLERA, *Roma moderna. Un secolo di storia urbanistica*, Turin 1972.
I. INSOLERA, *Roma. Immagini e realtà dal X al XX secolo*, Rome-Bari 1981.
R. KRAUTHEIMER (ed.), *Corpus basilicarum christianarum Romae*, 6 vols., Vatican City 1937-1980.
R. KRAUTHEIMER, *Roma. Profilo di una città*, Rome 1984.
R. LANCIANI, *Forma Urbis Romae*, Rome 1988.
F. MANCINELLI, *La Cappella Sistina*, Vatican City 1994.
F. MANCINELLI – A.M. DE STROBEL, *Michelangelo. Le lunette e le vele della Cappella Sistina*, Rome 1992.
S. MOSCATI, *L'Italia prima di Roma*, Milan 1987.
R. PANE, *L'architettura della Volta Sistina*, in G.C. ARGAN ET AL., *Michelangiolo architetto*, Turin 1964.
F. PAPAFAVA, *Vaticano*, Vatican City 1993.
L. PARTRIDGE – F. MANCINELLI – G. COLALUCCI, *La Cappella Sistina. Il Giudizio restaurato*, Novara 1998.
C. PAVOLINI, *Ostia*, Rome-Bari 2006.
P. PORTOGHESI, *Roma barocca*, Rome 1995 (Rome 1966).
M. PRAZ (ed.), *G.B. Piranesi. Vedute di Roma*, Rome 2000.
L. QUARONI, *Immagine di Roma*, Bari 1976.
S. QUILICI GIGLI, *Roma fuori le mura*, Rome 1985.

P. ROVAIOLI, *Le fontane di Roma. La storia e le immagini a colori delle fontane e fontanelle artistiche della 'Città Eterna'*, Rome 1995.
A. RAVAGLIOLI, *Vedere e capire Roma. Manuale per la scoperta della città*, Rome 1980.
G. TESEI, *Le Chiese di Roma*, Rome 1991 (Rome 1986).
G. TOMASSETTI, *La campagna romana antica, medioevale e moderna*, Rome 1910.
M.P. SETTE, *Il Restauro in Architettura*, Rome 2001.

Other useful works for understanding Rome:

The volume on *Rome* in the *Guide Rosse* of the Touring Club Italiano.
The *Illustrated Guide to Rome* published by Mondadori and the Touring Club Italiano.
The guides of the Soprintendenza Archeologica di Roma published by Edizioni Electa.
The series *Le chiese di Roma illustrate* of the Istituto di Studi Romani, and the *Guide Rionali di Roma* published by Palombi Editori.
The magazines *Roma Sacra* and *Roma Archeologica*, published by Elio de Rosa.
The magazines *Bella Roma* and *Bell'Italia* published by Giorgio Mondadori.
The magazine *Capitolium* published by the Comune di Roma.
The magazine *AR*, published every two months by the Order of Architects of the City and Province of Rome.

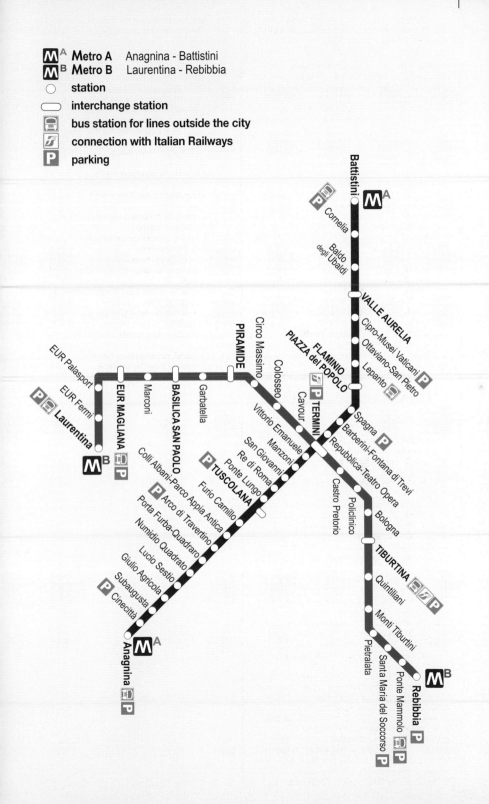

M^A **Metro A** Anagnina - Battistini
M^B **Metro B** Laurentina - Rebibbia
⭘ station
⬭ interchange station
🚌 bus station for lines outside the city
🚆 connection with Italian Railways
🅿 parking

© Copyright 2007
This book has been edited and published by
ATS Italia Editrice s.r.l.
via di Brava, 41/43 - 00163 Roma
tel. 0666415961 - fax 0666512461 - www.atsitalia.it
No part of this book may be reproduced

Text *Sonia Gallico*
Editorial co-ordination *Frida Giannini*
Editor *Paola Ciogli*
Photo research *Angela Giommi*
Graphic design, layout and cover *Sabrina Moroni*
Scanning and colour correction *Leandro Ricci*
Technical co-ordination *Flavio Zancla*
Translation *Piers Amodia*
Printing *Papergraf - Piazzola sul Brenta, Padova*
Photographs *Photographic archive Ats Italia Editrice*
Photographic archive Vatican Museums
Photographic archive Scala Group
Photographic archive Electa
Archive Arti Doria-Pamphilj

*The images from the Scala and Electa photographic archives reproducing
cultural assets that belong to the Italian State have been published
with the permission of the Italian Ministero dei Beni e le Attività Culturali*

*The publisher may be notified concerning
any unidentified iconographic sources*

Questo volume è disponibile anche in lingua italiana
Ce volume est disponible aussi en français
Dieser Band ist auch in deutscher Sprache erhältlich
Esta obra también está publicada en español

ISBN 978-88-7571-347-8